GEN. OGLETHORPE.

LIPPINCOTT'S

CABINET HISTORIES.

GEORGIA.

PHILADELPHIA
LIPPINCOTT, GRAMBO & Cº
1852.

Lippincott's

Cabinet Histories of the States.

GEORGIA.

THE

HISTORY OF GEORGIA,

FROM ITS

Earliest Settlement to the Present Time.

BY

T. S. ARTHUR

AND

W. H. CARPENTER.

PHILADELPHIA:
LIPPINCOTT, GRAMBO & CO.
1852.

STEREOTYPED BY L. JOHNSON AND CO.
PHILADELPHIA.
PRINTED BY T. K. AND P. G. COLLINS.

PREFACE.

A SERIES of State histories, which, without superseding the bulkier and more expensive works of the same character, might enter household channels from which the others would be excluded by their cost and magnitude, has long been wanted.

For some time past we have been making preparations to supply this want, by the publication, in separate and distinct volumes, of the history peculiar to each State in the Union.

The present volume on Georgia is one of the series. The merit we claim for it—and it will equally apply to the others—is point, condensation, and historical accuracy.

Our aim is to make the vital history of every State a portion of the knowledge of its people; to bring down the narrative to the present day;

and, while compressing all those dry details relating to legislative action, to present to the general reader every point of real interest in a clear, vivid, and picturesque manner.

CONTENTS.

CHAPTER I.

CHAPTER II.

CHAPTER III.

CHAPTER IV.

CHAPTER V.

CHAPTER VI.

CHAPTER VII.

CHAPTER VIII.

CHAPTER IX.

CHAPTER X.

CHAPTER XI.

CHAPTER XII.

CHAPTER XIII.

CHAPTER XIV.

CHAPTER XV.

CHAPTER XVI.

CHAPTER XXI.

CHAPTER XXII.

CHAPTER XXIII.

HISTORY OF GEORGIA.

CHAPTER I.

Introductory observations—Georgia discovered by Sir Walter Raleigh—His voyage along the coast—His conference with an Indian chief—Reasons for planting the colony—Jealousy of the Spaniards—A regiment of blacks formed at St. Augustine—Disagreement concerning the English and Spanish boundaries—A fort built by the Carolinians on the Alatamaha—A charter obtained for a new province—The proposed settlers to be persons in decayed circumstances—Their outfits and allotments—Stipulations with the adventurers—Negroes to be prohibited—Private contributions solicited—The first embarkation.

THAT portion of the United States of North America which now forms the State of Georgia was originally included in a patent granted to South Carolina; first, as a proprietary government, and afterwards, in 1719, as a regal one, bounded by the thirty-first and thirty-sixth degrees of north latitude.

For the first discovery of this portion of the North American continent, we are indebted to the zeal of the unfortunate Sir Walter Raleigh.

Being deeply interested in the adventures of his half brother, Sir Humphrey Gilbert, who had obtained a patent from Queen Elizabeth, granting him permission to possess and colonize such countries as he might discover, Sir Walter made a successful application for a similar grant, and on the 23d of April, 1584, despatched two ships, under the command of Captains Amadas and Barlow, for the purpose of visiting the countries of which he contemplated the future settlement.

To avoid the error of Gilbert in shaping his course too far to the north, Sir Walter took the route by the West India islands, and approached the North American continent at the Gulf of Florida, from whence he followed the coast, and touched the shore, occasionally, visiting and conversing with the natives, until he reached Pamlico Sound on the borders of North Carolina. From thence he proceeded northward along the coast, and returned to England in September of the same year.

There have been some doubts expressed by historians as to whether Sir Walter ever visited North America in person. But when James Edward Oglethorpe, the principal founder of the colony of Georgia, came over from England, he is said to have brought with him Sir Walter Raleigh's written journal, from which it appeared, by the latitude of Savannah and by the traditions of the natives, that Raleigh landed at the mouth of Savannah River, and visited the bluff on which the city was afterwards built.

According to the statement made by the Indians to Mr. Oglethorpe, Sir Walter was the first Englishman their forefathers ever saw. So favourable was the impression made by the gallant knight upon this rude forest people, that their chief king, before he died, desired to be taken to a high mound of earth, about half a mile from Savannah, in order that he might be buried at the spot where he talked with the great and good white stranger.

The policy of planting a new colony south of Savannah River was an object of great importance to South Carolina, in consequence of the differences existing between England and Spain in regard to the respective boundaries of their settlements in North and South America.

The rapid increase of population in North America, and its growing commercial importance, had long been viewed by Spain with a jealous eye. Already occupying, in right of discovery and possession, the territory of Florida; the Spanish government sought, by garrisoning the coast with troops, to command not only the Indian trade brought down the Mississippi, but also the trade of those large rivers to the north of it. These encroachments could not be made without seriously endangering the province of South Carolina, which at that time was numerously stocked with negroes, brought from Africa by British merchants, and sold to the rice-planters, whose wealth consisted almost entirely of slaves.

It being the interest of Spain to throw every obstacle in the way of the English planters, the most favourable means of doing so seemed that of enticing the negroes from the service of their masters, by pointing out to them the happiness of freedom, and promising them all the privileges enjoyed by the subjects of Spain.

To more effectually accomplish this sinister purpose, a black regiment was formed at St. Augustine, consisting entirely of runaway slaves from Carolina; and though there was no war existing at that time between the rival nations, all the remonstrances addressed to the Spanish governor were disregarded.

One cause of this vexatious state of things was the uncertainty in regard to the correct boundaries between the British provinces and Florida. These had never been settled by any public agreement, neither were they marked or well understood. To prevent negroes escaping from the Carolinas to St. Augustine, a fort was built on the Alatamaha river, and garrisoned. This gave offence to the Spanish governor, who complained of it to the court of Madrid as an encroachment on the dominions of his royal master. The Spanish ambassador at London was immediately authorized to demand that the troops should be removed and the fort demolished.

It was thereupon agreed, that the governors of

the respective nations in America should meet in an amicable manner, and adjust the boundaries between the British and Spanish dominions in that quarter.

Commissioners were accordingly appointed for that purpose. They met at Charleston, but the negotiation ended unsatisfactorily to both parties. The fort was soon after burned down, and the southern frontier of South Carolina again left exposed and defenceless.

Finding that the Spanish authorities in Florida still continued their acts of aggression, the people of South Carolina, alarmed at the danger to which they were continually exposed, endeavoured to protect their property in future by placing a more efficient barrier between themselves and their imperious neighbours in Florida.

With these views, they advocated the formation of a new colony between the Savannah and Alatamaha rivers; and encouraged a number of gentlemen, of wealth and station in England, to embark in the humane design of sending over a number of poor people, who had no means of supporting themselves and families in the mother country.

Accordingly, twenty-one persons petitioned the throne; and, on the 9th of June, 1732, obtained a charter for a separate and distinct province from Carolina, between the Savannah and Alatamaha rivers, by the name of Georgia, in honour of the king by whom the charter was granted.

Subsequently, the limits of Georgia were extended to the Chattahoochee river, which now forms its western boundary.

In pursuance of this charter, the trustees, with Lord Purcival at their head, met in London about the middle of July, for the purpose of fixing upon some fit person to superintend the settlement of the colony, and also to establish rules for its government.

In order to carry out the intents and purposes for which the charter was obtained, it was finally resolved, that none were to have the benefit of the charity fund, for their transportation and subsequent subsistence, except such as were in decayed circumstances, and thereby disabled from any profitable business in England; and such as, having large families, were in a measure dependent upon their respective parishes. No drunken or vicious persons were to be received.

The trustees consented to give to such persons as they sent upon charity—to every grown male, a watch-coat, musket and bayonet, hatchet, hammer, hand-saw, sod-shovel or spade, broad-hoe, narrow-hoe, gimlet, and drawing-knife; a public grindstone to each ward or village; and to each man, an iron-pot, pot-hooks, and frying-pan.

For his maintenance for one year, they allowed

him three hundred pounds of beef or pork, one hundred and fourteen pounds of rice, one hundred and fourteen pounds of peas, one hundred and fourteen pounds of flour, forty-four gallons of strong beer, sixty-four quarts of molasses, eighteen pounds of cheese, nine pounds of butter, nine ounces of spice, nine pounds of sugar, five gallons of vinegar, thirty pounds of salt, twelve quarts of lamp oil, and twelve pounds of soap. The same allowances, with the exception of beer, were extended to each of the mothers, wives, other females, and children over twelve years of age; half allowance for children of seven and under twelve; and one-third for those from two to seven; passage paid, and sea stores allowed extra.

Before embarkation, the emigrants were required to enter into the following covenants:

That they would repair on board such ship as should be provided for them; demean themselves well during the voyage, and go to such place in the province of Georgia as should be designated, and then obey such orders as should be given them for establishing and governing the said colony.

That for the first twelve months after landing in the province, they would labour in clearing their lands, making habitations and necessary defences, and on all other works for the common good and public benefit of the said province, according to such plans and directions as should be given them.

That after the expiration of the said twelve months, they would, during the next two succeeding years, inhabit the province of Georgia, and cultivate the lands allotted to them and their male heirs, according to their best skill and ability.

All such persons were to be settled in the same colony, either in new towns or villages. Those in the towns were to have, each of them, a lot sixty feet front by ninety deep, whereon they were to build a house, and as much land in the adjoining country as would, in the whole, make up fifty acres. Those in the villages were each of them to have a lot of fifty acres, upon which a house was to be built; and a rent-charge was placed alike upon all, of two shillings and sixpence sterling upon every fifty-acre lot, for the support of the colony.

By another provision, the trustees allowed every freeholder to take over with him one male servant, or apprentice, of the age of eighteen and upwards, to be bound for no less than four years. By way of loan to such freeholder, they agreed to advance the charges of passage for such servant or apprentice, and to furnish him with the following clothing and provisions:

A pallet, bolster, blanket, a frock and trousers of linsey-woolsey, a shirt, a frock and trousers of osnaburg, a pair of English shoes, two pairs of colonial shoes, two hundred pounds of meat, three hundred and forty-two pounds of rice, peas, or Indian corn. The expenses of passage, clothing, and provision, to be reimbursed to the trustees by the master, within the third year from their embarkation from England.

To each man-servant and his male heirs, upon a certificate of good behaviour from his master, were to be granted, after the expiration of the term of service, twenty acres of land, under the same rents and agreements as had been granted to any other man-servant in like circumstances.

The inhabitants of Georgia were to be considered as soldiers and planters, and provided with arms for defence, as well as tools for cultivation; occasional military exercise being held as requisite to the safety and prosperity of the colony, as the more peaceful labours of agriculture.

Towns were to be laid out for settlement, and lands allotted to each colonist as near as convenient; so that the towns, which were to be regarded in the nature of garrisons, might be easily reached, and each man arrive at his post of defence at a short notice in case of emergency.

As the object of the trustees—having in view the protection of the Carolinas—was to found a province partly military and partly agricultural, and as the military strength was particularly to be taken care of, it was deemed necessary to establish such tenures of lands as might most effectually preserve the number of planters, or soldiers, equal to the number of lots of land within a narrow compass; therefore, each lot of land was to be considered as a military fief, and to contain no more than was deemed sufficient for the support of the planter and his family. Fifty acres were judged sufficient, and provision was made to prevent any increase or diminution of this quantity, lest, on the one hand, the means of defence should be weakened, or, on the other, subsistence found to be too scanty.

In the infancy of the colony, the lands granted were to descend to male heirs only, as most likely to answer the purposes of the donors; and, in consideration of the service expected of the colonists, they were to be maintained at the public expense during their voyage, and their passage paid; and were to be provided (for the space of one year) with arms, implements, seeds, and other necessaries, from the general store.

To others, who should come over at their own charges, particular grants were agreed upon under the same tenure, and on the condition that they should settle in Georgia within twelve months from the date of their grants, bringing with them one man-servant for every fifty acres; should inhabit there for three years; clear and cultivate within the first ten years one-fifth of the land so granted; within the next ten years, clear and cultivate three-fifths more, and plant one thousand white mulberry trees upon every hundred acres cleared—the raising of raw silk being one of the principal objects contemplated by the founders of the colony. One particular restriction was placed upon all the colonists alike, and this was, that no negro should be employed or harboured within the limits of Georgia, on any pretence whatever, unless by special leave of the trustees.

The object of this prohibition was to present a military frontier to South Carolina consisting of Europeans only; to shield the slave population of the latter State from the artifices and allurements held out by the Spaniards, and to shut out from among the colonists of Georgia all those incentives to idleness which the introduction of a slave population is so apt to favour. It was further argued, that the introduction of negroes into Georgia would facilitate the desertion of the Carolina slaves, and instead of proving a frontier, would promote the evil which was intended to be checked, and give additional strength to the Spanish force at St. Augustine. In the execution of this laudable plan, the trustees, after having themselves contributed largely towards the scheme, undertook to solicit donations from others, and to apply the money towards clothing, arming, purchasing implements for cultivation, and trans-

3

porting such poor people as should consent to go over and begin a settlement.

To prevent any misapplication or abuse of the funds thus collected, they agreed to deposit the money in the Bank of England, to keep a correct list of the names of the donors, and the sum received from each; and bound themselves and their successors in office, to lay an annual statement of the moneys contributed and expended before the lord chancellor, the lords chief justices of the King's Bench and Common Pleas, the master of the rolls, and the lord chief baron of the Exchequer.

When this scheme of settlement was made public, the philanthropic motives of the trustees were warmly applauded in all parts of Great Britain. Perfectly disinterested themselves, neither desiring nor retaining any source of personal aggrandizement, but contented with the simple honour of benefiting the poorer classes at home by gratuitously providing them with the means of procuring a comfortable subsistence in a region where industry was sure to meet with a successful reward, the benevolent founders of the colony of Georgia are entitled to the high honour of having promoted a design at once generous and praiseworthy. They voluntarily offered their money, labour, and time, with the hope of alleviating the distressed condition of others; leaving themselves no other reward than the gratification arising from having performed a humane and virtuous action.

When the trustees, by their own contributions, aided by donations from several private persons, had accumulated a sum of money sufficient to commence the intended settlement, it was resolved to send over one hundred and fourteen persons, men, women, and children, being such as were in decayed circumstances, and thereby disabled from following any business in England.

James Edward Oglethorpe, esquire, one of the trustees, consented to accompany them at his own expense, for the purpose of forming the settlement. The trustees prepared forms of government agreeably to the powers given them. These preliminaries being arranged, on November 16, 1732, the Rev. Mr. Shubert, a clergyman of the Church of England, and a man from Piedmont, engaged by the trustees to instruct the people in the art of winding silk, and one hundred and fourteen persons, embarked on board the ship Anne, Captain Thomas, with every thing furnished them by the trustees, and nothing to risk but what might arise from casualties or a change of climate. Mr. Oglethorpe was clothed with power to exercise the functions of a governor over the new colony.

CHAPTER II.

Arrival of the colonists in Charleston—Oglethorpe visits the Savannah, and selects Yamacraw Bluff as the site for a town—His letter to the trustees—Treats with the Indians for their lands—Certain lands reserved by the Indians—Government assists the trustees in the settlement—Glowing descriptions of the new colony.

On the 13th of January, 1733, the ship Anne arrived safely in the harbour of Charleston, with the loss only of two children at sea.

After being hospitably entertained by the governor and council, Oglethorpe and his people, well furnished with provisions and stock by generous Carolinians, set sail for the new province of Georgia.

The authorities of Charleston furnished vessels to carry the additional supplies to the Savannah River, and also ordered some scout-boats, with a body of rangers, to accompany the adventurers, and protect them from any assault by the Indians, while the former were building houses and fortifications to defend themselves. They reached Beaufort on the 20th of January. Here Oglethorpe left his colonists, while he, accompanied by two experienced men from Carolina, explored the country in search of a suitable place for his intended settlement. As soon as the governor had selected an advantageous site, he addressed the following letter to the trustees in London:

"*Camp, near Savannah, Feb.* 10, 1733.

"GENTLEMEN:—I gave you an account in my last of our arrival in Charleston. The governor and assembly have given us all possible encouragement. Our people arrived at Beaufort on the 20th of January, where I lodged them in some new barracks built for the soldiers, whilst I went myself to view the Savannah River; I fixed upon a healthy situation about ten miles from the sea. The river here forms a half-moon, along the south side of which the banks are about forty feet high, and on the top a flat, which they call a bluff. The plain high ground extends into the country about six miles, and along the river-side about a mile. Ships that draw twelve feet water can ride within ten yards of the bank.

"Upon the river's side, in the centre of this plain, I have laid out the town, opposite to which is an island of very rich pasturage, which I think should be kept for the trustees' cattle. The river is pretty wide, the water fresh, and from the key of the town you see its whole course to the sea, with the island of Tybee, which forms the mouth of the river. For about six miles up into the country the landscape is very agreeable, the stream being wide, and bordered with high woods on both sides.

"The whole people arrived here on the first

of February: at night their tents were got up. Till the 10th we were taken up in unloading and making a crane, which I could not get finished, so took off the hands and set some to the fortifications, and began to fell the woods. I have marked out the town and common: half of the former is already cleared, and the first house was begun yesterday in the afternoon."

On the 20th of the same month, writing again to the trustees, he gives a further description of the site he had chosen, and his reasons for selecting it.

"I chose the situation for the town upon a high ground, forty feet perpendicular, above high-water mark; the soil, dry and sandy; the water of the river fresh, and springs coming out of the hill. I pitched upon this place not only for the pleasantness of the situation, but because, from the above-mentioned and other signs, I judged it healthy; for it is sheltered from the western and southern winds, (the worst in this country,) by vast woods of pine trees, many of which are a hundred, and few under seventy feet high. The last and fullest conviction of the healthiness of this place was, that an Indian nation who knew the nature of the country chose it for their situation."

Soon after this, a small fort was erected on the bank of Savannah River, as a place of refuge, and some guns mounted on it for the defence of the colony. The people were then employed in felling trees and building huts, while Oglethorpe encouraged and animated them by his presence and example. He formed them into a company of militia, appointed officers, and furnished them with arms and ammunition.

To awe the Indians, he frequently exercised the colonists in their presence; and as his people had been disciplined previously by the sergeants of the guards in London, they exhibited, under review, but little inferiority to the regular troops.

As soon as his little colony was comfortably sheltered and protected, the next object of Oglethorpe was to treat with the Indians for a portion of their lands.

The principal tribes occupying the territory he desired to obtain, were the Upper and Lower Creeks. The former were numerous and strong; the latter, reduced by war and disease, but a small band; though both tribes together were computed at about twenty-five thousand. As these Indians laid claim to the lands lying southwest of Savannah River, it became an object of the highest consequence to secure their friendship.

There was only one small tribe at Yamacraw, the Indian name of the bluff which Oglethorpe had selected as the site of his town. It was, therefore, thought expedient to open a communication with the Upper Creeks also, as more numerous, and prevail upon them to join in the treaty.

To accomplish this purpose, Oglethorpe selected a half-breed Indian woman named Mary, who had married a trader from Carolina by the name of Musgrove, and who could speak both the English and Creek languages. Perceiving that she had some influence among the Indians, and might be made serviceable to his views, he first purchased her friendship with presents, and then allowed her a salary of one hundred pounds a year.

By her assistance he summoned the chief men of the Creeks to meet him at Savannah, and about fifty of them attended. With these Oglethorpe concluded a treaty; and after he had distributed some presents, according to the Indian custom on such occasions, Tomochichi, one of the principal orators among the Creeks, rose and addressed him as follows:

"Here is a little present. I give you a buffalo's skin, adorned on the inside with the head and feathers of an eagle, which I desire you to accept, because the eagle is an emblem of speed, and the buffalo of strength. The English are swift as the bird, and strong as the beast; since, like the former, they flew over vast seas to the uttermost parts of the earth; and like the latter, they are so strong that nothing can withstand them. The feathers of the eagle are soft, and signify love; the buffalo's skin is warm, and signifies protection; therefore I hope the English will love and protect their little families."

The treaty—subject to the ratification of the trustees in England—was concluded to the satisfaction of both parties; and as the colonists appeared contented with their condition, every thing seemed to promise a long course of prosperity.

By this treaty, a full and complete right and title were granted the trustees for all the lands lying between the Savannah and Alatamaha Rivers, extending west to the extremity of the tide-water, and including all the islands on the coast from Tybee to St. Simons.

By a short-sighted policy, which was afterwards a source of great danger and annoyance, the Indians were allowed to reserve for themselves, within the limits of this tract, the islands of Sapelœ and St. Catharine's, for the purpose of hunting, bathing, and fishing; and also the tract of land lying between Pipe-maker's Bluff and Pally-chuckola Creek, above the new town of Savannah; these lands being retained by the Indians for an encampment, whenever they came to visit their beloved friends at Savannah.

The consequences arising from the admission of this unfortunate stipulation will be found narrated in a subsequent portion of this history.

The annual statement made by the trustees to the lord chancellor, on the 9th of June, 1734, showed that there had then been sent to Georgia, at the expense of the corporation, one hundred and fifty-two persons, of whom sixty-one were males capable of bearing arms; and that the money received from private contributions amounted to nearly four thousand pounds, of which two thousand two hundred and fifty-four pounds had been already expended for the purpose of settlement. In the mean time, the colonists had been kept busily employed. A public garden was laid off, as a nursery, to the eastward of the town, and planted with mulberry trees, vines, oranges, and olives, for the supply of the people. A beacon was erected on Tybee Island, at the mouth of the river. Fort Argyle was built at the narrows of the Ogechee, to protect the settlers against an inland invasion from St. Augustine, and a stockade fort built at Skidaway Narrows.

To aid the purposes of the trustees in rapidly strengthening their new colony, the British government sold some lands at St. Christopher, and applied ten thousand pounds to encourage the settlement.

In September and October, 1733, the trustees sent over two embarkations, amounting to three hundred and forty-one persons, principally persecuted Protestants from Saltzburg, in Germany. These settled further up the Savannah, at a place they called Ebenezer, and were soon followed thither by many others of their countrymen

During this year, the most glowing accounts of the climate of Georgia, and the prosperous condition of the colonists, were sent over by some of the immigrants to their friends in England. About the same time, a pamphlet also appeared in London, entitled, "A new and accurate Account of the Provinces of Carolina and Georgia," in which, after a high encomium of the trustees of the latter, the writer goes on to say:

"The air of Georgia is healthy, being always serene and pleasant, never subject to excessive heat or cold, or sudden changes of weather. The winter is regular and short, and the summer cooled by refreshing breezes. It neither feels the cutting northwest wind the Virginians complain of, nor the intense heats of Spain, Barbary, Italy, and Egypt.

"The soil will produce any thing with very little culture: all sorts of corn yield an amazing increase; one hundred fold is the common estimate, though the husbandry is so slight, that they can only be said to scratch the earth and cover the seed. All the best cattle and fowl are multiplied without number, and therefore without price.

"Vines are natives here; the woods near Savannah are easily cleared; many of them have no underwood, and the trees do not stand, generally, thick upon the ground, but at considerable distances asunder.

"When you fall timber to make tar, or for

any other use, the roots will rot in four or five years, and in the mean time you may pasture the ground. If you would only destroy the timber, it is done by a few strokes of an axe, surrounding each tree a little above the root. In a year or two the timber rots, and a brisk gust of wind fells many acres for you in an hour; of which you may make a bright bonfire.

"Such an air and soil can only be described by a poetical pen, because there is no danger of exceeding the truth; therefore take Waller's description of an island in the neighbourhood of Carolina, to give you an idea of this happy climate.

> "The spring, which but salutes us here,
> Inhabits there, and courts them all the year!
> Ripe fruits and blossoms on the same tree live;
> At once they promise what at once they give.
> So sweet the air, so moderate the clime,
> None sickly lives, or dies before his time.
> Heaven sure has kept this spot of earth uncursed,
> To show how all things were created first."

Speaking of the Indians, the author adds—

"They bring many a mile the whole of a deer's flesh, which they sell to the people who live in the country, for the value of *sixpence sterling;* and a wild turkey, of *forty pounds weight,* for the value of *twopence.*"

This florid picture excited a wonderful commotion among the peasantry of England. The trustees, however, represented that the description of the country was greatly exaggerated; and thus allayed the inflamed fancies of the people.

CHAPTER III.

Oglethorpe sails for England, taking with him several Indian chiefs—Speech of Tomochichi to the king—The king's reply—The Indians return to Georgia—Tomochichi's advice to his nation—Georgia found less healthy and productive than was supposed—Condition of the colonists during Oglethorpe's absence—Justice Causton—His arbitrary proceedings—The regulations of trustees found inoperative—Government assists the colony—Immigration of Scotch and Germans—John Wesley arrives in Georgia.

Having provided for the security and wants of the settlers during his absence, Oglethorpe sailed for England in April, 1734, taking with him the Indian chief Tomochichi, together with his wife, and several other influential Creeks.

On their arrival in London, the Indian chiefs were introduced to the king, in the presence of his nobility. Tomochichi, astonished at the grandeur of the British court, addressed the king in the following words:

"This day I see the majesty of your face, the greatness of your house, and the number of your people. I am come in my old days, though I cannot expect to see any advantage to myself; I am come for the good of the children of all the nations of the Upper and Lower Creeks, that they may be instructed in the language of the English.

"These are feathers of the eagle, which is the swiftest of birds, and which flieth round our nations: these feathers are emblems of peace in our land, and have been carried from town to town. We have brought them over to leave them with you, O great king, as a token of everlasting peace. O great king, whatever words you shall say unto me, I will faithfully tell them to all the chiefs of the Creek nation."

The king then replied:

"I am glad of this opportunity of assuring you of my regard for the people from whom you came. I am extremely well pleased with the assurances you have brought me from them, and accept very gratefully this present, as indicating their good dispositions to me and my people. I shall always be ready to cultivate a good correspondence between the Creeks and my subjects, and shall be glad on any occasion to show you marks of my particular friendship."

While these Indians remained in England, nothing was neglected that would impress them with just notions of the greatness and power of the British nation. They were allowed, during their sojourn in the country, twenty pounds a week by the government. They were feasted magnificently by the nobility; and when they returned to their own country, it was computed that they carried with them presents to the value of four hundred pounds sterling.

After staying four months they embarked for Georgia, highly pleased with the generosity and grandeur of the English nation, and promising perpetual fidelity to its interests.

On his return, Tomochichi told his people that the Great Spirit had given the English wisdom, power, and riches; so that they wanted nothing. He had given the Indians great extent of territories, yet they wanted every thing. He exerted his influence in prevailing on the Creeks to resign such lands to the English as were of no use to themselves, and to allow them to settle among them, that they might be supplied with useful articles for cultivation and the necessaries of life. He told them further, that the English would trade with them fairly; that they were brethren and friends, would protect them against danger, and go to war with them against their enemies.

Notwithstanding the enthusiastic praise which some of the settlers had bestowed upon the climate of Georgia, its fertility, salubrity, and the almost Arcadian life of those who had emigrated thither, it was soon found to be less healthy and productive than the imaginative had supposed. The colonists, too, partly owing to the absence of Oglethorpe, were neither happy nor prosperous.

When the governor sailed for England in April, 1734, he delegated his authority, mainly, to one Thomas Causton. Other magistrates were, indeed, associated with him, but, as Causton had sole charge of the public stores, they were dependent upon him for subsistence, and, consequently, entirely under his control.

This man, who was of low origin, soon became intoxicated with the powers vested in him. He grew proud, haughty, and cruel; assumed a sort of gubernatorial state; compelled eight freeholders, with an officer, to attend at the door of the court-house when it was in session, with their guns and bayonets, ordering them to rest their firelocks as soon as he appeared. He bullied the jurors, and threatened with the jail, stocks, and whipping-post, all who dared to oppose his arbitrary proceedings.

Among the victims of this tyrannical conduct was Captain Joseph Watson. He brought a charge against this militia officer of stirring up animosities in the minds of the Indians. Watson was indicted, and Causton appeared against him in the triple character of witness, prosecutor, and judge. The jury returned twice without finding the prisoner guilty of any crime, except that of using certain unguarded expressions. Causton commanded the jury to return, find him guilty of lunacy, and recommend him to the mercy of the court. They did so: Causton immediately ordered him to prison, and, without passing any sentence, confined him there for three years.

In December, 1734, Mr. Gordon was sent over by the trustees as chief magistrate, but old Causton's cunning soon devised an expedient to rid him of his adversary. Gordon was refused either money or provisions from the public store, and this refusal rendering him incapable of supporting himself and family, he was obliged, after a stay of six weeks, to return to England. After Gordon's resignation, two others were appointed; but the first died soon afterward, and the second soon became a pliant tool in the hands of Causton; so that the latter was eventually reinstated in his authority, and became as absolute as ever.

But the colony flourished no longer. The system of rules framed by the trustees was found to be but little adapted to the circumstances and situation of the poor settlers. The principal part of the people had been idlers and outcasts at home, and it was found impossible to make industrious farmers of them abroad. The tenure by which they held their lands offered no inducements to any extraordinary exertion, as, in default of male heirs, the lands reverted to the trustees at the death of the occupant. The restrictions placed upon the Indian trade injured Georgia, while it benefited Carolina, where the trade was carried on unshackled by conditions. In Carolina, too, the people could buy as many negroes as they pleased, possess by a fee-simple title several hundred acres of land, and choose it from the best that was vacant.

These comparisons between the two conditions

of provinces adjoining each other soon rendered the Georgians dissatisfied, and tempted many to cross the Savannah River and take up land under the more favourable auspices of Carolina.

In the year 1735, the British government having appropriated large sums of money to the settlement of Georgia, and deeming its rapid increase in population to be of the utmost importance to the other colonies, became more vigorous in its efforts.

Finding that the poorer classes, who formed the first settlers, were as idle and useless abroad as they had previously been at home, the trustees now sought for a hardy, bold, industrious race of men, accustomed to rural pursuits. Turning their eyes to Germany and Scotland, they resolved to send over a number of men from both those countries, to strengthen the infant colony.

A number of Highlanders immediately accepted the proposals, and were transported to Georgia. They were settled on the Alatamaha, where they built a town and called it New Inverness. It is at present known by the name of Darien. About the same time, one hundred and seventy Germans embarked with Oglethorpe, and joined their countrymen at Ebenezer. Thus in the space of three years, Georgia received six hundred inhabitants, one-third of whom were Germans.

Oglethorpe arrived in Georgia the 5th of February, 1736, bringing with him a number of guns for the forts and batteries already erected, or yet to be built at Savannah, Frederica, Augusta, and other places.

The town of Augusta, now to be garrisoned, had been laid off and partially settled the year previous. Several warehouses were already built, and furnished with goods suitable for the Indian trade. Boats, constructed by the inhabitants, and calculated to carry about ten thousand weight of peltry, made four or five voyages to Charleston annually. Augusta soon became a general resort for the Indian traders in the spring, where they purchased annually nearly two thousand pack-horse loads of peltry. It was estimated that six hundred white persons were engaged in this trade.

The celebrated John Wesley accompanied Oglethorpe to Georgia, with the intention of acting as a missionary among the Indians, as well as preaching to the colonists. Before he left England, Wesley and his followers were distinguished by a more than common strictness of religious life. They received the sacrament of the Lord's supper every week; observed all the fasts of the church; visited the prisons; rose at four o'clock in the morning, and refrained from all amusements. From the exact manner in which they disposed of every hour, they acquired the appellation of Methodists, by which title their followers have ever since been denominated.

Wesley soon gained a number of proselytes;

but, in doing so, was unfortunate in creating unpleasant divisions among the people. His enemies charged him with requiring from his converts too much of their time to attend prayer-meetings and sermons, fixed at improper hours, thus seriously interfering with their industrial pursuits. Other and more serious allegations were made; but we may justly conclude, from his subsequent irreproachable life, that they were either false, or exceedingly broad exaggerations of the truth. Finding himself involved, through the malice of ill-disposed persons, in difficulties of a mortifying nature, he abruptly left the province, and never afterward returned.

CHAPTER IV.

Oglethorpe makes a treaty with the Governor of East Florida —Confers with a commissioner from Havana—Embarks for England—Revival of discontents among the colonists—They petition the trustees for fee-simple titles, and the use of slaves—Counter-petition from the Germans and Scotch—The true condition of the settlers stated.

The presence of Oglethorpe in February, 1736, soon produced a good effect in allaying the internal dissensions of the colony, and strengthening it against the threatened hostility of the Spaniards. Finding that the Georgians were gradually acquiring ability to cope with the forces stationed at St. Augustine, the governor of that place, though still regarding his neighbours with a jealous eye, thought it expedient to enter into a negotiation with the English colony.

The terms upon which the treaty was concluded were just and reasonable to both the contracting parties. But it soon appeared that the Spanish ministry at home were far from being desirous that a fair understanding should be established between the two colonies. Their object was to compel the British government to relinquish the design of settling the colony of Georgia. Their ambassador at the court of London was instructed to present a memorial to the Duke of Newcastle, claiming it as indisputable that the colony of Georgia was settled upon his master's dominions. No plainer proof was needed to show that the Spaniards were determined, if possible, to compel the crown of Great Britain to surrender this settlement. This was soon made more clearly apparent.

In the course of the year, Oglethorpe was notified by a message from the governor of St. Augustine, that a Spanish commissioner from Havana had arrived in Florida to make certain demands of him, and would meet him at Frederica for that purpose. At the same time information was obtained that three companies of infantry had been landed with the commissioner at St. Augustine.

A few days afterward, Oglethorpe held a conference with the commissioner in Jekyl Sound. The latter demanded that the English should evacuate, without loss of time, all the territories to the southward of St. Helena Sound, as they belonged to the King of Spain, who was determined to maintain his right to them. Oglethorpe endeavoured to argue the matter; but as the demand continued positive and peremptory, the conference broke up without coming to any agreement.

Apprehensive of danger, Oglethorpe embarked immediately and sailed for England, for the purpose of obtaining a sufficient force to meet the enemy in case the colony should be invaded. On his arrival, he found the trustees disposed to suspend further proceedings, as war had not yet been formally declared between the two nations.

At length, late in the year 1737, the danger to the colony was found to be growing imminent. On the 10th of August, the trustees petitioned that the military strength of Georgia might be increased to an extent sufficient to protect the province from the additional forces thrown into Florida by the Spaniards.

On the 25th of the same month, Oglethorpe was appointed a colonel, with the rank of general, and commander-in-chief of the forces in South Carolina and Georgia; with orders to raise a regiment with all possible expedition for the protection of the frontiers of the colonies. This regiment reached Georgia in September, 1738.

During Oglethorpe's absence, the discontent of the people had ripened into a settled aversion to their condition. They discovered that their constitutions would not bear the cultivation of the swamp lands; and that the pine lands were unproductive. Instead of reaping the rich harvest of plenty, raising commodities for exportation, and rolling in wealth and affluence, as they had been taught to expect,—the labour of several years had not enabled them to provide a coarse, common subsistence for themselves and families. Under these discouragements, numbers of them withdrew to the Carolina side of the river, where the prospects of success were more promising.

Dispirited by a foresight of the depopulation of the colony, the magistrates joined the freeholders in and about Savannah, in drawing up a petition to the trustees, asking the latter to grant, as remedies for the grievances under which the settlers laboured, a fee-simple title to all lands held by them, and the use of negroes under proper limitations.

In this petition, the hardy, industrious Germans and Highlanders would not join. On the contrary, in counter-petitions, drawn up and presented to Oglethorpe soon after his arrival in 1738, while they were silent in regard to the restrictions under which their lands were held, they denounced in the strongest terms the introduction of slaves into the colony; the Scotch asserting that a white man could labour more usefully than the slave; and the Germans expressing themselves perfectly contented with their condition, while they denied emphatically the necessity of employing negroes in the culture of rice. The Highlanders and Germans both interceded for the introduction of more of their own countrymen, to assist them in their labours during the prevalence of peace, and strengthen them with their weapons in case they should be invaded.

In the German petition, they draw an excellent contrast between the land they had left and that of their adoption. It is well worthy of being preserved, as giving quite a picturesque glimpse of the habits of the period:

"Though it is here," they go on to say, "a hotter climate than our native country, yet it is not so extremely hot as we were told on our first arrival. Since we are used to the country, we find it tolerable, and for working people very convenient, setting themselves to work early in the morning till ten o'clock, and in the afternoon from three to sunset. Having business at home, we do it in our houses in the middle of the day, till the greatest heat is over. People in Germany are hindered by frost and snow in the winter, from doing any work in the fields and vineyards; but we have this preference, to do the most and heaviest work at such a time, preparing the ground sufficiently for planting in the spring. At first, when the ground has to be cleared of trees, bushes, and roots, and fenced in carefully, we undergo some hard labour; but it becomes easier and more pleasing when the hardest trial is over, and our plantations are better regulated."

It will be seen by the reader that Georgia contained two very different classes of men; one which laboured heartily, and was prosperous and contented; while the other charged the climate and soil with causing that deplorable condition of things which should have been ascribed to their own idleness and dissatisfaction.

Had the whole of the colonists consisted of such men as the Saltzburghers and the Highlanders, Georgia might have favourably compared with the most flourishing of her sister States, both in population and in wealth. But evil counsels prevailed. The idlers far outnumbered those who worked, and although the trustees stood out for a long time, slaves were eventually admitted, and the energies of the industrious whites correspondingly paralyzed.

On the one hand, it must be admitted that a portion of the settlers had just cause of complaint. The land about Savannah was granted indiscriminately. Some of the lots were rich and valuable, others poor. The farmer who was obliged to cultivate pine land could barely subsist by his labour; while the river and swamp land was so heavily clothed with timber, that it required twenty hands for one year to put forty acres in a good condition for cultivation. There is no doubt, also, that the air from the swamps generated intermittent and bilious fevers. The sea-breeze could not penetrate the thick forests sufficiently to agitate the air, which at some seasons is heavy and foggy, and at others clear, but close and suffocating.

CHAPTER V.

Difficulties between England and Spain still continue—Spanish encroachments—England declares war—Agents from St. Augustine deceive the Creeks—Oglethorpe's troubles—The trustees change the tenure of land in Georgia—Refuse to admit negroes or ardent spirits—Spanish perfidy—Conspiracy to murder Oglethorpe—His narrow escape—The ringleaders shot—Negro insurrection in Carolina quelled—Declaration of war—Oglethorpe projects an expedition to St. Augustine, which fails—Conduct of his enemies in Georgia and Carolina—Condition of Georgia in 1740.

SEVERAL years passed without England and Spain coming to an open rupture, yet there was not a good understanding between the two courts, either as regarded the privileges of navigation or the southern limits of Georgia. The British merchants claimed, by treaty, the privilege of cutting logwood in the Bay of Campeachy; and finding this tolerated by Spain, extended their claim to a traffic with the Spaniards, and supplied them with English manufactures.

To check this illicit trade, the Spaniards doubled their marine force on that station, and directed the seizure of all vessels carrying contraband commodities. At length, not only smugglers, but fair traders were searched and detained. This injustice produced remonstrances to the Spanish court, which were answered by evasive promises and vexatious delays.

In the mean time, considerable reinforcements were sent to the garrison at St. Augustine, and a surplus of arms, ammunition, and clothing, which were supposed to be intended for the Indians.

Georgia and Carolina now became seriously alarmed. The lieutenant-governor of the latter province despatched advice to England of the growing power of Spain in East Florida, and acquainted the trustees with the fact that such preparations were making there as evidently portended hostilities; and as the Spaniards pretended to have a claim to Georgia, there were strong grounds to believe that they would assert their claim by force of arms. The king resolved to maintain his rights and vindicate the honour of his crown. Instructions were despatched to the British ambassador at Madrid to demand, in absolute terms, a compensation for the injuries of trade. The Spanish government agreed to allow the demand, on condition of its claims upon the South Sea Company being deducted, and Oglethorpe's settlers recalled from Georgia.

These conditions were indignantly rejected by the court of Great Britain. The Spanish ambassador at London was informed that the King of England was determined on maintaining his right to every single foot of land within the province of Georgia; and that he must allow his subjects to make reprisals, since satisfaction for their losses in trade could be obtained in no other way.

The Hector and Blandford ships of war had been ordered to convey Oglethorpe's regiment to Georgia, where they arrived in September, 1738.

The general established his head-quarters on Jekyl and Cumberland Islands, to watch the motions of the enemy. During these preparations, Spanish agents from St. Augustine, knowing the attachment of the Creek Indians for Oglethorpe, went among them, and, impressing them with a belief that he was at St. Augustine, prevailed upon some of them, by promises of considerable presents, to visit him at that place.

Finding, on their arrival, that a deception had been practised upon them, they became highly offended. The Spanish governor, in order to cover the fraud, pretended that the general was sick on board of a ship in the harbour, and invited the chiefs to go there and see him. But the Indians, suspicious of some deep design, refused to go, rejected their presents and offers of alliance, and immediately left the place. When they reached their towns, they found an invitation from Oglethorpe to meet him at Frederica. They immediately repaired thither, and renewed, with an ardour increased by the conduct of the Spaniards, their former treaty of friendship and alliance.

But while thus watchful over the interests of the colony, Oglethorpe was continually harassed with unceasing complaints from the people in and around Savannah. Letters written in the boldest style, and couched in the most vigorous language, were addressed to him over the signature of "The Plain Dealer;" while petitions, numerously signed, were forwarded by the malcontents to the trustees in London. They were clamorous for rum, for the privilege of purchasing slaves, and for fee-simple titles to their lands.

Finding that the discontent and uneasiness among the settlers were not likely to be allayed until some favourable action was taken upon their petitions, the trustees met on the 15th of March, 1739, and removed the only real cause of complaint, by passing a resolution, that in default of male issue, any legal possessor of land might, by a deed in writing, or by his last will and testament, appoint his daughter as his successor, or any other male or female relation; with a proviso, that the successor should, in the proper court in Georgia, personally claim the lot granted or devised, within eighteen months after the decease of the grantor or devisor. This privilege was soon after extended to every legal possessor, who was empowered to appoint any other person to be his successor.

The petition for the introduction of negroes was at the same time rejected, out of consideration for the firm, but respectful remonstrances of the Scotch and German settlers.

All kinds of ardent spirits, however, in spite of prohibition, soon found their way, by secret channels, into the colony. So feeble or so imperfect were the exertions made to suppress their introduction, that Oglethorpe, while sitting in the apartments of respectable officers or settlers, would frequently observe them retire to an adjoining room to indulge privately in the use of the interdicted spirits, at the smell of which he would exclaim: "Wo to the liquor if it come to my sight!" That which he discovered was always thrown away.

The darling project of General Oglethorpe was to restrain the Spaniards to the south of St. John's; for which purpose he established a chain of forts from Augusta to the mouth of that river. But while he was thus preparing his colony for defence against the invasion of the enemy, a criminal scheme was concocted against him, which, had it been successful, would have involved the most dangerous consequences. Treason was discovered in the centre of his camp, and a deep-laid plot had been planned to assassinate him.

Two companies of his regiment had been drawn from Gibraltar, some of whom could speak the Spanish language. Detachments from these companies had been stationed on Cumberland Island, and the Spanish outposts on the other side could approach so near as to converse with them. One man of these companies had been in the Spanish service, and not only understood their language, but, being himself a Catholic, professed an aversion to the Protestant religion. The Spaniards found, through this villain, the means of corrupting the minds of several of the British soldiers, who united in forming a design to murder Oglethorpe, and then make their escape to St. Augustine.

Accordingly, the day was fixed. The soldiers who were concerned in the plot came up to the General, and made some extraordinary demands, as a pretext for executing their diabolical purpose. These, as they expected, being refused, at a signal previously concerted, one of them discharged his piece at the general, who was so near at the time, that the powder burned his face and singed his clothes, the ball passing harmlessly over his shoulder. Another conspirator then presented his piece and attempted to fire, but the powder only flashed in the pan; a third drew his hanger and attempted to stab him. The general, by this time, having drawn his sword, parried the thrust, and an officer, coming up, ran the ruffian through the body and killed him on the spot. The mutineers, discouraged by the failure of their efforts, attempted to escape by flight, but were caught and laid in irons. A court-martial was ordered to try the ringleaders of this desperate conspiracy, some of whom were found guilty and sentenced to be shot.

Another and more dreadful effort of Spanish policy was attempted to be practised about the same time in South Carolina. Emissaries had been sent from St. Augustine to Carolina, with a design to stir up an insurrection among the negroes, whose number amounted to forty thousand, while the entire white population of that province did not exceed more than five thousand.

This nefarious design was only partially successful. A number of negroes collected at Stono, hoisted their standard, and proclaimed open rebellion. They marched through the country, with drums beating and colours flying; plundered and burned several houses, and murdered men, women, and children. But for the circumstance of the English carrying their guns with them to church, an indiscriminate massacre of the whites must have ensued. Fortunately, the armed men from the church made a judicious attack upon the head-quarters of the negroes, and they were either killed or dispersed.

Oglethorpe, having been advised of the insurrection in the neighbouring province, redoubled his vigilance in Georgia, and seized all straggling negroes and Spaniards who were found passing through the colony.

In the mean time, matters were hastening to a rupture in Europe, and a war between England and Spain appeared to be inevitable. Plenipotentiaries met at Pardo in convention, but the conference terminated as before, unsatisfactorily to both parties. The spirit of the English people was now fully roused: hostile preparations were made; all the officers of the army and navy were ordered to their stations, and with the unanimous voice of the nation, war was declared against Spain, on the 23d of October, 1739.

Admiral Vernon was sent to take command of a squadron on the West India station, with orders to act offensively against the Spanish dominions in that quarter, so as to divide their force. General Oglethorpe was ordered to annoy the subjects of Spain in Florida, by every method in his power. Acting under these instructions, he projected an expedition against the Spanish settlement at St. Augustine, in which he was warmly seconded by the authorities of South Carolina. Owing to a combination of untoward circumstances, this expedition signally failed, and Oglethorpe returned to Frederica on the 10th of July, 1740.

His conduct during this short and unfortunate

campaign was bitterly censured, and maliciously criticised, by the news-mongers and pamphleteers of the province, by whom he was alternately charged with cowardice, despotism, cruelty, and bribery. That these charges were without the shadow of foundation in truth, the whole life of this amiable and energetic gentleman testified. Without any views to his own interests, his whole efforts were directed to the enlargement of the dominions of his country, the propagation of the Protestant religion, and providing for the wants and necessities of the indigent. He had voluntarily banished himself from the pleasures of a court, and exposed himself to the dangers of the ocean, in several perilous and tedious voyages. Instead of allowing himself the satisfaction which a plentiful fortune, powerful friends, and great merit entitled him to in England, he had inured himself to hardships and exposures, in common with the poor settlers; his food, boiled rice, mouldy bread, salt beef and pork; his bed the damp ground, and his covering the canopy of heaven.

The settlers of Georgia had not increased with that rapidity which had been anticipated by the trustees, nor was its condition by any means flourishing, considering the immense sums of money which had been expended. The number of colonists sent to Georgia, and supported at the expense of the trustees, was found, at the close of the eighth year, to be fifteen hundred and twenty-one, of whom six hundred and eighty-six were men capable of bearing arms. The amount expended in the settlement, up to the same period of time, were one hundred and twelve thousand pounds. Of this amount, ninety-four thousand pounds were appropriated by the British Parliament, and the balance raised by private contributions. Those who came at their own charges are not included in the above statement, nor is the number of them known.

CHAPTER VI.

Rev. George Whitefield arrives in Georgia—His piety and benevolence—His Orphan-house—Whitefield's character and life—His death.

The Rev. George Whitefield, who merits particular notice in the history of Georgia, arrived at Savannah in May, 1738. This celebrated field preacher was born in 1714, in Gloucester, England. At twelve years of age he was put to a grammar-school, and at sixteen he was admitted servitor in Pembroke College, Oxford, where he distinguished himself by the austerities of his devotion. At the age of twenty-one, the fame of his piety recommended him so effectually to Dr. Benson, Bishop of Gloucester, that he ordained him. Immediately after Mr. Whitefield's admission into the ministry, he applied himself with the most extraordinary and indefatigable zeal and industry to the duties of his calling, preaching daily in the prisons, fields, and open streets, wherever he thought there would be a likelihood of making religious impressions. Having at length made himself universally known in England, he applied to the trustees for establishing the colony of Georgia, for a grant of a tract of land near Savannah, with the benevolent intention of building an orphan-house, designed as an asylum for poor children, who were to be clothed and fed by charitable contributions, and educated in the knowledge and practice of Christianity. In his efforts for the propagation of religion, Whitefield several times crossed the Atlantic Ocean to convert the Americans, whom he addressed in such manner as if they had been all equally strangers to the privileges and benefits of religion, with the aborigines of the forest. However, his zeal never led him beyond the maritime parts of America, through which he travelled, spreading his faith among the most populous towns and villages. Wherever he went in America, as in Britain, he had multitudes of followers. When he first visited Charleston, Alexander Garden, who was an Episcopal clergyman in that place, took occasion to point out the pernicious tendency of Whitefield's doctrines and irregular manner of life. He represented him as a religious impostor or quack, who had an excellent way of setting off, disguising, and rendering palatable his poisonous tenets. On the other hand, Mr. Whitefield, who had been accustomed to stand reproach and face opposition, retorted in his own peculiar way. On one occasion, Alexander Garden, to keep his flock from going after this strange pastor, expatiated on these words of Scripture: "Those that have turned the world upside down are come hither also." Mr. Whitefield, with all the force of comic humour and wit for which he was distinguished, by way of reply enlarged upon these words: "Alexander the copper-smith hath done me much evil: the Lord reward him according to his works."

Mr. Whitefield commenced the building of his orphan-house in Georgia in 1740, on a sandy bluff near the sea-shore, on a tract of land granted to him for the purpose by the trustees; the house was built of wood, and was seventy feet by forty. To this house poor children were sent, to be supported partly by charity, and partly by the products of the land cultivated by negroes.

Mr. Whitefield took the healthiness of the place for granted, from its similarity of situation to that of Frederica, and having formed the project, he determined to persevere, priding himself on surmounting every obstacle and difficulty. He travelled through the British empire, setting forth the excellence of his design, and obtained from charitable people money, clothes, and books, to forward his undertaking and supply his poor orphans in Georgia. The house was finished, and furnished with an excellent library; but, owing most probably to the unhealthiness of the situation, the institution never flourished to the extent of his expectations and wishes, though a great sum of money was expended in bringing it to maturity.

The talents of Mr. Whitefield were extraordinary. His influence and weight at that day certainly made him one of the most useful men in America. He had many friends and admirers among men of the first influence and respectability, and followers from all classes. He was so popular in preaching, that his churches or places of religious resort were crowded a long time before he appeared. Often when he preached in a church, a line was extended outwards, there being no room to go in; and at the door pious persons were soliciting for leave "only to see his blessed face," though they could not hear him. Such were the respect, enthusiasm, and regard he had inspired, owing to his sincerity, faith, zeal, and truly great and extraordinary talents. It is related of the accomplished Lord Chesterfield, that he once observed, "Mr. Whitefield is the greatest orator I have ever heard, and I cannot conceive of a greater." His writings are said to afford no idea of his oratorical powers: his person, his delivery, his boldness, his zeal and sincerity of purpose in the propagation of the gospel, made him a truly wonderful man in the pulpit, while his printed sermons give the impression of only an indifferent preacher. It is not an easy task to delineate his character. He was in the British empire not unlike one of those strange and erratic meteors which appear now and then in the system of nature. He often lamented that in his youth he was gay and giddy; so fondly attached to the stage, that he frequently recited difficult pieces while he was at school, with such great applause, that Garrick observed of him that the stage had lost an ornament. Then he probably acquired those gestures, which he practised under his clerical robes with great success and advantage upon the feelings of his hearers.

After receiving his ordination in the Church of England, he refused submission to the regulations either of that or any other particular church, but became a preacher in churches, meeting-houses, halls, fields, in all places and to all denominations, without exception. Though not distinguished for his learning, he had a lively imagination, much humour, and had acquired a great knowledge of human nature and the customs of the world. He possessed a large share of humanity and benevolence; but frequently displayed an excessive warmth of temper when roused by opposition and contradiction. His reading was inconsiderable, but he had an extraordinary memory, and mankind being one of the great objects of his study, he could, when he pleased, raise the passions and excite the emotions of the human heart with admirable skill and fervour. By his affecting eloquence and address, he impressed on the minds of many, especially of the more soft and delicate sex, such a strong sense of sin and guilt as often plunged them into dejection and despair. While he was almost worshipped by the lower order, men of superior rank and erudition found him the polite gentleman, and the facetious and jocular companion. Though he loved good cheer, and frequented the houses of the rich and hospitable, yet he was an enemy to all manner of excess and intemperance. While his disposition to travel led him from place to place, his natural discernment enabled him to form correct opinions of the characters and manners of men, wherever he went. Though he gave a preference to no particular established church, yet good policy winked at all his eccentricities, as he everywhere supported the character of a steady friend to civil government. He had great talents for exciting the curiosity of the multitude, and his roving manner stamped a kind of novelty on his instructions. When exposed to the taunts of the irreligious scoffer and the ridicule of the flagitious, he remained firm to his purpose, and could retort upon his deriders with astonishing ease and dexterity, and render vice abashed under the lash of his satire and wit. In short, though he was said to have had many oddities, yet few will undertake to deny that religion in America was greatly indebted to the zeal, diligence, and oratory of this extraordinary man. After a long course of peregrination, his fortune increased as his fame extended among his followers, and he erected two very extensive buildings for public worship in London, under the name of tabernacles: one in Tottenham Court road, and the other at Moorfields, where, by the help of some assistants, he continued several years, attended by very crowded congregations. By being chaplain to the Countess-dowager of Huntingdon, he was also connected with two other religious meetings: one at Bath, and the other at Tunbridge, chiefly erected under that virtuous lady's patronage.

In America, which had engaged much of his attention, Mr. Whitefield was destined to close his eyes. He died at Newburyport, Massachusetts, in 1770. When the report of his decease reached the legislature of Georgia, honourable mention was made of him, and a sum of money was appropriated, with a unanimous voice, for bringing his remains to Georgia, to be interred at his orphan-house; but the inhabitants of Newburyport, being much attached to him when living, objected to the removal of his body, and the design was relinquished.

In a letter from Dr. Franklin to Dr. Jones, mentioning Mr. Whitefield, he says, "I cannot forbear expressing the pleasure it gives me to see an account of the respect paid to his memory by your assembly: I knew him intimately upwards of thirty years; his integrity, disinterestedness, and indefatigable zeal, in prosecuting every good work, *I have never seen equalled, I shall never see excelled.*"

CHAPTER VII.

Description of Frederica—Its fortifications—Zeal and energy of Oglethorpe—Descent of the Spaniards upon Georgia—Lukewarmness of the Carolinians—Indians and Highlanders assist Oglethorpe—Spanish fleet enter the harbour and land—The Spaniards defeated in three engagements—Oglethorpe's successful stratagem—The Spanish defeated at Bloody Marsh—The enemy retreats from Georgia—Spanish commander tried and disgraced—The provincial governors congratulate Oglethorpe—Charges brought against him by Colonel Cook—He is tried and acquitted—Cook disgraced—Civil government established.

FREDERICA, the head-quarters of General Oglethorpe, was settled in 1736, on the island of St. Simons, south of the Alatamaha, and on the west side of that island about the centre. It stands upon a high bluff, compared with the marshes in its front. The shore is washed by a fine river, which communicates with the Alatamaha, and enters the ocean through Jekyl Sound, at the south end of the island. The river forms a bay before the town, and is navigable for vessels of large burden. The town was defended by a pretty strong fort of tappy, and several eighteen-pounders were mounted on a ravelin in front, which commanded the river. The fort was surrounded by regular ramparts, had four bastions of earth, stockaded and turfed, and a palisaded ditch, which included the storehouses; two large and spacious buildings of brick and timber, with several pieces of ordnance mounted on the rampart. The town was also surrounded by a rampart, with flankers of the same thickness as that round the fort, in form of a pentagon, and a dry ditch. The whole circumference of the town was about a mile and a half.

The town had two gates, called the town and water posts; next to the latter was the guardhouse, under which was a prison handsomely built of brick.

At the north end the barracks were built of tappy, and near them the magazine. A road was opened to the southward, to the plantations of Captain Demere, Mr. Hawkins, and General Oglethorpe; the latter, at a little distance, resembled a neat little country village: farther on were several families of Saltzburghers. A lookout of rangers was kept at Bachelor's Bluff, on the main. A corporal's guard at Pike's Bluff on the north, and a canal was cut through the general's island to facilitate communication with Darien. Frederica was laid out with spacious streets, named after the officers, and margined with orange trees.

At the south point of the island was the little town of St. Simons; near it a small battery was built as a watch-tower to discover vessels at sea, and upon such discovery an alarm-gun was fired, and a horseman despatched to head-quarters about nine miles distant. In case an enemy appeared, the number of guns fired indicated the number of vessels.

Forts and batteries were also erected on the north end of Jekyl Island, (where a brewery was established to make beer for the troops,) on the north end of Cumberland Island, near St. Andrew's Sound, and at the mouth of St. John's River. A stronger proof cannot be given of General Oglethorpe's zeal and indefatigable industry, than that all these fortifications were erected in seven months.

The time was now advancing when these defences were to be found useful. The squadron of Admiral Vernon had, for some time, occupied so much the attention of the enemy in the West Indies, that none of the Spanish fleet could be spared to contest their supposed right to the southern portion of Georgia. But no sooner had the greatest part of the British fleet left those seas and returned to England, than the Spaniards commenced their preparations for a descent upon Oglethorpe's settlement.

Accordingly, two thousand troops, commanded by Don Antonio de Rodondo, embarked at Havana, and arrived about the first of May, 1742, at St. Augustine; but before they had reached their destination, they were discovered by the captain of an English cruiser, who notified Oglethorpe of the impending danger. The latter immediately sent intelligence to Governor Glen of South Carolina, requesting his military assistance with all possible expedition, and at the same time he despatched a sloop to the West Indies to acquaint Admiral Vernon with the expected invasion.

But though the Carolinians had found great advantage from the settlement of Georgia, and were equally interested with their neighbours in making a vigorous defence, they had but little confidence in Oglethorpe's abilities after his unsuccessful expedition against St. Augustine.

The inhabitants of Charleston declared against sending him any assistance. They determined to fortify their town and defend themselves upon their own ground, leaving Oglethorpe to stand or fall against a far superior force.

In the mean time, the general sent messages to his faithful Indian allies, who gathered to his assistance in the hour of danger.

Captain McIntosh's Highlanders, burning to revenge the loss of their companions who had been overwhelmed by the Spaniards at the recapture of Fort Moosa, marched from Darien and joined Oglethorpe on the first intimation of the enemy's approach. With these, and his regiment at Frederica, the general determined to stand his ground, still hoping for reinforcements from Carolina, and expecting their arrival every hour.

On the 21st of June, nine sail of Spanish vessels came into Amelia Sound, but were repulsed by a brisk cannonade from Fort William.

When Oglethorpe was advised of this attack, he resolved to support the fortifications on Cumberland, and set out with a detachment on board of his boats. He sent Captain Horton with his company of grenadiers in front, and was himself obliged to fight his way, in two boats, through fourteen sail of Spanish vessels, which endeavoured to intercept him in St. Andrew's Sound. Owing to the cowardice of Lieutenant Tolson, who commanded the boat of the greatest strength, and was afraid to follow the general, fears were entertained for the safety of the latter, but he succeeded in returning the next day to St. Simons.

On the 28th of June, the Spanish fleet, amounting to thirty-six sail, and carrying upwards of five thousand men, under the command of Don Manuel Monteano, came to anchor off St. Simon's

Bar, where they remained until the 5th of July, sounding the channel. After finding a depth of water sufficient to float the ships, they came in on the flood-tide. They were received with a brisk fire from the batteries and the vessel. All the attempts of the Spaniards to board the ships in the harbour were repulsed with considerable loss. In this engagement, which lasted upwards of three hours, the enemy lost seventeen killed and ten wounded.

The fleet anchored about a mile above Oglethorpe's works, on the south end of the island, hoisted a red flag at the mizzen topmast head of the largest ship, landed their forces upon the island, and erected a battery, on which twenty eighteen-pounders were mounted.

Among their land forces, they had a fine regiment of artillery, under the command of Don Antonio de Rodondo, and a regiment of negroes. The negro commanders were clothed in lace, bore the same rank with the white officers, and with equal freedom and familiarity, walked and conversed with the commander-in-chief. When Oglethorpe found that his batteries at St. Simon's had become useless, he spiked the guns, destroyed the stores, and fell back upon his head-quarters at Frederica. So great was the disparity of the opposing forces, that he plainly saw his only hope of safety lay in acting upon the defensive. He kept scouting parties in every direction, to watch and annoy the enemy, while his main body made the fortifications as strong as circumstances would permit. His little army did not exceed seven hundred men. To animate them with a spirit of perseverance, he exposed himself to the same hardships and fatigues as were experienced by the common soldiers.

In the mean time, the Spaniards had made several attempts to pierce the woods, with a view to attack the fort, but met with such opposition from the deep morasses and dark thickets, defended by the Indians and Highlanders, that every effort failed with considerable loss.

On the 7th of July, the general was warned that a body of the enemy had approached within two miles of Frederica; he ordered four platoons of the regiment to follow him immediately, and marched with some rangers, Highlanders, and Indians, who were then under arms, and attacked and defeated the enemy, who lost one hundred and twenty-nine men in killed and prisoners. After heading the pursuit two miles, Oglethorpe halted until a reinforcement came up. He posted them with the Highlanders in a wood, with a large savanna in front, over which the Spaniards must pass on their way to Frederica, and then hastened to the fort to have an additional force in readiness, in case of emergency. By the time this arrangement was completed, three hundred of the enemy's best troops attacked the party he had left. Oglethorpe hurried to their relief, rallied three platoons which had retreated in disorder, and led them to the assistance of the gallant Highlanders, and the only platoon which had nobly remained firm. When he reached them the conflict was over, and the enemy in retreat. In this action, Don Antonio de Barba was mortally wounded, and several of the enemy killed and taken. In these two actions and the previous skirmishes, the Spaniards acknowledged a loss of two hundred and sixty-nine men.

On the 12th, an English prisoner escaped from the Spaniards, and brought advice to Oglethorpe of a difference subsisting between the troops from Cuba and those from St. Augustine; and that in consequence of this misunderstanding, they encamped in separate places. Oglethorpe instantly decided to attempt a surprise upon one of the encampments. With the advantage of his knowledge of the woods, he marched out in the night, with three hundred regular troops, the Highland company, rangers, and Indians. Having advanced within two miles of the enemy's camp, he halted, and set forward with a small party to reconnoitre their position. While most desirous of concealing his approach, a Frenchman from his party fired his musket, deserted to the enemy, and gave the alarm. Oglethorpe, finding his design thus defeated, thought it prudent to return to Frederica. Apprehensive that the traitor would discover his weakness to the enemy, he resorted to a stratagem, with the hope of shaking the confidence of the Spaniards in the deserter's story. For this purpose he wrote a letter, and addressed it to the Frenchman, in which he desired him to acquaint the Spaniards of the defenceless condition of Frederica, and how easy and practicable it would be to cut him and his small garrison to pieces. He requested the deserter to use every art in urging them forward to an attack, and to assure them of success. If he could not prevail upon them to make the attempt, he was to use every influential argument to detain them two or three days longer upon the island, as within that time he (Oglethorpe) would receive a reinforcement of two thousand land forces, and six British ships of war. He closed this letter by cautioning the renegade not to subject himself to suspicion, reminding him of the great reward he was to receive in the event of success attending the plan, and urging the necessity of profound silence respecting Admiral Vernon's intentions against St. Augustine. This letter was given by Oglethorpe to one of the Spanish prisoners, who, for the sake of liberty and a small reward, promised to deliver it to the French deserter privately, and conceal the circumstance from every other person. With these injunctions, the soldier was liberated, and, as Oglethorpe wished and expected, the letter was delivered to the Spanish commander-in-chief.

The conjectures and speculations occasioned by this letter were various; and the Spanish commandant was not a little perplexed to know what inference he ought to draw from it.

In the first place, he ordered the supposed spy to be placed in irons to prevent his escape, and then called a council of war to consider what was most proper to be done, in consequence of intelligence so puzzling and alarming. Some officers were of opinion that the letter was intended as a deception to prevent them from attacking Frederica; others thought that the circumstances mentioned in it wore such an appearance of truth, that there were good grounds to believe that the English general wished them to take place, and, therefore, gave their voice for consulting the safety of St. Augustine, and relinquishing a plan of conquest attended with so many difficulties, and putting to hazard the loss of both army and fleet, and perhaps the whole province of East Florida.

While the Spanish officers were employed in these embarrassing deliberations, three vessels of small force, which the Governor of Carolina had sent out to watch the motions of the enemy, appeared at some distance on the coast. This, corresponding with part of Oglethorpe's letter, induced the Spanish commander to give credit to its entire contents. It was, therefore, determined to attack Oglethorpe at his stronghold at Frederica before the expected reinforcement should arrive; and accordingly the whole Spanish army was put in motion.

Captain Noble Jones, with a detachment of regulars and Indians, being out on a scouting party, fell in with a small detachment of the enemy's advance, who were surprised and made prisoners, not deeming themselves so far in front of the main army. From these prisoners information was received that the whole Spanish army was advancing: this was immediately communicated by an Indian runner to the general, who detached Captain Dunbar with a company of grenadiers, to join the regulars and Indians, with orders to harass the enemy on their approach. These detachments, having formed a junction, observed at a distance the Spanish army on the march; and, taking a favourable position near a marsh, formed an ambuscade.

The enemy fortunately halted within a hundred paces of this position, stacked their arms, made fires, and were preparing their kettles for cooking, when a horse observed some of the party in ambuscade, and frightened at the uniform of the regulars, began to snort and gave the alarm. The Spaniards ran to their arms, but were shot down in great numbers by Oglethorpe's detachment, who continued invisible to the enemy. After repeated attempts to form, in which some of their principal officers fell, they fled with the utmost precipitation, leaving their camp equipage on the field, and never halted until they had got under cover of the guns of their battery and ships. General Oglethorpe had detached Major Horton with a reinforcement, who arrived only in time to join in the pursuit.

So complete was the surprise of the enemy, that many fled without their arms; others in a rapid retreat, discharged their muskets over their shoulders at their pursuers; and many were killed by the loaded arms which were left on the ground. Generally the Spaniards fired so much at random that the trees were pruned by the balls from their muskets. Their loss in killed, wounded, and prisoners, was estimated at five hundred. The loss in Oglethorpe's detachment was very inconsiderable. From the signal victory obtained over the enemy and the great slaughter among the Spanish troops, the scene of action just described has ever since been denominated the "*Bloody Marsh*." On the 14th, the Spaniards burned all the works and houses on the south end of St. Simon's and Jekyl Islands. They then sailed to the southward, with Oglethorpe following close on their rear. At daylight, twenty-eight sail of the Spanish line appeared off Fort William, which was commanded by Ensign Stuart. Fourteen of these vessels came into the harbour, and demanded a surrender of the garrison: Stuart replied, that it should not be surrendered, nor could it be taken. They attacked the works from their galleys and other vessels, and attempted to land, but were repulsed by a small party of rangers who had arrived by a forced march down the island. Stuart, with only sixty men, defended the fort with such bravery, that after an assault of three hours, the enemy discovered the approach of Oglethorpe, and put to sea with considerable loss. Two galleys were disabled and abandoned, and the Governor of St. Augustine proceeded with his troops by the inland passage. Ensign Stuart was rewarded, by promotion, for the bravery of his defence.

Thus was the province of Georgia delivered, when brought to the very brink of destruction by a formidable enemy. Don Manuel de Monteano had been fifteen days on the small island of St. Simon's, without gaining the least advantage over a handful of men; and in the several skirmishes, had lost a considerable number of his best troops; while Oglethorpe's loss was very inconsiderable.

When the Spanish troops returned to the Havana, their commander was arrested and tried by a court-martial, found guilty, and dismissed with disgrace, for his improper conduct on an expedition, the result of which proved so shameful and inglorious to the Spanish arms.

The Carolinians, surprised at a success so triumphant, achieved without their assistance, were still divided in their opinions respecting the military character of Oglethorpe. The more magnanimous among them acknowledged his signal services, and poured out the highest encomiums on his courage and military skill. There were others, however, who still continued to censure his conduct and detract from his merit. The authorities of South Carolina neither praised nor blamed. The Governors of New York, New Jersey, Pennsylvania, Maryland, Virginia, and North Carolina, congratulated the general in the warmest terms, and offered their humble thanks to the Supreme Governor of the universe for placing the fate of the southern colonies under the direction of one so well qualified for the important task.

But in the midst of his glorious achievements, envy and detraction busied themselves with defaming his honour and integrity. Lieutenant-colonel Cook exhibited nineteen charges against him, and named several officers and citizens in Georgia, who were to be summoned to prove his guilt. Indignant at the calumnious misrepresentations of his accuser, Oglethorpe embarked for England, and reached there in 1743. A general court-martial was ordered for his trial; several days were spent in examining the various articles of complaint lodged against him, and, after the most mature deliberation, the court adjudged the charges to be false, malicious, and groundless;

and his honourable acquittal was reported to the king. Lieutenant-colonel Cook was dismissed from the service in consequence, and declared incapable of serving his majesty in any military capacity whatever. Oglethorpe never afterward returned to Georgia; but upon all occasions, zealously exerted himself in behalf of its prosperity and improvement.

From its first settlement, the colony had been under a military government, executed by the general and such officers as he chose to appoint. But now the trustees thought proper to establish a sort of civil government, and committed the charge of it to a president and four councillors or assistants, who were to act agreeably to the instructions they should receive from the trustees; and to be accountable to them for their public conduct. Under these new regulations, William Stephens received the appointment of president.

CHAPTER VIII.

Slavery introduced—Daring scheme of Thomas Bosomworth—Malatche made Emperor of the Creeks—Signs a deed to Mary Bosomworth for the Indian reserved lands—Mary assumes the title of empress—She threatens destruction to the colony—March of the Creeks—The president prepares for defence—The Indians reach Savannah—Bosomworth and Mary seized and confined.

After the signal defeat of the Spaniards, the affairs of the province passed on without any important occurrences for several years. The cultivation of the vine and mulberry, being found unprofitable, was neglected, although the trustees made strenuous efforts to encourage the manufacture of silk by offers of bounty for its production.

After bearing with the unceasing complaints of the colonists for a long time, the restrictions placed upon the introduction of slaves were partially abandoned; and, although slavery had not yet been formally introduced into the province, the planters were tacitly permitted to hire negro servants in Carolina. Finding that this plan of evading the law succeeded, negroes were hired for a hundred years, or during life, and a sum equal to the value of the slave paid in advance;

the former owner in Carolina binding himself to exhibit his claim whenever the Georgian authorities should interfere. Finally, purchases were openly made in Savannah; some seizures took place, but the magistrates and the courts for the most part joined in evading the operation of the law. Matters had now reached a crisis. The trustees, finding that any further resistance to the introduction of slavery would endanger the peace and prosperity of the colony, yielded to the publicly expressed wishes of a majority of the people, and in the year 1747 all previous restraints upon the purchase of negroes were removed. In December of this year, a daring scheme of self-aggrandizement was devised by a clergyman named Bosomworth, which came very nearly involving the destruction of the whole province.

It will be recollected that at the first settlement of the colony, Oglethorpe had employed a half-breed woman, called Mary Musgrove, as an interpreter between himself and the Creeks. By the generosity of Oglethorpe, who had allowed her a liberal salary for her services, she obtained great influence over the minds of the Indians. After the death of her first husband, Bosomworth, who had been a chaplain in Oglethorpe's regiment, married this woman, and taking advantage of the respect in which she was held by the neighbouring tribes, conceived a plan of acquiring, through her means, a fortune equal to any in America.

An Indian king, by the name of Malatche, of an age and standing in the Creek nation well suited to Bosomworth's purpose, was present at Frederica with sixteen others, who called themselves kings and chiefs of the different towns. While at Frederica, Bosomworth suggested to Malatche the idea of having himself crowned by his companions. Accordingly, a paper was drawn up, acknowledging Malatche Opiya Meco to be the rightful natural prince and emperor of the dominions of the Creek nation; vesting him with power to declare war, make laws, frame treaties, convey lands, and transact all affairs relating to the nation; the chiefs binding themselves, on the part of their several towns, to abide by and fulfil all his contracts and engagements.

This paper having been duly signed and witnessed, Bosomworth obtained a deed in the name of Mary, his wife, from Malatche for all the islands and lands reserved by the Indians in their first treaty with Oglethorpe.

For two years after the making of this deed, Bosomworth remained silently waiting an opportunity to profit by it. In 1749, he determined that his wife should assert her claim to the Indian reservations of the islands of Sapelo, Ossabaw, and St. Catharine's. To render this claim still stronger, he encouraged his wife into the pretence of being the eldest sister of Malatche, and of having descended in a maternal line from an Indian king, who held from nature the whole territory of the Creek.

Accordingly, Mary assumed the title of an independent empress, and disavowed all allegiance or subjection to the King of Great Britain, otherwise than by way of treaty and alliance. She summoned a meeting of all the Creeks, to whom she set forth the justice of her claim, and the great injury they had sustained by the loss of their territories, and urged them to a defence of their rights by force of arms.

The Indians, thus artfully addressed, rose up, and pledged themselves, to a man, to stand by her to the last drop of their blood, in defence of her royal person and their lands. Thus supported by the whole force of the tribe, Queen Mary, escorted by a large body of her savage subjects, set out for Savannah, to demand from the president and council a formal acknowledgment of her rights in the province.

President Stephens and his council, alarmed at her high pretensions and bold threats, and sensible of her influence with the Indians, from her having been made a woman of consequence as an interpreter, were not a little embarrassed as to what steps to take for the public safety. They thought it best to use soft and healing measures until an opportunity might offer of privately laying hold of her and shipping her off to England.

In the mean time, the militia were ordered to hold themselves in readiness to march to Savannah, at the shortest notice. The town was put in the best possible state of defence, but its whole force amounted to only one hundred and seventy men able to bear arms. A message was sent to Mary, while she was yet several miles distant from Savannah at the head of her mighty host, to know whether she was serious in such wild pretensions, and try the influence of persuasion to induce her to dismiss her followers and drop her audacious design; but finding her inflexible and resolute, the president resolved to put on a bold countenance, and receive the savages with firmness and resolution.

The militia were ordered under arms to overawe them as much as possible; and as the Indians entered the town, Captain Noble Jones, at the head of a troop of horse, stopped them, and demanded whether their visit was with hostile or friendly intentions; but receiving no satisfactory answer, he required them to ground their arms, declaring that he had orders not to suffer one armed Indian to set foot in the town, and that he was determined to enforce the orders at the risk of his own life and that of his troops.

The savages with great reluctance submitted; and, accordingly, Thomas Bosomworth, in his canonical robes, with his queen by his side, followed by the kings and chiefs according to rank, marched into the town on the 20th of July, making a most formidable appearance.

The inhabitants were struck with terror at the sight of this ferocious tribe of savages. When they advanced to the parade, they found the militia drawn up under arms to receive them, by whom they were saluted with fifteen cannon, and conducted to the president's house. Bosomworth being ordered to withdraw, the Indian chiefs in a friendly manner were required to declare their intention in paying this visit in so large a body, without being sent for by any person in authority. The warriors, as they had been instructed, answered that Mary was to speak for them, and that they would abide by whatever she said; that they had heard that she was to be sent like a captive over the great waters, and they were come to know on what account they were to lose their queen; that they intended no harm, and begged that their arms might be restored to them; and after consulting with Bosomworth and his wife, they would return and amicably settle all public affairs. To please them, their guns were accordingly returned, but strict orders were issued to allow them no ammunition, until the council should see more clearly into their dark designs.

On the day following, the Indians, having had some private conferences with Mary, were observed to march in a tumultuous manner through the streets, evidencing a hostile temper, and apparently determined on mischief. All the men being obliged to mount guard, the women and children were terrified and afraid to remain in the houses by themselves, expecting every moment to be murdered and scalped. During this confusion, a false rumour was circulated, that they had cut off President Stephens's head with a tomahawk, which so exasperated the inhabitants that it was with difficulty the officers could restrain the troops from firing upon the savages: perhaps the exercise of the greatest prudence was never more requisite to save the town from being deluged with blood. Orders were given to lay hold of Bosomworth, to whom it was insinuated that he was marked as the first victim of vengeance in case of extremities; and he was carried out of the way and closely confined, upon which Mary, his beloved queen, became outrageous and frantic, and threatened the thunder of her vengeance against the magistrates and the whole colony. She ordered all white persons to depart immediately from her territories, and at their peril to refuse; she cursed Oglethorpe and his fraudulent treaties, and furiously stamping her foot upon the earth, swore that the whole globe should know that the ground she stood upon was her own. To prevent any ascendency by bribes over the chiefs and warriors, she kept the leading men constantly under her eye, and would not suffer them to utter a sentence on public affairs, but in her presence.

The president, finding that no peaceable agreement could be made with the Indians while under the baleful influence of their pretended queen, privately laid hold of her, and put her with her husband in confinement. This step was found necessary, before any reasonable terms of negociation would be heard.

Having secured the royal family, who were unquestionably the promoters of the conspiracy, the president employed men acquainted with the Indian tongue to entertain the warriors in the most friendly and hospitable manner, and directed that explanations should be made to them of the wicked designs of Bosomworth and his wife. Accordingly a feast was prepared for all the chiefs and leading warriors, at which they were informed that Bosomworth had involved himself in debts which he was unable to pay, and that he wanted not only their lands, but a large share of the king's presents, which had been sent over for the chiefs and warriors; that his object was to satisfy his creditors in Carolina at their expense; that the king's presents were only intended for the Indians, as a compensation for their useful services and firm attachment to him during the war against their common enemy; and that the lands adjoining the town were reserved for them to encamp upon when they should come to visit their beloved friends in Savannah, and the three maritime islands to fish and hunt upon when they should come to bathe in the salt waters: that neither Mary nor her husband had any right to those lands, but that they were the common property of the whole nation: that the great King George had ordered the president to defend their right to them, and expected that all his subjects, both white and red, would live together like brethren, and that the great king would suffer no one to molest or injure them; and had ordered these words to be left on record, that they might not be forgotten by their descendants, when they were dead and gone.

This policy produced a temporary effect, and many of the chiefs, being convinced that Bosomworth had deceived them, declared they would no longer be governed by his advice: even Malatche, the leader of the lower Creeks, and the pretended relation of Mary, seemed satisfied, and was not a little pleased to hear that the king had sent them some valuable presents. Being asked why he acknowledged Mary as the empress of the great nation of the Creeks, and resigned his power and possessions to a despicable old woman, while he was universally recognised as the great chief of the nation, and that too at the very time when the president and council were to give him many rich clothes and medals for his services,—he replied, that the whole nation acknowledged her as their queen, and none could distribute the royal presents but herself, or one of her family, as had been done heretofore.

The president, by this answer, saw more clearly the design of Bosomworth's family. To lessen their influence and consequence, and show the Indians that he had power to divide the royal bounty among the chiefs, he determined to take the task upon himself, and immediately dismiss them, on account of the growing expenses of the colony, and the hardships the people underwent in keeping guard night and day for the defence of the town.

CHAPTER IX.

Fickleness of Malatche—His speech—The president's reply—Bosomworth and Mary threaten vengeance against the colony—The Indians prevailed on to return home—Bosomworth and Mary released—Bosomworth reasserts his claims by a suit at law—Decision of the English Courts—Another suit instituted.

In the mean time, Malatche, whom the Indians compared to the wind, because of his fickle and variable temper, having at his own request obtained admission to Bosomworth and his wife, was again drawn over to support their chimerical claims. While the Indians were gathered together to receive their respective shares of the royal bounty, he stood up in the midst of them with a frowning countenance, and in violent agitation delivered a speech fraught with the most dangerous insinuations and threats. He declared that Mary possessed the country before General Oglethorpe; that all the lands belonged to her as queen and head of the Creeks; that it was by her consent that Englishmen were at first permitted to settle on them; that they still held the land as her tenants at will; that her words were the voice of the whole nation, consisting of three thousand warriors, every man of whom would raise the hatchet in defence of her rightful claim. Then pulling a paper out of his pocket, he delivered it to the president in confirmation of what he had said. This was evidently the production of Bosomworth, and served to discover in the plainest manner his ambitious views and wicked intrigues. The preamble was filled with the names of Indians, called kings of all the towns in the upper and lower Creeks, none of whom, however, were present except two. The substance of the paper corresponded with Malatche's speech, styling Mary the rightful princess of the whole nation, invested with full power and authority to settle and finally determine all public affairs and causes relative to land and other things, with King George and his men on both sides of the sea; and asserting that whatever should be done by her, they would abide by as if done by themselves. Bosomworth probably did not intend that this paper should have been shown, nor was Malatche aware of the consequences of putting it in the hands of the president.

After reading this paper in council, the members were struck with astonishment; and Malatche, perceiving their uneasiness, begged to have it again, declaring that he did not know it was a bad talk, and promising that he would immediately return it to the person from whom he had received it. To remove all impressions made on the minds of the Indians by Malatche's speech, and convince them of the deceitful and dangerous tendency of this confederacy, into which Bosomworth and his wife had betrayed them, had now become a matter of the highest consequence: happy was it for the province, that this, though difficult, was practicable. As ignorant savages were easily misled on the one side, it was practicable to convince them of their error on the other. Accordingly, having gathered the Indians together, the president determined to adopt a bold and decided tone, and addressed them with the following speech:—

"Friends and brothers:—When Mr. Oglethorpe and his people first arrived in Georgia, they found Mary, then the wife of John Musgrove, living in a small hut at Yamacraw; he had a license from the Governor of South Carolina to trade with the Indians; she then appeared to be in a poor ragged condition, and was neglected and despised by the Creeks; but General Oglethorpe, finding that she could speak both the English and Creek languages, employed her as an interpreter, richly clothed her, and made her a woman of the consequence she now appears; the people of Georgia always respected her until she married Bosomworth, but from that time she has proved a liar and a deceiver. In fact, she was no relation of Malatche, but the daughter of an Indian woman of no note, and a white man. General Oglethorpe did not treat with her for the lands of Georgia, for she had none; but with the old and wise leaders of the Creek nation, who voluntarily surrendered their territories to the king; the Indians at that time having much waste land, which was useless to themselves, parted with a share of it to their friends, and were glad that white people had settled among them to supply their wants. He told them that the present discontents of the Creeks had been artfully infused into them by Mary, at the instigation of her husband; that he demanded a third part of the royal bounty, in order to rob the naked Indians of their right; that he had quarrelled with the president and council of Georgia, for refusing to answer his exorbitant demands, and therefore had filled the heads of the Indians with wild fancies and groundless jealousies, in order to ferment mischief, and induce them to break their alliance with their best friends, who alone were able to supply their wants and defend them against their enemies."

Here the Indians desired him to stop, and put an end to the contest, declaring that their eyes were now opened, and that they saw through the insidious design of Bosomworth; but though he desired to break the chain of friendship, they were determined to hold it fast and disappoint him; and begged, therefore, that all might smoke the pipe of peace. Accordingly, pipes and rum were brought, and they joined hand in hand, drank and smoked together in friendship, every one wishing that their hearts might be united in like manner as their hands. The royal presents, except ammunition, with which it was judged imprudent to trust them, until they were some distance from town, were brought and distributed among them; the most disaffected and influential received the largest presents: even Malatche himself seemed fully satisfied with his share, and the savages in general, perceiving the poverty and insignificancy of Bosomworth and his wife, and their total inability to supply their wants, apparently determined to break off all connection with them.

While the president and council were congratulating themselves on the re-establishment of friendly intercourse with the Creeks, Mary, drunk with liquor, and disappointed in her royal views, rushed in among them like a fury, and told the president that these were her people, that he had no business with them, and that he should soon be convinced of it to his cost. The president calmly advised her to retire to her lodgings and forbear to poison the minds of the Indians, otherwise he would order her again into close confinement. Upon this, she turned about to Malatche in great rage, and repeated, with some ill-natured comments, what the president had said. Malatche started from his seat, laid hold of his arms, and, calling upon the rest to follow his example, dared any man to touch the queen.

The whole house was filled in a moment with tumult and uproar. Every Indian having his tomahawk in his hand, the president and council expected nothing but instant death. During this confusion, Captain Jones, who commanded the guard, very seasonably interposed, and ordered the Indians immediately to surrender their arms. Such courage was not the only requisite to overawe them; great prudence was, at the same time, necessary, to avoid coming to extremities. With reluctance the Indians submitted, and Mary was conveyed to a private room, where a guard was placed over her, and all further communication with the Indians denied to her during their stay in Savannah. Her husband was sent for, in order to reason with him and convince him of the folly of his chimerical pretensions, and of the dangerous consequences which might result from his persisting in them; but no sooner did he appear before the president and the council, than he became outrageously abusive, and in defiance of every argument which was used to persuade him to submission, he remained contumacious, and protested he would stand forth in vindication of his wife's right to the last extremity, and that the province of Georgia should soon feel the weight of her power and vengeance.

Such conduct justly merited a course which it would have been impolitic in the council to pursue; but finding that fair means were fruitless and ineffectual, they determined to remove him out of the way of the Indians until they were gone, and then humble him by force.

After having secured the two leaders, it only remained to persuade the Indians to leave the town and return to their homes. Captain Ellick, a young warrior, who had distinguished himself in discovering to his tribe the base intrigues of Bosomworth, being afraid to accompany Malatche and his followers, consulted his safety by setting out among the first. The rest followed him in different parties, and the inhabitants, tired out with constant duty, and harassed with frequent alarms, were at length happily relieved.

It affords a striking evidence of the weakness of the colonists, and their fear of Indian retaliation, when we relate, that after passing through this terrible ordeal, the provincial authorities did not dare to molest either Bosomworth or his wife. It is true, that the reasons given for their pardon were said to have been in consideration of the intercession of Adam Bosomworth, a brother of the culprit, and a letter from Bosomworth himself, acknowledging the title of his wife to be groundless, and craving forgiveness on the plea of her present remorse and past services to the province. But the real cause of their not being severely dealt with was, undoubtedly, a dread of the consequences that might ensue.

In 1751, the restless intriguer revived his claim. It was litigated in the English courts for many years, and at length partially decided in his favour; but one Levy claiming a moiety of the lands by previous purchase of Bosomworth, a new suit was instituted, which, from Levy dying not long after, has never been legally settled.

CHAPTER X.

Condition of the province—Hostile attitude of the Cherokees—Trustees resign their charter—Georgia formed into a royal government—Quarrel between the Virginians and Cherokees—Treachery of Occonostota—Captain Coytmore killed—Indian hostages massacred—The savages desolate the frontiers—Colonel Montgomery sent against them—Defeats them and burns all the lower towns—Returns to Fort Prince George—Enters the nation again—Bloody battle near Etchoe town—Returns to Fort Prince George—Siege and capitulation of Fort Loudon—Treachery of the savages—Attakullakulla rescues Captain Stewart—Hostilities encouraged by the French—Grant marches against the Indians, and defeats them—Treaty of peace concluded.

The condition of the province of Georgia in 1751 was indeed deplorable. Eighteen years had now passed off, and the colonists had not, in any one year, furnished subsistence enough for its own consumption. Commerce had barely commenced; numbers, in disgust at the unpromising state of things, had left the country, and settled in Carolina; the white servants fled from their masters and took refuge in Carolina, and the country was rapidly dwindling into insignificance.

In this enfeebled condition, the Cherokee Indians assumed a hostile attitude. At the first signal of alarm, a number of Quakers, who had settled, during the preceding winter, on a body of land west of Augusta, abandoned their plantations and fled the country. Other planters also sought protection in the towns, and the province was placed in the best state of defence which its weakened condition admitted. The difficulty, however, blew over for a time.

The trustees, finding that the province did not flourish under their patronage, and wearied out with the complaints and murmurs of the people, for whose benefit they had devoted so much time and expended so much money, resigned their charter on the 20th of June, 1752, and the province was formed into a royal government.

For two years after the resignation of the trustees, the province of Georgia remained in an unprotected condition. On the 1st of October, 1754, the king appointed John Reynolds, an officer in the navy, Governor of Georgia, and granted legislative powers similar to those of the other royal governments in America. Several years elapsed, however, before Georgia began to prosper.

During the year 1759, war between France and Great Britain having been previously declared, General Abercrombie, commanding the British forces in America, threatened the French stronghold on the Ohio, westward of Virginia. To assist in carrying out his designs, he invited the Cherokees to join him in the capture of Fort Duquesne. The French garrison fled to the south, and taking advantage of an unfortunate quarrel between the Virginians and Cherokees, were successful in detaching the latter from the British cause, and exciting them into a bloody and remorseless war against their former friends.

The occasion which gave rise to the feud was this. A number of Indians returning home through the back parts of Virginia, having lost their own horses in the expedition against Duquesne, caught such as came in their way; never imagining that they belonged to any individual in the province. The Virginians, resenting the injury, followed the savages, killed fourteen of them, and took several prisoners. The Cherokees, naturally indignant at such conduct from their allies, flew immediately to arms, and murdered and scalped a number of people on the frontiers.

Captain Coytmore, commanding Fort Prince George, on the bank of Savannah River, near the Cherokee town of Keowee, despatched messengers to the Governors of Georgia and South Carolina, warning them of the dangers which were threatening. Governor Lyttleton immediately hastened to the fort, with a body of militia, and succeeded in forming a treaty of peace with six of the chiefs on the 26th of December, 1759. By this treaty, thirty-two Indian warriors were left in the fort as hostages for the fulfilment of certain stipulated conditions. The small-pox breaking out in Lyttleton's camp, he was obliged to return to Charleston. He had scarcely reached the seat of his government, when war again broke out.

The Indians had contracted an invincible antipathy to Captain Coytmore, who commanded in the fort; the imprisonment of their chiefs had converted their desire for peace into the bitterest rage for war.

Occonostota, a chieftain of great influence, had become a most implacable and vindictive enemy: he collected a strong party of Cherokees, surrounded the fort, and compelled the garrison to keep within their works; but finding that he could make no impression on them, nor oblige the commander to surrender, he contrived the following stratagem for the relief of his countrymen, confined in it as hostages. As the underwood was well calculated for his purposes, he placed a party of savages in a dark canebrake by the river-side, and then sent an Indian woman whom he knew to be always welcome at the fort, to inform the commander that he had something of consequence to communicate to him, and would be glad to speak to him at the river-side. Captain Coytmore imprudently consented, and without any suspicion of danger, walked to the river, accompanied by Lieutenants Bell and Foster. Occonostota appeared on the opposite side, and told them that he was going to Charleston to procure the release of the hostages, and would be glad of a white man to accompany him as a safeguard. The better to cover his design, he had a bridle in his hand, and added that he would go and hunt for a horse. The captain replied, that he should have a guard, and wished that he might find a horse, as the journey was very long, and performing it on foot would be fatiguing and tedious: upon which the Indian turned quickly, swung the bridle round his head as a signal to the savages placed in ambush, who instantly fired upon the officers, shot the captain dead upon the spot, and wounded the other two. In consequence of this, orders were given to put the hostages in irons, to prevent any further danger from them; but, while the soldiers were attempting to execute these orders, the Indians stabbed the first man who laid hold of them, and wounded two more, upon which the garrison, exasperated to the highest degree, fell upon the unfortunate hostages and butchered them in a manner too shocking to relate.

There were few men in the Cherokee nation that did not lose a friend or relation by this massacre; and, therefore, with one voice all declared for war.

The consequences were dreadful. From the different towns, large parties of warriors took the field, and commenced an indiscriminate slaughter among the defenceless families upon the frontiers, ravaging and burning wherever they went.

In this extremity, application for immediate assistance was made to the commander of the British forces in New York, and to the Governors of North Carolina and Virginia.

Seven companies of rangers were raised to patrol the frontiers, and prevent the savages from penetrating farther down the settlements, and the best possible preparations made for chastising the enemy as soon as the regulars should arrive from New York.

In April, 1760, Colonel Montgomery landed in Carolina, with a battalion of Highlanders and four companies of Royal Scots. As the conquest of Canada was the grand object of this year's campaign in America, he had orders to strike a sudden blow for the relief of the southern provinces, and return to head-quarters at Albany without loss of time.

After having been joined at the Congarees by the military strength of South Carolina, he marched rapidly in the night with a party of his men to surprise the Indian town of Estatoe. On his way thither, he entered suddenly the town of Little Keowee, and put every Indian in it to the sword, sparing only the women and children. He next proceeded to Estatoe and burned it to ashes; but the savages, with the exception of a few, had already fled. Sugartown, and every other settlement eastward of the Blue Ridge, shared the same fate. In the lower towns, one hundred Indians were killed or taken prisoners, and the rest driven to seek for shelter in the mountains.

Having finished this business with the loss of only three or four men, he marched to the relief of Fort George, which had been invested for some time by the savages. Happily succeeding in his object, he despatched from thence messengers to the upper and lower Cherokee towns, offering to treat with them for peace. Finding the enemy still implacable, he determined to chastise them a little farther; but in order to reach the savages, he was now compelled to penetrate a wilderness of dark thickets, rugged paths, and dangerous passes.

On the 27th of June, when he had advanced within five miles of Etchoe, the nearest town of the middle settlements, he entered a low valley, covered so thick with brush that a soldier could scarcely see the length of his body, and in the middle of which there was a muddy river with steep clay banks. Through this dark place, where it was impossible for any number of men to act together, the army must necessarily march. Captain Morison, who commanded a company of rangers, was ordered to scour the thickets. They had scarcely entered it, when a number of savages sprang from their ambuscade, fired on them, killed the captain, and wounded several of his party; upon which the light grenadiers were ordered to advance and charge the enemy. The firing then became general, though the soldiers, for some time, could only discover the enemy by the report of their guns.

Montgomery, finding that the Indians were in large force, ordered the Royal Scots to advance between the savages and a rising ground on the right, while the Highlanders marched to the left, to support the light infantry and grenadiers. Undismayed by the war-whoops and horrible yells of the savages, the troops pressed forward. At length, the Indians gave way, and in their retreat, falling in with the Royal Scots, suffered severely. As soon as Montgomery saw that the enemy continued to retreat as his troops advanced, he gave orders for the line to face about and march directly for the town of Etchoe. The Indians immediately retreated behind the hill, and hastened to provide for the safety of their wives and children.

In this desperate battle, Montgomery had twenty men killed, and seventy-six wounded. The loss of the enemy was never ascertained.

This action, though it terminated in favour of the British, had so burdened them with wounded, that the commander judged it most prudent to return to Fort George. Accordingly, orders were given for a retreat, which was made with great regularity, although the enemy continued hovering around and annoying the troops whenever a favourable opportunity presented itself.

In the mean time, the distant garrison of Fort Loudon, consisting of two hundred men, was reduced to the dreadful alternative of perishing by hunger or submitting to the mercy of the enraged Cherokees. For a long time they had entertained hopes of being relieved by the Virginians; but the latter, foreseeing the difficulty of marching an army burdened with supplies, through a barren wilderness, where the passes and thickets were ambuscaded by the enemy, had given over all thoughts of the attempt. Driven to despair, the men threatened to leave the fort and die at once by the hands of the savages, rather than perish slowly by famine. In this extremity, a council of war was called, when it was finally agreed to surrender the fort to the Cherokees on the best terms that could be obtained. For this purpose, Captain Stewart, an officer much beloved by all the Indians who remained in the British interest, was sent to Chote, one of the principal towns in that neighbourhood, where he obtained terms of capitulation. One of the conditions assented to by the Indians was, that the garrison, with a sufficiency of arms and ammunition, should be permitted to march unmolested to Fort Prince George or Virginia, under the escort of a number of Indians, by whom they were to be supplied with provisions during their march.

Accordingly, the fort was given up on the 7th of August, 1760, and the garrison, accompanied by Occonostota and several other Indians, set out on their way to Fort Prince George. At the first halting-place for the night their treacherous escort deserted them, and early next morning they were attacked by a large body of warriors, who killed Captain Demere, the commander, the other officers, and twenty-six men, and took the remainder as prisoners back to Fort Loudon.

Among those who deplored this shameful breach of faith, was a noble-hearted chief by the name of Attakullakulla. No sooner did he learn that his friend Captain Stewart had escaped death, than he hastened to the fort and purchased him from his Indian captor, giving the latter his rifle, his clothes, and every thing he could command. Soon after this, he learned from Captain Stewart that Occonostota, meditating an attempt upon Fort Prince George, had determined that Stewart and a party of his companions should assist in the reduction of the fort; and that in the event of Stewart's refusal to act against his own countrymen, the prisoners should be burned one after another before his face.

Upon hearing this savage resolve of Occonostota, the aged Attakullakulla resolved to save the life of Captain Stewart at once, and at every hazard. Accordingly, he signified to his people that he intended to go hunting for a few days, and carry his prisoner with him to eat venison: at the same time Captain Stewart went among his soldiers, and told them that they could never expect to be ransomed by their government if they gave the smallest assistance to the Indians against Fort Prince George.

Having settled all matters, they set out on their journey, accompanied by the old warrior's wife, his brother and two soldiers, who were the only persons of the garrison that knew how to convey great guns through the woods. For provisions they depended upon what they might kill by the way. The distance to the frontier settlements was great, and the utmost expedition necessary to prevent any surprise from Indians pursuing them. Nine days and nights did they travel through a dreary wilderness, shaping their course by the sun and moon for Virginia, and traversing many hills, valleys, and paths that had never been travelled before but by savages and wild beasts. On the tenth they arrived at Holston's river, where they fortunately fell in with a party of three hundred men sent out by Colonel Bird for the relief of such soldiers as might make their escape that way from Fort Loudon. On the fourteenth day the captain reached Colonel Bird's camp, on the frontiers of Virginia, where having loaded his faithful friend and his party with presents and provisions, he sent him back to protect the unhappy prisoners until they should be ransomed, and to exert his influence among the Cherokees for the restoration of peace.

Having glutted their vengeance, the Cherokees would have been disposed to listen to terms of accommodation, had not several French emissaries crept in among the upper towns, and fomented their ill-humour against the southern provinces.

Louis Latinac, a French officer, was among these, and proved an indefatigable instigator to mischief. He furnished the Indians with arms and ammunition, and urged them to war, persuading them that the English had nothing less in view than the extermination of their race from the face of the earth. At a great meeting of the nation, he pulled out his hatchet, and sticking it into a log, cried out, "Who is the man that will take this up for the King of France?" Saloue, a young warrior of Estatoe, laid hold of it and cried out, "I am for war! The spirits of our brothers who have been slain still call upon us to revenge their death—he is no better than a woman who refuses to follow me." Many others seized the tomahawk yet dyed with the stains of innocent blood, their hearts burning with ardour for the field.

Canada being now reduced, General Amherst, responding to the repeated calls from the south for assistance, despatched Colonel Grant to Charleston, with a force of regulars amply sufficient to meet the emergency. In the spring, Grant took the field with two thousand six hundred men, and on the 27th of May, 1761, arrived at Fort Prince George.

On the 7th of June, he marched from thence into the Cherokee country, carrying with him thirty days' provisions. On the 10th, various circumstances concurred to awaken suspicion, and orders were given for the first time to load and prepare for action, and the guards to march slowly forward, doubling their vigilance.

As they frequently spied Indians around them, all were convinced that they should that day have an engagement. At length, having advanced near the place where Colonel Montgomery was attacked the preceding year, the Indian allies in the vanguard, about eight in the morning, observed a large body of Cherokees posted upon a hill on the right flank of the army, and immediately gave the alarm. The savages rushed down and commenced a heavy fire upon the advanced guard, which being supported, the enemy was soon repulsed, and again formed upon the heights: under this hill the army was obliged to march a considerable distance.

On the left was a river, from the opposite bank of which a large number of Indians fired briskly on the troops as they advanced. Colonel Grant ordered a party to march up the hill and drive the enemy from the heights, while the line faced about and gave their whole charge to the Indians who annoyed them from the side of the river. The engagement became general, and the savages seemed determined obstinately to dispute the lower grounds, while those on the hill were dislodged only to return with redoubled ardour to the charge. The situation of the troops was in several respects unfavourable: fatigued by a tedious march in rainy weather; surrounded with woods, so that they could not discern the enemy; galled by the scattered fire of the savages, who when pressed always kept aloof, but rallied again and returned to the ground; no sooner did the army gain an advantage over them on one quarter, than they appeared in force on another.

While the attention of the commander was occupied in driving the enemy from their lurking-place on the river-side, the rear was attacked, and so vigorous an effort made to take the flour and cattle, that he was obliged to order a party back to the relief of the rear-guard. From eight o'clock in the morning until eleven, the savages continued to keep up an irregular and incessant fire, sometimes from one place and sometimes from another, while the woods resounded with the war-whoop, and hideous shouts and yells, to intimidate the troops. At length the Cherokees gave way, and being pursued for some time, scattered shots continued until about two o'clock, when the enemy disappeared.

The loss sustained by the enemy in this action was not accurately ascertained. Colonel Grant's loss was between fifty and sixty killed and wounded. Orders were given not to bury the slain, but to sink them in the river, to prevent their being dug up from their graves and scalped. The army then proceeded to Etchoe, a large Indian town, which they reached about midnight, and next day reduced to ashes. All the other towns in the middle settlement, fourteen in number, shared the same fate. The corn, cattle, and other stores of the enemy were likewise destroyed, and the savages, with their families, were driven to seek shelter and subsistence among the barren mountains.

After remaining thirty days in the heart of the Cherokee territories, Grant concluded to return to Fort Prince George, and await there, recruiting the strength of his men, until he saw whether the enemy were yet sufficiently humbled to sue for peace.

To represent the situation of the savages, when reduced by this severe correction, would be difficult. Even in time of peace, they were destitute of that foresight which, in a great measure, provides for future events; but in time of war, when their villages were destroyed, and their fields plundered, they were reduced to the extreme of want. Driven to barren mountains, the hunters being furnished with ammunition, might, indeed, obtain a scanty subsistence for themselves; but women, children, and old men, suffered greatly, when almost deprived of the means of supporting life.

A few days after Colonel Grant's arrival at Fort Prince George, Attakullakulla, attended by several chiefs, came to his camp and expressed a desire for peace. Severely had they suffered for breaking their alliance with the English, and giving ear to the deceitful promises of the French. Convinced at last of the weakness and perfidy of the latter, who were neither able to assist them in time of war, nor to supply their wants in time of peace, they resolved to renounce all connection with them forever: accordingly, terms of peace were drawn up and proposed, which were no less honourable to Colonel Grant than advantageous to the southern provinces.

The different articles being read and interpreted, Attakullakulla agreed to them all, excepting one, a cruel provision, by which it was demanded, that four Cherokee Indians should be delivered up to Colonel Grant at Fort Prince George to be put to death in the front of his camp, or four green scalps be brought to him within twelve days. Attakullakulla declared that he had no such authority from his nation, that he thought the stipulation unreasonable and unjust, and that he could not voluntarily grant it. Colonel Grant wisely withdrew this offensive article; after which peace was formally ratified, and their former friendship being renewed, all expressed a hope that it would last as long as the sun should shine and the rivers run.

10*

CHAPTER XI.

Wright appointed governor—Prosperity of Georgia—Emigration continues—Political aspect of the colony overclouded—Dr. Franklin appointed agent in England—The legislature define their rights and demand redress—Corresponding committees nominated—Georgia charged with lukewarmness—Defence of the same—Republican spirit manifested—Powder magazine in Savannah broken open and its contents secreted—Cannon spiked on the battery—Delegates appointed to the Congress at Philadelphia—Munitions of war seized—Georgia declares her independence—Governor Wright imprisoned—Escapes in the night—Troops ordered to be raised—Bill of credit issued—Nine merchant vessels burned or dismantled—Patriotism of the citizens of Savannah.

On the 30th of October, 1760, Sir James Wright was appointed Governor of Georgia, and under his auspices the colony soon began to flourish. By the peace which was soon after made with Spain, the boundaries were extended to the Mississippi on the west, and on the south to latitude 31° and the St. Mary's River. East and West Florida were also given up by Spain, and though of themselves but little more than a barren waste, formed an important acquisition to Georgia.

No province on the continent felt the happy effects of public security sooner than Georgia. The able and energetic exertions of the governor soon developed resources which had hitherto lain dormant. Commerce extended rapidly; agriculture flourished. The planters, having the strength of Africa to assist them, laboured with success, and the lands every year yielded greater and greater increase. Many emigrations now took place from Carolina, and settlements were made about Sunbury and the Alatamaha. The planters situated on the other side of the Savannah River found in the capital of Georgia an excellent market for their commodities; and, at length, the shipments of produce from the province to Europe equalled, in proportion to its population, those of its more powerful and opulent neighbours.

Nothing of any marked interest interfered with the progress of the colonies for several years. The brief but bloody wars of the Indian nations among themselves occasioned at times a temporary alarm among the colonists residing on the frontiers, but by a cautious policy on the part of the governors, and the watchfulness of the Indian agents, all real danger was for the most part averted.

Emigrants continued to flock into the country. In 1765, four additional parishes were laid off between the Alatamaha and the St. Mary's rivers. Within the space of ten years from 1763, the exports of the province increased from twenty-seven thousand, to one hundred and twenty-one thousand six hundred pounds sterling. The number of negroes in 1773 was estimated at fourteen thousand. The political aspect of the colony was, however, far from being unclouded.

When the offensive stamp act of the 22d of March, 1765, received the royal assent, it produced a tumult in every province in America. It was no sooner repealed than it was succeeded by the revival of another act equally offensive, for quartering his majesty's troops on the inhabitants, and supplying them in their quarters; so that wherever they were stationed, no expense should be brought upon the crown. These and similar grievances occasioned a spirit of discontent, which the systematic neglect of all petitions for relief in no wise tended to allay.

In 1768, Doctor Franklin was recognised as the agent of Georgia in England, but his subsequent letters afforded only faint hopes of adequate relief.

The people now determined to speak out for themselves. At a meeting of the legislature in the province of Georgia, in February, 1770, they took into consideration the authority by which the parliament of Great Britain claimed, to bind the people of America by statutes in all cases; their imposition of taxes on the Americans under various pretences, but in truth for the purpose of raising a revenue; their establishing of a board of commissioners with unconstitutional powers, and extending the jurisdiction of courts of admiralty, not only for collecting the duties imposed by these acts, but for trial of causes arising within the body of a county. Standing armies were also kept up in America in time of profound peace; and by the revival of a statute made in the thirty-fifth year of Henry the Eighth, colonists might be transported to England, and tried there upon accusations for treason, or misprisions or concealments of treason, committed in the colonies; and by a late statute, such trials had been directed in cases therein mentioned. Moreover, the governor had frequently taken upon himself to dissolve the assemblies, contrary to the rights of the people, when they attempted to deliberate on grievances, in conformity to the custom of their ancestors, for ascertaining and vindicating their rights and liberties.

In consequence of these infringements, the House of Assembly, after defining their rights by the laws of nature, the principles of the English constitution, and the several charters or compacts, resolved, "that the exercise of legislative power in any colony by a council appointed during pleasure by the crown, may prove dangerous and destructive to the freedom of American legislation: all and each of which, the commons of Georgia, in general assembly met, do claim, demand, and insist on, as their indubitable rights and liberties, which cannot be legally taken from them, altered, or abridged by any power whatever, without their consent."

After detailing a list of the acts of Parliament which the members of the assembly considered as infringing upon and violating the rights of the colonies, they demanded the repeal of the same, and closed their deliberations by resolving "that ———, ———, be deputies to represent this province in the intended American continental congress, proposed to be held at the city of Philadelphia on the 10th of May next, or at any other place or time as may hereafter be agreed on by the said congress."

Letters from Doctor Franklin, during the course of this year, held out some feeble prospects that, gradually, every obstruction to that cordial amity so necessary to the welfare of the whole empire would be removed. But the arbitrary conduct of the provincial governors and other crown officers, and the blind obstinacy of the British ministry, prevented such pleasing anticipations from being realized.

In 1772, corresponding committees were nominated in all the colonies, and the crisis approached when it was necessary for them to decide whether they would submit to taxation by the British Parliament, or make a firm stand for the support of their principles.

During the intervening period, Georgia had been charged with lukewarmness in the cause of freedom by her sister provinces; but though there appeared to be some grounds for the obnoxious accusation, her course was justified by all impartial minds, when the difficulties of her position came to be better understood.

Her situation was a peculiar one. Governor Wright, with that political forecast which led him to anticipate the subsequent events, had secured to the interest of the king as many men of wealth, talents, and influence, as he could find willing to hold offices. John Stuart, superintendant of Indian affairs, had taken the same precaution in the selection of his agents with the different tribes of Indians. Many of the most wealthy inhabitants foresaw that their pecuniary ruin would be the inevitable consequence of participating with the other colonies in resistance to the aggressions of the crown; while another class, composed of the idle and dissipated, who had little or nothing to risk, perceived their advantage in adhering to the royal government.

The situation of Georgia was inauspicious. It was but thinly inhabited, on a territory about one hundred and fifty miles from north to south, and about thirty miles from east to west. It presented a western frontier of two hundred and fifty miles. It had on the northwest the Cherokees; on the west, the Creeks; on the south, a refugee banditti in Florida; and on the east, the influence of Governor Wright, who controlled the king's ships on the sea-coast. The population of the eastern district of the province was composed of white people and negro slaves; the latter the most numerous, the former but few in number. A great majority of the inhabitants were favourable to the cause of the colonies; yet, from surrounding dangers, their measures were to be adopted with cautious circumspection.

Under these depressing circumstances, the strength of the republican party was of slow growth. The committees of safety, though cautious, were active and efficient; and the more daring of the patriots took advantage of every opportunity of serving the cause of freedom, and testifying their abhorrence of the royal domination.

On the night of the 11th of May, 1775, a number of gentlemen, principally members of the council of safety, and zealous in the American cause, broke open the magazine at the eastern extremity of the city of Savannah, took out the powder, sent a part of it to Beaufort, in South Carolina, and concealed the remainder in their cellars and garrets. Governor Wright issued a proclamation, offering a reward of one hundred and fifty pounds sterling for apprehending the offenders and bringing them to punishment; but the secret was not disclosed until the Americans had occasion to use the ammunition in defence of their rights and property.

On the 1st of June, Governor Wright and the loyal party at Savannah ordered preparations to be made for the celebration of the king's birthday. On the night of the 2d, a number of the inhabitants of the town collected, spiked up all the cannon on the battery, and hurled them to the bottom of the bluff. With difficulty a few of the spikes were drawn and drilled out, and the guns re-mounted to perform the usual ceremonies.

A general election was held for delegates, to meet at Savannah on the 4th day of July. The members accordingly assembled; and on the 15th of that month they appointed the honourable Archibald Bulloch, John Houstoun, John Joachim Zubly, Noble Wimberly Jones, and Lyman Hall, esquires, to represent this province in Congress, at Philadelphia. The resolution for this measure was signed by fifty-three members, who pledged themselves for its support; and their proceedings were communicated to Congress, then in session, accompanied by a declaration that this province was determined to unite in, and adhere to the common cause of the provinces.

During the session of the delegates in Savannah, Captain Maitland, from London, arrived at Tybee, with thirteen thousand pounds of powder, and other articles for the use of the British troops, and for the Indian trade. It was determined to obtain possession of that valuable prize without loss of time. Accordingly, about thirty volunteers, under the command of Commodore Brown and Colonel Joseph Habersham, embarked on board of two boats, proceeded down the river Savannah to the ship, took possession of her, and discharged the crew. A guard was left on board of the ship, and the powder brought to town and secured in the magazine. Five thousand pounds of the powder were sent to the patriots near Boston.

Owing to a variety of causes, but mainly to a dread of being involved in a war with the Cherokees, who were already desolating the frontiers of South Carolina, Georgia took no farther open and decided part in the contest, until the meeting of the provincial assembly on the 20th of January, 1776.

Then it was that President Ewin, of the committee of safety, laid before the house a variety of documents, representing the oppression of the other colonies to the north, and the united zeal with which the British troops had been opposed. Among other papers was the address of the House of Commons to the king, at the opening of parliament, on the 28th of October, 1775. In this address the English members expressed the greatest satisfaction in having learned that the king had increased his naval establishment, and greatly augmented his land forces; and that he had adopted the economical plan of drawing as many regiments from outposts as could be spared, to subdue the American colonies, and bring them to a proper sense of their dependence upon the British government.

After the documents were read, the house entered into a resolution to embark with the other colonies in the common cause with the utmost zeal; to resist and be free. Orders were given to arrest Governor Wright and his council. Accordingly, on the 28th of January, Joseph Habersham, Esq., who was then a member of the house, raised a party of volunteers, took Governor Wright prisoner, paroled him to his house, and placed a sentinel at his door, prohibiting all intercourse with the members of his council, the king's officers, or any other persons who were supposed to be inimical to the American cause.

On the night of the 11th of February, the governor effected his escape, and passing down the river in a boat, took refuge on board the Scarborough man-of-war, which, with four other armed ships, was lying at Tybee, in the mouth of the Savannah River.

Previous to this occurrence, the assembly had passed a resolution to raise a battalion of continental troops; and on the 4th of February, the following field officers were appointed to command it: Lachlan McIntosh, Colonel; Samuel Elbert, Lieutenant-colonel; and Joseph Habersham, Major. About the same time, Archibald Bulloch, John Houstoun, Lyman Hall, Button Gwinett, and George Watson, esquires, were elected to represent the province in Congress, at Philadelphia. Bills of credit were issued in the form of certificates, and resolutions entered into for the punishment of those who refused to receive them in payment of debts, or at par, for any article which was offered for sale.

In direct opposition to a law of Congress, prohibiting commercial intercourse between the colonies and the British dominions, a number of wealthy loyalist planters, early in March, freighted in Savannah River eleven merchant vessels with rice, and prepared for a sea voyage. To favour this design, the armed ships at the mouth of the river, moved up and threatened the town. The militia under the command of Colonel McIntosh were immediately called out; and with the assistance of five hundred Carolinians, commanded by Colonel Bull, succeeded in dislodging the enemy, burning three of the merchant vessels, and dismantling six. The other two escaped to sea.

Upon this trying occasion, the patriotism of the citizens of Savannah was tested, by a resolution which was offered by one of the members of the committee of safety; the purport of which was, that the houses in Savannah which were owned by those whose motto was "Liberty or Death," including houses which belonged to widows and orphans, should be appraised; and in the event of the enemy's gaining possesion of the city, the torch was to be applied in every direction, and the town to be abandoned in smoking ruins. To the astonishment, even of those who made the proposition, when the republican party was convened, there was not one dissenting voice. Among the number where this resolution originated, were many of the most wealthy inhabitants of Savannah, and some whose *all* consisted of houses and lots. The houses of those persons who were inimical to the American cause were not to be noticed in the valuation. Committees were accordingly appointed, and in a few hours returns were made to the council of safety. There are many instances of conflagration by order of a monarch, "who can do no wrong," but there are few instances upon record, where the patriotism of the citizen has urged him on to the destruction of his own property, to prevent its becoming an asylum to the enemies of his country.

CHAPTER XII.

Loyalists take refuge in Florida—Their predatory incursions—Treachery of the McGirth's—Expedition against the Cherokees—Treaty of peace with that nation—Unsuccessful invasions of Florida—Howe's attempt—The American army retreats—Georgia attacked on the south—Skirmish at Bulltown Swamp—Battle at Medway—Scriven mortally wounded—White retreats to the Ogechee—Sunbury invested—Heroic reply of Colonel McIntosh—The enemy retreats.

DURING the period in which the republican party in Georgia maintained the ascendency, many of the loyalists fled from the latter province and from the Carolinas, and found a secure retreat in East Florida. The southern frontiers of Georgia were thus exposed to the predatory incursions of these banditti, who bore the appellation of "Florida Rangers," and whose place of rendezvous and deposite was a fort on St. Mary's River. The destruction of this receptacle became, therefore, an object of great consequence.

Accordingly, during the year 1776, Captain John Baker collected seventy mounted militia, and marched to St. Mary's with the hope of surprising and demolishing the fort.

Unfortunately, when he was within a short distance of the fortress, he was discovered by a negro, who gave the garrison notice of his approach. The enemy were immediately on the alert, and Baker, finding his design frustrated, retreated eight or nine miles and encamped for the night. While his party were sleeping in fancied security, Daniel and James McGirth, two privates who had been placed on guard, stole the greater part of the horses and deserted with them to the enemy. For this act of treachery, Daniel McGirth received the appointment of lieutenant-colonel of the Florida Rangers, and his brother that of captain in the same corps. These traitors afterward distinguished themselves above all others, by the energy, audacity, and cruelty with which their predatory incursions were marked.

The subsequent operations of this and the succeeding year consisted of an expedition against the Cherokees, which resulted in a treaty of peace with that nation; of numerous skirmishes between the loyalists and patriots, wherein victory inclined sometimes to the one side and sometimes to the other; and of several abortive attempts made by the Americans to conquer East Florida; which, being planned with rashness, and executed without skill, depressed the ardour of the patriots and gave increased confidence to the enemy.

Early in the year 1778, Major-general Robert Howe, to whom the command of the southern forces had previously been confided, removed his head-quarters from Charleston to Savannah.

The project of reducing Florida being still a favourite one, Governor Houstoun of Georgia consented to co-operate with Howe for that purpose.

Accordingly, on the 20th of May, the latter reached the Alatamaha, where he halted till his reinforcements should come up. On the 25th, Howe crossed the river and landed at Reid's Bluff. Here the mischievous effects of a divided command became first apparent. Governor Houstoun had issued orders in regard to his galleys which it was impossible for them to execute; neither of the commanders was willing to submit to the dictation of the other, and as unanimity of action was no longer to be expected, the American forces were compelled to return without effecting any thing of importance.

These repeated failures were probably among the causes which induced the enemy to become assailants in their turn.

General Augustine Provost, who commanded at St. Augustine, was informed by the British general at New York, that a number of transports with troops on board would sail from thence direct for the coast of Georgia, and was ordered by him to send detachments from his commmand to annoy the southern frontier of that state, and divert the attention of the American troops from

Savannah. By these measures, the possession of that town would be obtained with little loss, the retreat of the American troops cut off, and their capture rendered probable. Reinforcements were promised to insure success to the enterprise.

In obedience to these orders, Provost despatched a portion of his troops, with some light artillery, by water, to Sunbury, where Colonel John McIntosh was stationed with one hundred and twenty-seven men. The command of the British detachment was given to Lieutenant-colonel Fuser, who had orders to possess himself of that important post. Another detachment under Lieutenant-colonel James Mark Provost, consisting of one hundred regular troops, sailed by the inland navigation to Fort Howe on the Alatamaha, where he was joined by the infamous McGirth, with three hundred refugees and Indians.

On the 19th of November, Lieutenant-colonel Provost advanced into the settlements, making prisoners of all the men found on their farms, and plundering the inhabitants of every valuable article that was portable.

As soon as Colonel John Baker received intelligence of the advance of Provost and McGirth, he assembled a party of mounted militia with the intention of annoying the enemy on their march. He had not proceeded farther than Bulltown

Swamp, when he fell into an ambuscade prepared by McGirth, and after a short skirmish was compelled to retreat.

In the mean time, Colonel John White had collected about one hundred continental troops and militia. With two pieces of light artillery he took post at Medway meeting-house. He constructed a slight breastwork across the road, at the head of the causeway over which the enemy must pass, where he hoped to keep them in check until he should be reinforced by Colonel Elbert from Savannah.

On the 24th, General James Scriven, with twenty militia, joined Colonel White. While the enemy was approaching it was determined to meet them in ambush, about a mile and a half south of Medway meeting-house, where the main road was skirted by a thick wood. But the design was already anticipated by McGirth.

When the Americans approached the ground they intended to occupy, General Scriven, accompanied by his aid-de-camp, Lieutenant Glascock, inclined to the right to make a reconnoisance, while Colonel White arranged his plan of attack. The British and Americans arrived on the ground, and were preparing their snares for each other about the same time. A firing commenced. General Scriven had advanced but a short distance, when he received a mortal wound, of which he died the ensuing day. Major Baker, who commanded the left flank, pressed the enemy with such vigour that they gave way, but they were soon reinforced and returned to the contest.

As Colonel Provost was crossing the road, a shot from one of the field-pieces passed through the neck of his horse and he fell. On seeing him fall, Major Roman advanced quickly with the field-pieces to take advantage of the confusion which ensued; and Major James Jackson called out "Victory," supposing the enemy was retreating. But Provost was soon remounted, and advanced in force.

Finding himself opposed by far superior numbers, Colonel White ordered a retreat to the meeting-house, which he effected in good order by throwing out small parties to annoy the front and flanks of the enemy, and by breaking down the bridges as he retired.

When he had regained his position, he learned that the force opposed to him consisted of five hundred men. This great superiority of numbers compelled him to retreat to the Ogechee River, but fearful of being pressed too closely by the enemy, he endeavoured by a stratagem to check the ardour of their pursuit.

He prepared a letter as though it had been written to himself by Colonel Elbert, directing him to retreat, in order to draw the British as far as possible; and informing him that a large body of cavalry had crossed over Ogechee River, with orders to gain the rear of the enemy, by which their whole force would be captured.

This letter was dropped in such a way as to insure its getting to Colonel Provost's hand, and to attach to it the strongest evidence of its genuineness. It was found, handed to Provost, and was supposed to have been so far effectual as to deter the enemy from advancing more than six or seven miles. When White reached the Ogechee, he found Colonel Elbert already there with a reinforcement of two hundred men.

The latter now assumed the command. He despatched by Major John Habersham a flag to Colonel Provost, requesting permission to furnish General Scriven with medical aid. The messenger was also to propose some general arrangements to secure the country against pillage and conflagration. The attendance of surgeons was allowed, but Colonel Provost refused to make any stipulations for the security of the country.

Learning from Major Habersham—whom he put upon his honour to answer truly—that no British reinforcements had arrived off the coast of Georgia, he retreated early next morning toward St. Augustine, burning and plundering as he went.

The British detachment under Colonel Fuser, being delayed by contrary winds, did not reach Sunbury before the 1st of December. On that day, Fuser anchored off Colonel's Island. After making the necessary preparations to attack the fort by land and water, he demanded a surrender; threatening, in case of refusal, to put the whole garrison to the sword. The force under Fuser amounted to five hundred men, well supplied with battering cannon, artillery, and mortars. The garrison at the fort did not exceed one hundred and twenty-seven men. Against a well-conducted attack the works would not have been tenable for an hour; but expecting immediate relief from Savannah, Colonel McIntosh determined on opposition to the last extremity. When, therefore, Fuser summoned the garrison to surrender the fort, McIntosh, undeterred by the bloody threat of extermination, answered in four bold defiant words, "Come and take it." This heroic reply deterred Fuser from making an attack, until he should be joined by the forces under Provost. Learning soon afterward that the latter had retreated, Fuser, alarmed by the tidings of troops advancing from Savannah, and hearing nothing of the expected reinforcements from the north, supposed that Provost had fallen back before a superior force. He therefore raised the siege and returned to St. John's River, where he met Provost, and where each attributed the failure of the expedition to the misconduct of the other.

When Fuser retreated from Sunbury, he left the regular troops of his command at Frederica, on St. Simon's Island, where the old military works of General Oglethorpe were temporarily repaired for defence. The loyalists proceeded with Fuser to St. John's, and thence to St. Augustine, where the booty was deposited in safety, and preparations made to return to Georgia with a more formidable force.

General Provost, having been disappointed in this expedition, determined to suspend further operations until he should receive certain information of the arrival of the transports from New York. In the mean time, he held himself in readiness for that event.

CHAPTER XIII.

Defensive operations of General Howe—Approach of the British fleet—Exposed condition of Savannah—British army land at Brewton's Hill—Capture of Savannah—Provost takes Sunbury—The Rev. Moses Allen drowned—Lincoln assumes command of the southern army—Provost unites with Campbell—Proclamations of the enemy—Unsuccessful conference for the exchange of prisoners.

During the interval that elapsed between the retreat of Provost and Fuser into Florida, and the arrival of British reinforcements from New York, General Howe endeavoured to place the province of Georgia in the best state of defence that circumstances would admit.

From his letters to Congress, the attempt appears to have been both difficult and unsatisfactory. He complained that all the military works were in ruins; that there were no tools, nor any apparent disposition to make the necessary repairs; that the militia came and went as they pleased; and that he had more trouble with the officers than with the men.

On the other hand, the people of Georgia charged Howe with military incapacity; and the influence of the state was exerted to remove him from the chief command; but as Congress had, as yet, seen nothing to justify this exercise of its power, the request, from motives of delicacy, was not complied with.

It was during this untoward state of affairs in the province that tidings reached Savannah of the approach of the enemy.

On the 27th of December, the transports, escorted by a squadron of the fleet, under the command of Commodore Sir Hyde Parker, crossed the bar and came up to Cockspur Island.

The British land forces consisted of the seventy-first regiment of Royal Scots, two battalions of Hessians, four battalions of provincials, and a detachment of artillery. They were commanded by Lieutenant-colonel Archibald Campbell, an officer of acknowledged skill and bravery.

Having made arrangements for landing, the Vigilant man-of-war, Keppel brig, Greenwich sloop-of-war, and the Comet galley, came up the river with a strong tide and favourable breeze, followed by the transports in three divisions. About five o'clock in the afternoon of the 28th, the Vigilant opened the reach at Four-mile Point, and was cannonaded by the American galleys Congress and Dee, but without much effect. Night coming on, some of the transports grounded on a mud flat, but got off at high-water, and proceeded up, in the morning, above Five-fathom Hole, opposite to Brewton's Hill, where the first division of light infantry debarked, and marched up to take possession of the high ground, so as to cover the landing of the troops from the other transports.

Savannah, at this time, was in the most defenceless condition imaginable. With the exception of a few guns mounted upon a battery at the eastern end of the city, and only calculated to defend the approach by water, every other part of the town was exposed, and the ground offered no advantage against an equal force.

General Howe had formed his encampment southeast of the town of Savannah, anxiously waiting the arrival of reinforcements of miltia and the continental troops from South Carolina, under the command of Major-general Benjamin Lincoln. Howe's army had not yet recovered from the fatal effects of the Florida campaign, the preceding summer: about one-fourth were confined by disease, and many of his convalescents yet too feeble to encounter the fatigues of a battle. The dread of a climate, where disease had produced more terrors, and proved not less fatal than the sword, retarded the progress of militia, and prevented many from returning who were absent on furlough. On the day of battle, Howe's army, exclusive of militia, amounted to six hundred and seventy-two, rank and file. The force of the enemy was two thousand one hundred, including land troops, seamen, and marines; but it was thought by Howe that the enemy exhibited the appearance of greater numbers than what was really possessed, and that the opposing armies were nearly equal.

The town of Savannah is situated on high, level, sandy ground, forty feet above the surface of the water, on the south bank of the river, and approachable by land at three points;—from the high ground of Brewton's Hill and Thunderbolt, on the east by a road and causeway over a morass, with rice-fields on the north side of the causeway to the river, and the morass with wooded swamps from the causeway southward several miles; from the south, by the roads from White Bluff and Ogechee Ferry, which unite near the town; and from the westward, by a road and causeway over the deep swamps of Musgrove's Creek, with rice-fields from the causeway to the river on the north, and by Musgrove's Swamp leading in from the southward. From the eastern causeway to that on the west is about three quarters of a mile.

On the morning of the 29th, Colonel Elbert suggested to Howe the advantage of occupying Brewton's Hill, and offered to defend it with his regiment; but his proposition was rejected. About the same time, Colonel Walton informed the general of a private way through the swamp, by which the enemy could march from the high grounds of Brewton's Hill and gain the rear of the American right; but though it admitted of easy defence, General Howe did not avail himself of the advantage which would have resulted from its occupation. By this pass, so blindly neglected, Colonel Campbell approached.

Howe formed for battle on the southeast side of the town. His centre was opposed to the head of the causeway by which he believed the enemy must advance; his left with the rice-fields in front, and flanked by the river; his right with the morass in front, and flanked obliquely by the wooded swamp, and one hundred of the Georgia militia.

Having made his disposition, Howe detached Captain John C. Smith, of South Carolina, with his company of forty infantry, to occupy Brewton's Hill and the head of the causeway. The force was altogether inadequate to its object. Smith defended his post with gallantry, but was compelled to retreat, which he accomplished without loss of men. The enemy lost in this affair one captain and two privates killed, and five privates wounded.

Ignorant as yet of the force of the enemy, but now believing it to be greatly superior to his own, Howe called a council of his field officers to advise him whether to retreat or defend Savannah. Very rashly they resolved to defend the town to the last extremity. General Howe certainly ought not to have risked an action with superior numbers, when he had certain information that General Lincoln was advancing with a body of troops to reinforce him, and with whom he could have formed a junction in two days.

The consequences were disastrous in the extreme. After Colonel Campbell had formed his army on Brewton's Hill, he moved forward and took a position within eight hundred yards of the American front, where he manœuvred to excite a belief that he intended an attack on their centre and left. At the same time a body of infantry and New York volunteers, under the command of Major Sir James Baird, filed off, unperceived, from the rear, and, under the guidance of an old negro, penetrated the swamp by the pass which Howe had so carelessly neglected, and fell suddenly upon the American rear. At this moment Campbell moved forward and attacked the front. Hemmed in between two fires, the American line was almost immediately broken, and the men retreated in great disorder towards the only practicable outlet across Musgrove's Swamp, west of the town. Before they gained the head of the causeway, they found, to their dismay, that the enemy already occupied a position which enabled them to dispute the passage.

At length, however, by the extraordinary exertions of Colonel Roberts, the American centre gained the causeway and accomplished their retreat. The right flank suffered severely. The left, under Colonel Elbert, continued the conflict until a retreat was impracticable. He attempted to escape with a part of his troops, under a galling fire from the high grounds of Ewensburg, through the rice-fields between the causeway and the river; but as it was high-tide when they reached the creek, only those who could swim were enabled to cross it; the others were made prisoners or drowned.

About one hundred Georgia militia, under Colonel Walton, posted on the south common of the town, made a gallant defence until their colonel was wounded and taken prisoner. The way of retreat being cut off, most of the men were killed, wounded, or taken. Some of them, who were citizens of Savannah, were bayoneted in the streets by their victorious pursuers. General Howe retreated with the remains of his army to Cherokee Hill, about eight miles from the field of battle, where he halted till the rear came up.

He then marched up the Savannah River to the Sister's and Zubley's ferries, and crossed over into South Carolina.

Few conquests have ever been made with so little loss to the victor. The enemy had only seven killed, and nineteen wounded.

The American army lost eighty-three men killed, and thirty-eight officers; and four hundred and fifteen non-commissioned officers and privates, including the sick, wounded, and the aged inhabitants of the town and country, were made prisoners. The fort, with forty-eight pieces of cannon, and twenty-three mortars and howitzers, with all the ammunition and stores belonging to them, a large quantity of provisions, the shipping in the river, and the capital of Georgia, all fell into the possession of the British army, in the course of a few hours. The private soldiers who were made prisoners on this occasion were alternately persuaded and threatened to induce them to enlist into the British army: those who resolutely refused were crowded on board of prison-ships, and during the succeeding summer, four or five of them died every day: the staff-officers, particularly those of the quarter-master's and commissary's departments, were treated in a similar way. Many gentlemen who had been accustomed to ease and affluence were consigned to these abominable prison-ships: among the number was the venerable Jonathan Bryan, bending under the weight of years and infirmities, whose daughter, when she was entreating with Commodore Sir Hyde Parker to soften the sufferings of her father, was treated by him with vulgar rudeness and contempt.

When General Howe halted at Cherokee Hill, he despatched Lieutenant Tennill with orders to Lieutenant Aaron Smith of the third regiment of South Carolina, who commanded at Ogechee Ferry, and to Major Joseph Lane, who commanded at Sunbury, to evacuate their posts, retreat across the country, and join the army at the Sister's Ferry. Lieutenant Smith immediately complied; but Major Lane, influenced by Captain Dollar, who commanded a corps of artillery, and many others of the inhabitants whose pecuniary ruin was at stake, resolved to defend his post. On the 6th of January, 1779, he was attacked by General Provost, with an army of two thousand men from Florida, and after a short conflict compelled to surrender at discretion. By this rash and unwarrantable conduct, the Americans lost twenty-four pieces of artillery, ammunition, and provisions, and the garrison, consisting of seventeen commissioned officers and one hundred and ninety-five non-commissioned officers and privates. During this assault one captain and three privates were killed and seven wounded. The British loss in killed and wounded was only four men.

The Washington and Bulloch galleys were stranded and burned by their crews, who took passage for Charleston on board of Captain Salter's sloop, but were captured by a British tender and taken to Savannah.

For this disobedience of orders, Lane was subsequently tried by a court-martial, and dismissed the service.

After Sunbury fell into the possession of the British troops, the continental officers who were made prisoners at Savannah were sent to that place on their parole, except the Rev. Moses Allen, who had accepted a commission as chaplain in the Georgia brigade.

This gentleman was refused the privileges allowed to the other officers, and confined on board a prison-ship. His animated exertions on the field of battle, and his patriotic exhortations from the pulpit, had exposed him to the particular resentment of the enemy. Wearied by long confinement, and hopeless of speedy release, he determined to regain his liberty, or lose his life in the attempt. In pursuance of this hazardous resolution, he leaped overboard with the hope of being able to swim to one of the islands, assisted by the flood-tide, but was unfortunately drowned. The death of Mr. Allen was greatly lamented by the friends of independence, and particularly by his brethren in arms, who justly admired him for his bravery, exemplary life, and many virtues.

Major-general Benjamin Lincoln, who had been previously appointed by Congress to take the command of the southern army, reached Purysburg, a few miles above Savannah, on the 3d of January. His troops, consisting of levies from North and South Carolina, amounted to twelve hundred men.

On the 4th, he was joined by the remnant of Howe's army, which had been placed under the orders of Colonel Huger.

Finding himself in no condition to advance against the enemy, Lincoln established his head-quarters at Purysburg, and waited for the expected reinforcement.

When General Provost had united his troops with those under Campbell, his force consisted of nearly four thousand men. He determined to complete the subjugation of Georgia, and establish military posts as far as the populous settlements in the back country extended. He confided the garrison of Savannah and the police of the neighbouring country to Lieutenant-colonel Innes; he established a fort at Ebenezer, twenty-five miles above Savannah, and advanced Lieutenant-colonel Campbell at the head of eight hundred infantry to capture Augusta, and take advantage of circumstances in completing the conquest of the province. With the main body he watched the movements of the American general. The inhabitants of Savannah and the surrounding country were ordered by proclamation to bring in their arms and accoutrements of every description, and to discover where arms, accoutrements, stores, and effects were buried or otherwise concealed.

Regulations were established; places designated for the landing of boats; and, to prevent property from being carried away, no departure was allowed without a permit from the superintendent of the port.

A joint proclamation was also issued by the commanders of the royal army and navy, offering peace, freedom, and protection to the king's subjects in America, desiring them to repair without loss of time and unite their forces under the royal standard; reprobating the idea of forming a league with the French; promising freedom from the imposition of taxes by the British Parliament, and securing them in the enjoyment of every privilege consistent with the mutual interests of the colonies and the mother country. Ample protection was offered to the persons and effects of all who would immediately come in and acknowledge their allegiance to the British crown and support it with their arms. Deserters of every description were invited to return within three months, and such inhabitants as were inclined to enjoy the benefits of the proclamation were desired to repair to head-quarters at Savannah, and take the oath of allegiance.

On the 11th of January, another proclamation was issued, offering a reward of two guineas for every citizen who adhered to the American cause, and ten guineas for every committee or assembly-man, who should be taken and delivered to the commanding officer of any of the king's garrisons.

The families of those who adhered to the cause of their country, whether in the camp or on board of prison-ships, were stripped by the British of every article of property, even to the common necessaries of life. From this cause many of them were reduced to the most deplorable extremities.

Upon a representation of the suffering of the Americans in captivity being made to General Lincoln at Purysburg, the general wrote to Lieutenant-colonel Campbell, then on his march to Augusta, and proposed a conference with him at Zubley's Ferry, for an exchange of prisoners, and the parole of the officers until exchanged. A negotiation was consented to, and Lieutenant-colonel James M. Provost was nominated to confer with Major Thomas Pinckney on the subject. They had an interview on the 31st of January, and terms were proposed; but being such as Major Pinckney could not in honour allow, the negotiation terminated in a disagreement.

CHAPTER XIV.

Position of Lincoln—His force—Moultrie defeats Gardiner—Skirmishes in Burke county—Campbell occupies Augusta—Pickens and Dooley besiege Hamilton at Carr's Fort—Pursuit of Boyd—Battle of Kettle Creek—Death of Boyd—British outpost surprised and captured.

THE position chosen by General Lincoln at Purysburg was an excellent one. It enabled him to watch the movements of General Provost, and wait for reinforcements.

The freshets in Savannah River at that season of the year overflowed the swamps from two to four miles in breadth, and upwards of one hundred miles in length from the sea, so that neither general could assail the other with any prospect of advantage.

By a field return, on the 1st of February, General Lincoln had three thousand six hundred and thirty-nine men, composed of about six hundred continental troops, five hundred new levies, and one thousand three hundred effective militia. The residue were invalids, and without arms. If the American troops had been all effective and veteran, General Lincoln would have been about equal to his antagonist; but his numbers were principally made up by militia, on which no dependance could be placed, when opposed to a veteran army. From the equality of the militia with their officers, and independence at home, they were unwilling to submit to the requisite discipline of a camp: they must know where they were to go, what they were going to do, and how long they were to be absent, before they would move; and if not satisfied on these points, and permitted to do very much as they pleased, they would be off, knowing that their punishment for desertion would be light.

Early in February, a party of the enemy, commanded by Major Gardiner, embarked at Savannah, and proceeded by the inland passage to Beaufort, in South Carolina; they effected a landing, but were soon after attacked and defeated by General Moultrie, with an equal force, nearly all militia of Charleston. In this engagement forty of the enemy were killed and wounded: they fled to their boats, and returned to Savannah.

While Lieutenant-colonel Campbell was advancing to take possession of Augusta, he detached Colonels Brown and McGirth, with four hundred mounted militia, to make a forced march to the jail in Burke county, and form a junction with Colonel Thomas and a party of loyalists. On his way thither, Brown fell in with a party of two hundred and fifty militia under Colonels Few and Twiggs, and in the attack which ensued, he was defeated with the loss of several men. Expecting that Brown would be reinforced by Campbell, Twiggs and Few retreated the ensuing day.

Brown rallied his troops during the night, and having been strengthened in the mean time by some refugees from South Carolina, and a detachment under Major Gardiner, he determined to renew the attack. He was defeated with greater loss than before, himself being among the wounded. In this skirmish Captain Joshua Inman killed three of the enemy with his own hand.

Shortly after this, Twiggs and Few being joined by a detachment of troops under General Elbert, the united commands crossed the Savannah River, and skirmished with Campbell; but not receiving the reinforcements they expected, were compelled to retire, and Campbell took possession of Augusta about the last of January, where he established a post, and placed it under the orders of Colonel Brown.

About the 1st of February, Campbell spread his military posts over the most populous parts of Georgia, and all opposition ceased, though for a few days only. The oath of allegiance was administered to the inhabitants who remained, and the torch applied to the habitations of those who had fled into Carolina.

When the families of the latter were placed in security, the men assembled under their leader, Colonel John Dooley, and took a position on the Carolina shore of the Savannah River, about thirty miles above Augusta. McGirth, with three hundred loyalists, occupied a position on the Georgia shore, five miles below. Dooley returned into Georgia with a part of his men, but being closely pressed by one of McGirth's detachments under Major Hamilton, was compelled to recross the Savannah River.

Hamilton then encamped at Waters's plantation, three miles below Petersburg, and Dooley opposite to him in Carolina, where he was joined by Colonel Andrew Pickens, with two hundred and fifty men of his regiment.

With this united force it was determined to assault Hamilton's detachment. But the latter had already marched across the country, and was in possession of Carr's Fort before the main body of the Americans came up with them. The baggage and horses of the enemy fell into the hands of their pursuers.

Hamilton was summoned to surrender, but refused. Knowing that the garrison were without food or water, a siege was determined upon, under the confident belief that they could not hold out twenty-four hours. But disappointment awaited the besiegers. An express arrived from Captain Pickens, with the information that Colonel Boyd, at the head of eight hundred loyalists, was passing through Ninety-six district, on his way into Georgia, ravaging and burning all before him.

The Americans instantly raised the siege, and

started in pursuit of Boyd. In the mean time, Captain Anderson, with eighty men of Pickens's regiment, having learned that the enemy were advancing, took post about five miles above Cherokee Ford, and disputed Boyd's passage into Georgia.

In the skirmish which ensued the American loss was sixteen killed and wounded, and the same number taken prisoners. Boyd acknowledged a loss of one hundred in killed, wounded, and missing; many of this number deserted him, and returned to their homes. After the skirmish, Anderson retreated, and joined Pickens and Dooley in pursuit of the enemy.

On the 12th of February, the Americans passed over Savannah River into Georgia, and advanced to Fishdam Ford on Broad River. Captain Neal, with a party of observation, was ordered to gain the enemy's rear, and occasionally send a man back with the result of his discoveries, so as to keep the main body well informed of the enemy's movements. To avoid danger, Boyd at first shaped his course to the westward, and on the morning of the 13th, crossed Broad River near the fork, at a place now called Webb's Ferry, and thence turned toward Augusta, expecting to form a junction with McGirth at a place appointed on Little River. The corps of observation under Captain Neal hung close upon the enemy's rear, and made frequent communications to Pickens and Dooley. The Americans crossed Broad River, and encamped for the night on Clark's Creek, within four miles of the enemy.

Early on the morning of the 14th, the Americans resumed their march with a quickened pace, and soon approached the enemy's rear, but with such caution as to remain undiscovered. The line of march was the order of battle, wherever the face of the country admitted of it. Colonel Dooley commanded the right wing, and Lieutenant-colonel Clarke the left, each consisting of one hundred men. The centre, commanded by Colonel Pickens, consisted of two hundred, and an advance guard one hundred and fifty yards in front. Under three leaders whose courage and military talents had been often tested, this inferior number, of four against seven, looked forward to a victory with great confidence. Early in the morning they passed the ground where the enemy encamped the preceding night.

Colonel Boyd, unapprehensive of danger, had halted at a farm on the north side of Kettle Creek. His horses were turned out to forage among the reeds in the swamp; some bullocks were killed, and corn parched to refresh his troops, who had been on short allowance for three days. The encampment was formed on the edge of the farm next to the creek, on an open piece of ground, flanked on two sides by the cane-swamp. The second officer in command was

Lieutenant-colonel Moore, of North Carolina, who, it is said, possessed neither courage nor military skill: the third in command, Major Spurgen, is said to have acted with bravery, and gave some evidence of military talents.

After the Americans had marched three or four miles, the enemy's drums were heard to beat. They halted for a few minutes, examined their guns, and primed them afresh. Captain McCall had been ordered in front to examine the enemy's situation and condition. He reported the situation of the encampment and the nature of the adjacent ground. The enemy were, apparently, unsuspicious of danger, he having passed their flank within musket-shot, and in full view. Satisfied upon these points, the Americans advanced to the attack. As the camp was approached, the enemy's pickets fired and retreated. Boyd ordered the line to be formed in the rear of his camp, and advanced at the head of one hundred men, who were sheltered by a fence and some fallen timber. The American centre filed off a little to the right, to gain the advantage of higher ground. Boyd contended for the fence with bravery, but was overpowered and compelled to order a retreat to the main body. On his retreat he fell under two wounds through the body, and one through the thigh, which proved mortal. The other two divisions were embarrassed in passing through the cane, but by this time had reached their points of destination, and the battle became warm, close, and general, and some of the enemy who had not formed fled into the cane and passed over the creek, leaving behind them their horses, baggage, and some of their arms. Colonel Clarke observed a rising ground on the opposite side of the creek, in the rear of the enemy's right, on which he believed they would attempt to form. After a warm contest, which lasted an hour, the enemy retreated through the swamp over the creek.

Clarke ordered his division to follow him across the creek; at the same moment his horse was shot, and fell under him; he was quickly remounted, and fortunately fell into a path which led to a fording-place on the creek, and gained the side of the hill. His division had not heard, or had not understood the order, in consequence of which not more than one-fourth of it followed him. While Major Spurgen was forming the enemy upon one side of the hill, Colonel Clarke attacked him upon the other side, which gave intimation to the remainder of his division, by which he was soon joined. Colonels Pickens and Dooley pressed through the swamp with the main body in pursuit, and when they emerged from the cane, the battle was again renewed with great vigour. For a considerable time the contest was obstinate and bloody, and the issue doubtful. The Americans finally gained the summit of the hill, when the enemy began to retreat in some confusion, and fled from the field of battle.

This engagement lasted one hour and forty-five minutes, and for the last half hour was close and general. Great credit is given to Colonel Clarke for his foresight in speedily occupying the rising ground on the west side of the creek. Considering the inequality of the troops in point of military experience and equipment, and that the numbers in the ranks of the enemy were seven to four, the result of this engagement reflects great honour and credit on the American officers and soldiers who were engaged in it, and it was justly considered a brilliant victory.

About seventy of the enemy were killed and died of their wounds, and seventy-five were taken prisoners, including the wounded who could be carried off the ground. The American loss was nine killed, and twenty-three wounded—two mortally. The prisoners that Boyd had taken at the skirmish on Savannah River were in charge of a guard in advance, which consisted of thirty-three men, including officers, with orders, in case of disaster, to move towards Augusta. When the guard heard the result of the engagement, they voluntarily surrendered themselves prisoners to those whom they had in captivity, upon a promise of their influence for pardon and permission to return home. This promise was complied with, upon condition that they would take the oath of allegiance to the American government.

After the action was ended, Colonel Pickens went to Colonel Boyd and tendered him any services which his present situation would authorize, and observed, that as his wounds appeared to be mortal, he would recommend those preparations which approaching death required. Boyd thanked him for his civilities, and inquired what had been the result of the battle. Upon being informed that victory was with the Americans, he observed that it would have been otherwise if he had not fallen. He said that he had marched from his rendezvous with eight hundred men; that one hundred of that number were killed and wounded, or had deserted at Savannah River; and that on the morning of the action, he had seven hundred men under his command. He had the promise of Colonel Campbell, that McGirth, with five hundred more, should join him on Little River, about six miles from the field of battle, on that evening or the ensuing morning. He concluded by saying that he had but a few hours to live, and desired that Colonel Pickens would leave two men with him to furnish him with water, and bury his body after he died. He also asked Colonel Pickens to write to Mrs. Boyd, informing her of his fate, and to send her a few articles which he had about his person. He expired early in the night, and his requests were faithfully complied with.

The insurgents taken at Kettle Creek were conveyed to South Carolina and tried by the laws of the state; found guilty of treason, and sentenced to death. Five of the most atrocious offenders suffered accordingly; the others were pardoned.

Of those who fled from the scene of action, some took refuge in Florida; some in the Creek and Cherokee nations; and a remnant, under command of Colonel Moore, retreated to Augusta, where they met with nothing but humiliation, scorn, and neglect.

In the engagements at Carr's Fort and Kettle Creek, the Americans took as booty about six hundred horses and their equipments, with a quantity of arms, accoutrements, and clothing. Shortly after this action, Colonel Twiggs, and Lieutenant-colonel John McIntosh, with some militia from Richmond county, surprised one of the British outposts at Herbert's, consisting of seventy men; killed and wounded several, and compelled the remainder to surrender.

CHAPTER XV.

Campbell evacuates Augusta—Lincoln proposes the recovery of Georgia—Ash defeated at Brier Creek—Force of the British in Georgia—Campbell leaves for England—Censure of Ash by a court of inquiry—Embarrassed condition of Lincoln—Shameful treatment of the American prisoners—Lincoln marches into Georgia—Provost advances towards Charleston—Battle at Stono River—Cooper defeats a British detachment—Spencer captures a British cutter—Sir James Wright resumes the government of Georgia.

UPON the approach of General John Ash with a body of North Carolina militia to reinforce General Elbert, Colonel Campbell precipitately abandoned Augusta, and fell back to a fortified camp at Hudson's Ferry, about fifty miles from Savannah.

Ash passed the river at Augusta on the 28th of February, and pursued Campbell as far as Brier Creek, where he halted and encamped. His force was seventeen hundred men. General Lincoln was encamped at Purysburg with three thousand men; General Rutherford at Black Swamp with seven hundred; and General Williamson at Augusta with twelve hundred. By concentrating these scattered forces, General Lincoln believed he would be sufficiently strong to commence active operations against the enemy. A council was therefore summoned to meet at General Rutherford's quarters on the 1st of March. At this council, it was inquired of Ash if his position was secure, and such that his troops could act with the best advantage? General Ash expressed himself confidently, as to the safety of his command, against any force it was in the power of the enemy to bring against it.

He observed that the enemy appeared to be afraid of him, believing his numbers to be greater than they were; he only asked for a detachment of artillery with two field-pieces, which General Lincoln ordered to his assistance.

Strange as it may appear, while Ash was thus boasting of the complete security of his troops, they were encamped in a position the best calculated for their defeat of any he could possibly have chosen. On the left of his army was a deep creek, on the right a lagune, and on the rear the Savannah River; while the front offered an open and uninterrupted entrance to the enemy.

Always prompt to take any advantage of any unskilful conduct on the part of his adversaries, Lieutenant-colonel Campbell determined to strike at Ash before Williamson—who was already on the march to join him—should be able to come to his assistance. Masking his real design by advancing a battalion of the seventy-first regiment and a party of South Carolina loyalists to Buck Creek, three miles south of Brier Creek bridge, he ordered Lieutenant-colonel Provost, with a force of regulars and provincials amounting to some seventeen hundred men, to march by a circuitous route of about forty miles, gain the rear of General Ash, and surprise and attack him in his camp.

In the mean time, Ash, having learned that Campbell was manœuvring on his front, sent out various detachments to reconnoitre, until he had reduced his force in camp to eight hundred men.

From Williamson's advanced parties Ash obtained the first intelligence that Provost was approaching his rear. These startling tidings being soon afterward confirmed by Colonel Smith, who was in command of the baggage-guard some eight miles up the river, General Ash ordered the beat to arms. Strange as it may appear, at that late hour cartridges were to be distributed to the militia, some of whom had rifles, some shotguns, a few had muskets, while some were without arms.

Thus equipped, without any preconcerted plan, General Ash ordered his troops into the line of battle in three divisions; the right, under the command of Colonel Young, and the centre under the command of General Bryant. The left was committed to the care of General Elbert and Lieutenant-colonel John McIntosh, and consisted of about sixty continental troops and one hundred and fifty Georgia militia, to which a light field-piece was attached.

At three o'clock P. M. the enemy's advance-guard attacked and drove back the American pickets, and took some prisoners, who gave information that the Americans were unadvised of an enemy in force being near. Provost made his disposition for action: the light infantry with two field-pieces was formed on the right, with orders to penetrate by a road leading toward the American camp: the centre was composed of the second battalion of the seventy-first regiment, with some rangers and Carolina loyalists on its left, and with a howitzer and two field-pieces in front; the left consisted of one hundred and fifty dragoons, with orders to turn the American right; the reserve was formed four hundred yards in the rear, composed of three companies of grenadiers and a troop of dragoons; and fifty riflemen were placed in ambuscade at a pass, by which it was supposed the Americans might turn their left and attack their rear. At four P. M. the British moved forward and commenced the attack.

When General Ash had formed his line, he advanced about a quarter of a mile in front of his encampment, with his left at the creek, and his right extending within half a mile of the river swamp. The British, advancing in three columns of six in front, opened their fire at the distance of one hundred and fifty yards from their cannon. The American centre, which was in advance, began to retreat in about five minutes, and the right broke and ran the instant they were attacked. Colonel Young, who commanded the right, said that it was not his intention to retreat; but, perceiving that the enemy intended to turn his right, he wished to file off to the right to prevent it; but his troops construed his intentions into an order to retreat. The centre and right fled in the utmost confusion. General Elbert, with the left, maintained his ground with so much gallantry, that the British reserve was ordered to support their right; and, notwithstanding the great superiority of the enemy, Elbert supported the conflict until every avenue of a retreat was cut off. Finding that further resistance would be temerity, he ordered his gallant little band to ground their arms and surrender. Nearly the whole of his command was killed, wounded, or made prisoners.

The Americans who fled entered the river swamp, which was two or three miles in extent, to escape from the enemy; such of them as could swim crossed the river, but many who made the attempt were drowned.

The American loss was estimated at one hundred and fifty killed and drowned; twenty-seven officers, and one hundred and sixty-two non-commissioned officers and privates, were taken prisoners; seven pieces of field artillery, a quantity of ammunition, provisions, and baggage, and five hundred stand of arms, were lost or fell into the possession of the victors. The British loss was one commissioned officer and fifteen privates killed and wounded. Generals Ash and Bryant, with two or three hundred of the fugitives, were stopped at Bee's Creek bridge, twenty miles from the scene of action, in the evening of the same day, by Captain Peter Horry, who was marching with a detachment to join the camp; some with and some without arms.

The loss of General Elbert and his command, of Neal's dragoons, and many of Pirkins's regiment of North Carolina, was seriously calamitous to Georgia, which had more than one thousand men, including nearly all the regular troops of the state, in captivity with the British.

The defeat of Ash disconcerted the plans of General Lincoln. If the army had been concentrated, as was intended, the American forces, including the reinforcements about to join them, would have amounted to seven thousand men; an army sufficient, as it was believed, to have driven the British troops out of Georgia. The wavering and disaffected would have joined the American standard, and South Carolina would not have been invaded. The parties of militia, who were on their march to join the army, heard of the disaster and returned home; while many who were previously undecided in their politics now joined the enemy.

The different corps composing the British army in Georgia amounted to upward of four thousand men. Five thousand additional troops were daily expected from New York, under General Vaughan. After these arrived, the capital of South Carolina was intended as the object of future operations. The command of the southern British army was offered to Lieutenant-colonel Campbell, but he declined it. He appears to have been dissatisfied with General Provost's having taken the chief command and government of Georgia, after he had made the conquest.

Colonel Campbell was an officer at all points; circumspect, quick, brave, and profound in military knowledge. He was beloved for his courtesy and humanity, and admired for the elegance of his manners. The departure of such an officer from the southern states excited joyful sensation among the friends of freedom and independence. He sailed soon after for England.

In addition to the British force already stated, five hundred Indians were assembled on the Alatamaha River, and there was a proffer of all the aid of the Creek and Cherokee Indians, under the influence of Stuart and Cameron, to engage in any enterprise which might be required of them.

Hudson's Ferry and Paris Mill were well fortified, cannon mounted at each, and strongly garrisoned. Ebenezer and Sister's ferries were put in a state of defence, and all the passes of Savannah River secured by the British. The light troops were held prepared to move to any point, on short notice.

After the defeat of Ash at Brier Creek, that general, finding he was viewed by all grades of the army with contempt and disrespect, demanded a court of inquiry, which was granted.

The court was convened on the 9th day of March. The conclusions they came to, after having maturely considered the matter before them, were,—"That General Ash did not take all the necessary precautions, which he ought to have done, to secure his camp and obtain timely intelligence of the movements and approach of the enemy."

While Lincoln was thus, most unfortunately, thwarted in his project to attempt the recovery of Georgia, the British army received the expected reinforcements from New York. Shortly after this, the forces of the American general were rendered still less effective; the term of service for which the North Carolina militia had been drafted having expired, without any immediate prospect of others arriving to replace them. In this condition of things several of the inhabitants of Georgia, who had left their families, represented to General Lincoln that all their property had been plundered and destroyed by the enemy, and desired him to point out to them any possible means by which their families could be secured against want. They expressed their willingness to yield to the loss of property and every other privation, if their wives and families could be guarantied the necessaries of life; but that they should be left to suffer from the want of food, and under the continued insolence of their enemy, was rather more than their feelings could be expected to endure. The general consented that such men as had families should return to their homes, and remain quiet until a change should take place.

Some of the Georgia prisoners, who were exchanged for a like number sent from Charleston, were so much emaciated when they arrived in camp, that they were obliged to be carried from the boats in which they were brought from the prison-ships. They complained bitterly of the ill-treatment which they had experienced on board these filthy floating dungeons, of which their countenances and emaciated bodies exhibited condemning testimony. They asserted that they had been fed on condemned pork, which nauseated the stomach, and oatmeal so rotten that swine would not have fed on it; that the staff officers and the members of council from Savannah shared in common with the soldiery; even the venerable Bryan was obliged to partake such repasts, or die of hunger.

The Jews of Savannah were generally favourable to the American cause, and among this persuasion was Mordecai Sheftall, commissary-general, and his son, who was his deputy; they were confined in common with the other prisoners, and by way of contempt to their offices and religion, condemned pork was given them for the animal part of their subsistence. In consequence of such food, and other new devices of mal-treatment, five or six died daily. Their bodies were conveyed from the prison-ships to the nearest marsh and buried in the mud, whence they were soon exhumed by the washing of the tides; and at low water, the prisoners beheld the carrion crows picking the bones of their departed companions.

General Lincoln, having removed his quarters from Purysburg to Black Swamp, was soon afterward reinforced by seven hundred militia from North Carolina. His army being thus increased to five thousand men, he determined once more to attempt the recovery of Georgia. He left General Moultrie, with one thousand men, to defend Purysburg and the passes of the Savannah River, with orders to maintain his post as long as possible, and if the enemy should force their way toward Charleston to retreat before them, skirmishing with their front and destroying the boats and bridges on the way.

On the 20th of April, Lincoln, with two thousand men, marched for Augusta. Five days after his departure, General Moultrie received intelligence that the enemy were in motion, and that some parties of them had passed over into South Carolina below the town of Savannah.

Moultrie filed off toward Charleston for the purpose of keeping in the enemy's front, and sent an express to General Lincoln to apprize him of their movements, and his intention to harass and retard their progress, until he received reinforcements. General Provost's army consisted of two thousand chosen troops, and seven hundred loyalists and Indians. Moultrie, to oppose him, had but one thousand militia; and, instead of his numbers increasing, his troops wasted away by desertion. When he had retreated to Ashley River Ferry, he had only six hundred men.

Lincoln, imagining that Provost only intended a feint on Charleston, to divert him from his purpose toward Savannah, continued his march on the south side of the Savannah River, and sent three hundred light troops and the legion of Pulaski, which had been stationed at the ridge forty-five miles north-east from Augusta, to reinforce Moultrie.

Every advantageous pass was disputed with the enemy by the latter officer, and he so effectually retarded their progress, by frequent skirmishes, that they did not reach Charleston until the 11th of May.

When Provost appeared before Charleston, he

made the apparent dispositions for a siege, and demanded a surrender. Calculating that Lincoln was in pursuit of the enemy, it was deemed important to gain time. The reinforcement sent by General Lincoln and the legion of Pulaski had arrived; and the greatest exertions were used to place the town in a state of defence. Twenty-four hours were spent in negotiations, which terminated in bidding the enemy defiance. Having failed in his expectations, and fearing that Lincoln would fall upon his rear, Provost retreated precipitately over Ashley Ferry, and formed a fortified encampment on Stone River, within reach of some small armed vessels and transports, by which he could secure a retreat toward Savannah, if he should be pressed by a force with which he was unable to contend. He collected all the boats which fell in his way, to facilitate the transportation of his troops from one island to another, or through the inland navigation, as might be advisable.

When Lincoln arrived at Ashley River, he was doubtful of the issue of a general engagement with the enemy; for, although he was superior to his antagonist in numbers, he was far inferior in the quality of his troops and equipments, and was aware of the certain consequences of a defeat. It was, therefore, necessary for him to proceed with caution, and not risk a battle, if the result appeared in the least doubtful. He was apprehensive of the consequences of drawing his forces to one point, for a general attack, and leaving Charleston unprotected; and to prevent the enemy from retreating by land to Savannah, he was obliged to guard the passes by strong detachments. Thus situated, the two armies lay within thirty miles distance, for forty days, watching the motions of each other.

The British army was encamped on John's Island, near Stono Ferry. To preserve a communication with the main land, they had constructed some redoubts and lines of communication, on which some field artillery was advantageously placed, with an abatis in front, on the main land at the ferry, and a garrison of eight hundred men to defend it, under Lieutenant-colonel Maitland. In the event of its being attacked, the main encampment was sufficiently near to afford reinforcements.

At length, on the 20th of June, an attack was made on the redoubts at the ferry. General Moultrie, with a body of the Charleston militia, was to have made a feint on the British encampment, from James's Island; but from the difficulty of procuring boats, he was unable to reach the place of destination in time to make the diversion required. When the Americans advanced to the attack, two companies of the seventy-first regiment of Scots sallied out to support the pickets; Lieutenant-colonel Henderson, with the light infantry, charged them, and only nine of their number returned within their intrenchments. All the men at the field-pieces between their redoubts were killed or wounded. Major Handley, who commanded the remnant of the Georgia continental troops, was attached to Colonel Malmady's command, and carried that part of the British works against which they acted. The failure of General Moultrie in the diversion assigned to him enabled General Provost to reinforce the redoubts, and made it necessary for General Lincoln to withdraw his troops; a general sortie was made on the retiring Americans; but the light infantry, commanded by Malmady and Henderson, held the enemy in check, and enabled the Americans to remove their wounded, and retire in good order.

Soon after the action at Stono, the British commenced their retreat, and passed from island to island, until they arrived at Port Royal, where Provost established a post with eight hundred men, under the orders of Lieutenant-colonel Maitland, and thence returned to Savannah.

While Lincoln was employed in South Carolina against Provost, Colonels Dooley and Clarke were actively engaged in defending the frontiers of Georgia; and Colonels Twiggs, Few, and Jones were watching the British outposts, to cut off supplies of provisions from the country. Private armed vessels were also employed along the seacoast.

On the 24th of June, Captain Spencer, who commanded an American privateer, surprised Colonel Cruger and a party of British officers at a house on the river Medway, and took them prisoners of war.

On the 28th, Colonel Twiggs, being informed that a detachment of forty mounted grenadiers under Captain Muller was advancing to attack him, sent forward Major Cooper with thirty men to meet the enemy. Cooper formed his command across a rice-dam upon which Muller was advancing, and after a short, but fierce conflict, during which Muller was mortally wounded, the whole of the enemy were either killed, wounded, or taken prisoners. The American loss was only two officers wounded.

The situation of the wounded required the assistance of a surgeon, and Savannah being the nearest place where one could be obtained, William Myddleton offered his services to carry a flag for that purpose. Captain Muller died before the surgeon's arrival. While Myddleton was in Provost's quarters, a British officer requested him to narrate the circumstances attending the skirmish. After he had given the particulars, the officer observed, that "If an angel was to tell him that Captain Muller, who had served twenty-one years in the king's guards, had been defeated by an equal number of rebels, he would disbelieve it." Myddleton requested the officer's address, and observed that they were not then on equal terms, but hoped to have it in his power at a future time to call him to an account for his rudeness. Colonel Provost rebuked the officer for using such improper language to the bearer of a flag.

On the 3d of August, Captain Samuel Spencer sailed into Sapelo Sound, when one of the enemy's vessels, of six guns, ran down and attacked him. The engagement was well supported for fifteen minutes, when the enemy was boarded and surrendered. Spencer had one man wounded: the British, one killed, five wounded, and twelve made prisoners. Spencer divided his crew, and collected a number of negroes and other property, which he carried in safety to the owners, who had fled to Carolina. The prisoners were paroled and landed on Sapelo Island.

Ten days previous to the above gallant little affair, Sir James Wright returned from England and resumed the government of Georgia; but he was not suffered to remain long in the quiet performance of his official duties.

CHAPTER XVI.

France acknowledges the independence of the United States —D'Estaing agrees to co-operate with Lincoln—British preparations for defence—French forces disembarked—D'Estaing demands the surrender of Savannah—Truce granted —Provost reinforced—Siege of Savannah—Assault—Repulse of the combined armies—Jasper wounded—Count Pulaski wounded—Force of the allied army—Force of the British—Siege raised—Lincoln retreats to Ebenezer.

WHILE Georgia was thus ineffectually struggling in the grasp of her conquerors, an event occurred which, while it roused the timid and recalled the wavering, inspired all those who still clung fearlessly to the cause of freedom, with the liveliest hopes of eventual success.

France acknowledged the independence of the United States, and on the 6th of February, 1778, negotiated with the American commissioners at Paris a treaty of alliance, offensive and defensive.

Having thus become a party to the war, preparations were made to render the colonies that assistance which, from the increased efforts of Great Britain to recover her lost authority, was now becoming imperatively necessary.

A fleet was fitted out, and an army sent to the West Indies, under the orders of the Count D'Estaing. They made the conquest of the islands of St. Vincent and Grenada, and retired to Cape Francois.

As the recovery of Georgia was of the utmost importance, the co-operation of the French forces in the West Indies was solicited for that purpose. Count D'Estaing immediately returned a favourable response, and sailed from Cape Francois on the 20th of August, 1779, after despatching to Charleston two ships of the line and three frigates in advance, to concert a plan of operations with the American general.

General Lincoln made every exertion to collect an army, and was sanguine in his hopes of success in the execution of the concerted plan. The 11th of September was the time appointed for the rendezvous of the two armies at Savannah, and preparations were made to invest the place.

The militia took the field with alacrity, supposing that nothing further would be necessary than to march to Savannah and demand a surrender. Colonel Maitland, with eight hundred men, retained his position at Beaufort, and General Lincoln had fixed his quarters at Sheldon, to prevent them from spreading into the country to obtain provisions: thus occupied, General Lincoln could not march to Savannah until the French troops were ready to land.

As soon as the probability of an attack in force became known at Savannah, Provost called in his outposts, and endeavoured to make his fortifications as strong as possible. Thirteen redoubts and fifteen batteries were completed, and mounted with seventy-six pieces of cannon. The guns and batteries were manned by the seamen from the ships of war, transports, and merchant vessels in the harbour. A number of field-pieces, protected by intrenchments, were placed in reserve.

In the mean time, General McIntosh pressed forward from Augusta toward Savannah accompanied by the infantry under his command, and a body of cavalry under Count Pulaski. Before the enemy were apprized of his approach, the latter cut off one of their pickets, killed, wounded, and captured eleven men, and opened a communication to the sea-shore.

McIntosh advanced toward Ogechee Ferry, but so soon as a body of French troops had landed, he returned and halted three miles from Savannah, until Lincoln should arrive.

On the 6th of September, the French fleet appeared off Savannah bar; but it was not until the morning of the 16th, that Count D'Estaing was able to approach within three miles of the town, and demand a surrender.

In answer to the summons, Provost proposed a suspension of hostilities for twenty-four hours, to which D'Estaing agreed. The latter had not then formed a junction with the American forces under Lincoln, and was entirely ignorant of the advantages which would have accrued from an immediate attack.

Lincoln reached Millen's plantation on the Ogechee the same day, and proceeded directly to pay his respects to the Count D'Estaing, and fix on the plan of future operations. The latter suggested that no time should be lost, as it was necessary for the fleet to leave the coast as early as possible, from the dangerous character of the hurricanes which usually visited it at that season of the year. Measures were thus precipitated, which, under other and more fortunate circumstances, would have been arranged with greater coolness and system.

General Provost exercised great military judgment in soliciting twenty-four hours for consideration, because he calculated with great certainty that within that time Colonel Maitland would arrive with eight hundred troops from Beaufort. There is but little doubt that on this event rested all his hopes of saving the garrison. When the fleet first appeared off the coast, the enemy had but twenty-three pieces of cannon mounted upon the redoubts and batteries, to defend an extent by land and water of near three miles.

On the evening of the 16th, Maitland arrived at Dawfuskie; guided by some negro fisherman, he was enabled to avoid the Savannah River, and by passing through various creeks in small boats, gained the town in safety.

The acquisition of this formidable reinforcement effected a complete change in the condition of the desponding garrison. A signal was made, and three cheers given, which rang from one end of the town to the other. In the afternoon of the 17th, Provost notified D'Estaing of his determination to defend the place.

Mortified at receiving a defiance when he was confidently anticipating a surrender, and the favourable moment for reducing the fortress by assault having been suffered to pass away, no prospect of success now offered but the tedious operations of a siege. This was what the enemy wished. The principal engineer had declared that if the allied army would once resort to the spade, he would pledge himself for the success of the defence.

To prevent the French frigates from coming so near the town as to aid the operations by land, two ships and four transports were sunk in a narrow part of the channel below, while similar obstructions were placed above the town, to prevent the galleys which passed up the North river from assailing them in that direction. One of the frigates and two galleys anchored near the wrecks; but the enemy's guns, mounted upon batteries forty feet above the surface of the water, soon compelled them to retire.

From this time until the evening of the 7th of October, the siege was vigorously pressed by the allied forces, and as vigorously resisted on the part of the enemy.

Count D'Estaing having been a month on the American coast, and the fleet close in shore, his naval officers remonstrated with him on the dangerous situation it was in, and the hazard of being attacked by the British fleet while theirs was in bad condition, and while many of their officers and men were on shore. To these remonstrances were added the commencement of an extraordinary disease in the French camp, and the approach of the hurricane season, usually so destructive on the southern sea-coast of the United States. These considerations determined Count D'Estaing to call a council of war, in which it was the opinion of the engineers that it would require ten days more to work into the enemy's lines; upon which it was determined to try to carry them by an assault.

Accordingly, on the 8th of October, General Lincoln issued his orders for the attack, which was to be made at four o'clock the following morning.

He divided the infantry into two bodies; the first, consisting of the light troops under Colonel Laurens, to which the grenadiers were attached. The second, composed of the continental battalions and the Charleston militia.

Pulaski, who commanded the cavalry, had orders to penetrate the enemy's lines between the battery on the left of the Spring Hill redoubt, and the next toward the river. He was to be supported by the light troops and grenadiers, and reinforced, if necessary, by the first South Carolina regiment.

The militia of the first and second brigades, together with General Williamson's and the two battalions of Charleston militia, were ordered to the trenches, and to subject themselves to the commanding officer there. Previous to this, however, five hundred of the militia were to be drafted and placed under the command of General Huger, who was directed to march to the left of the enemy's lines, and make his attack as near to the river as possible. This was intended only as a feint, but Huger was authorized, if an opportunity offered, to convert it into a positive attack and push into the town.

On the night of the 8th, a sergeant of the Charleston grenadiers deserted, and communicated to the British general the plan of attack and the time when it was to be made. Being apprized that the Spring Hill redoubt and batteries was the point where the principal effort was to be sustained, and that the menace on the left of the works by Huger was but a feint, he made his dispositions accordingly. He removed the principal part of his force from the left of his works to the right, near to the Spring Hill, and placed that part of the defences under the orders of Lieutenant-colonel Maitland.

By one of those strange fatalities which seemed to accompany every attempt made by the Americans to release Georgia from the grasp of the British, the attack, which was ordered to take place at four o'clock on the morning of the 9th, was delayed until clear daylight. An opportunity was thus afforded the garrison of directing their fire upon the assailants with terrible effect, while the latter were in the act of advancing toward the works. The French columns passed the abatis, crowded into the moat, and ascended to the town under a galling fire in front and flank. The carnage was awful, but no useful impression made.

Lieutenant-colonel Laurens, with the light troops, advanced by the left of the French column, attacked Maitland's redoubt, and succeeded in gaining the parapet, where Lieutenants Bush and Hume set the colours of the second regiment of South Carolina: both those gallant officers were immediately shot down. Lieutenant Gray supported the colours, and was mortally wounded. Sergeant Jasper, seeing Gray fall, seized the colours and supported them, until he also received a wound, which proved mortal. At this point, the assault and resistance were of the most daring character.

McIntosh, at the head of the left column of

the American troops, forced his way into the ditch of the works north of the Maitland redoubt.

Count D'Estaing, early in the assault, received a wound in the arm, but remained at his post until a wound in his thigh made it necessary to bear him off the field.

Count Pulaski, while attempting to pass the works into the town, received a cannon-shot in the groin, of which he fell near the abatis. Huger made his attack as directed, and having accomplished the object of his orders, retired with the loss of twenty-eight men.

Finding it impossible to make any impression upon the works of the enemy, the commanding generals ordered a retreat. On the retreat, it was recollected by his corps that Count Pulaski had been left near the abatis; some of his men immediately forced their way through the firing and bore him off, though the heroic Pole was wounded mortally.

The loss of the allied army in this most rash but spirited assault was nearly eleven hundred men killed and wounded. Among the latter were the Count D'Estaing, Major-general De Fontange, the Chevalier D'Ernonville, and Count Pulaski. D'Ernonville was taken prisoner, his arm being broken by a ball. If he had consented to an amputation, he would probably have survived. When urged to the measure by General Provost, he refused; saying, that with but one hand, he could not serve his prince in the field, and if so disabled, life was not worth preserving. He died on the 25th of December, and was buried with all the honours of war.

The loss of the British during the assault was only fifty-five killed and wounded. How many they lost during the siege is not known.

The combined force employed against Savannah was four thousand nine hundred and fifty men. That of the enemy, twenty-eight hundred and fifty, including Indians and armed slaves.

General Lincoln urged that Count D'Estaing would agree to continue the siege of Savannah; but the reasons which the count gave for proposing the assault still obtained: it was further urged, that the troops of France were reduced by the consequences of the siege, in killed and wounded, and by disease, which was increasing, to less than fifteen hundred men fit for duty, on the 18th of October; and that the American troops under General Lincoln did not exceed twelve hundred effectives. In addition, there were good reasons for a belief that the British fleet at New York, with an army on board, was preparing for a southern expedition; and in the present sickly condition of the crews of the fleet, and the reduced force of the combined troops, who were not more than equal to the besieged, it would be highly imprudent to remain and risk the consequences. The count notified General Lincoln of his determination to raise the siege.

General Lincoln retreated to Ebenezer, and on the 19th of October he left the army for Charleston, with orders to march to that place.

There was great dissatisfaction expressed by the citizens of Georgia at the determination of D'Estaing to raise the siege. Many of them had been under British protection, and having resumed their arms in opposition to the royal government, they were apprehensive of the consequences if they again fell into the enemy's hands. Notwithstanding these murmurs, General Lincoln by prudent management silenced the expressions of discontent, and the allied forces separated with mutual assurances of esteem and affection.

CHAPTER XVII.

Heroic instances of devotion to freedom—The grenadiers of Count Dillon—Anecdote of Lieutenant Lloyd—Sergeant Jasper—His daring bravery at Fort Moultrie—His roving commission—Captures ten men near Savannah—Presented with a sword by Governor Rutledge—Plants the colours on Spring Hill redoubt—Is mortally wounded—Count Pulaski—His early life—Confederates with others for the redemption of Poland—Captures Stanislaus—Seeks refuge in France Appointed a brigadier-general in the American service—His death.

IF the siege of Savannah was unfortunate in many respects, it yet afforded many cheering instances of heroic devotion to the cause of freedom.

Count Dillon, commander of the Irish brigade in the service of France, and who led on the third column of the allied armies in their assault of the British garrison, anxious that his regiment should signalize itself, offered one hundred guineas as a reward to the first of his grenadiers that should plant a fascine in the fosse, which was exposed to the whole fire of the garrison. Not one offered to advance. The count, mortified and disappointed beyond measure, began upbraiding them with cowardice, when the sergeant-major made the following noble reply :—"Had you not, sir, held out a sum of money as a temptation, your grenadiers would, one and all, have presented themselves." They did so instantly, and out of one hundred and ninety-four, of which the company consisted, only ninety returned alive.

Previous to the assault, some Georgia officers who had no commands, and other private gentlemen to the number of thirty, formed themselves into a volunteer corps, under Colonel Marbury. Of this little party eleven were either killed or wounded. Among the latter was Lieutenant Edward Lloyd, whose arm had been carried away by a cannon-ball. While a surgeon was employed in dressing the remaining stump of this young officer's arm, Major James Jackson observed to him, that his prospect was unpromising, from the heavy burden which hard fate had imposed upon him, as a young man who was just entering into life. Lloyd answered that, unpromising as it was, he would not willingly exchange it for the feelings of Lieutenant Stedman, who had fled at the commencement of the assault.

The conduct of Sergeant Jasper merits still more particular notice. At the commencement of the Revolutionary war, Sergeant Jasper enlisted in the second South Carolina regiment of infantry, commanded by Colonel Moultrie. He distinguished himself in a particular manner at the attack which was made upon Fort Moultrie, on Sullivan's Island, on the 25th of June, 1776.

In the warmest part of the contest the flagstaff was severed by a cannon-ball, and the flag fell to the bottom of the ditch on the outside of the works: this accident was considered by the anxious inhabitants of Charleston as putting an end to the contest by striking the American flag to the enemy.

The moment Jasper made the discovery that the flag had fallen, he jumped from one of the embrasures, and seizing the colours, which he had tied to a sponge-staff, supported them on the parapet until another flag was procured. His subsequent activity and enterprise induced Colonel Moultrie to give him a sort of a roving commission to go and come at pleasure; confident that he was always usefully employed.

He was privileged to select such men from the regiment as he should choose to accompany him in his enterprises. His parties consisted generally of five or six, and he often returned with prisoners before Moultrie was apprized of his absence. Jasper was distinguished for his humane treatment when an enemy fell into his power. His ambition appears to have been limited to the characteristic of bravery, humanity, and usefulness to the cause in which he was engaged.

When it was in his power to kill but not to capture, it was his practice not to permit a single prisoner to escape. By his sagacity and enterprise, he often succeeded in the capture of those who were lying in ambush for him. In one of his excursions, an instance of bravery and humanity is recorded by the biographer of General Marion, which would stagger credulity, if it were not well attested.

While he was examining the British camp at Ebenezer, all the sympathy of his breast was awakened by the distresses of Mrs. Jones, whose husband, an American by birth, had received the king's protection, and had been confined in irons for deserting the royal cause after he had taken the oath of allegiance. Her well-founded belief was, that nothing short of the life of her husband would atone for the offence with which he was charged.

Jasper secretly consulted with his companion, Sergeant Newton, whose feelings for the distressed female were equally excited with his own, upon the practicability of releasing Jones from his impending fate.

Though they were unable to suggest a plan of operation, they were determined to watch for the most favourable opportunity, and make the effort. The departure of Jones and several others (all in irons) to Savannah, for trial, under a guard consisting of a sergeant, corporal, and eight men, was ordered upon the succeeding morning.

Within two miles of Savannah, about thirty yards from the main road, is a spring of fine water, surrounded by a deep and thick underwood, where travellers often halt to refresh themselves with a cool draught from the pure fountain. Jasper and his companion considered this spot the most favourable for their enterprise. They accordingly passed the guard, and concealed themselves near the spring.

When the enemy came up, the corporal, with his guard of four men, conducted the prisoners to the spring, while the sergeant, with the other four, having grounded their arms near the road, brought up the rear. The prisoners, wearied with their long walk, were permitted to rest themselves on the earth. Two of the corporal's men were ordered to keep guard, and the other two to give the prisoners drink out of their canteens.

The last two approached the spring where our heroes lay concealed, and resting their muskets against the tree, dipped up water; and having drunk themselves, turned away, with replenished canteens, to give the prisoners also. "Now, Newton, is our time!" said Jasper. Then bursting from their concealment, they snatched up the two muskets that were rested against the tree, and instantly shot down the two soldiers that kept guard.

By this time the sergeant and corporal, a couple of brave Englishmen, recovering from their panic, had sprung and seized up the two muskets which had fallen from the slain: but before they could use them, the Americans, with clubbed guns, levelled each at the head of his antagonist the final blow. Then securing their weapons, they flew between the surviving enemy and their arms, grounded near the road, and compelled them to surrender.

The irons were taken off, and arms put in the hands of those who had been prisoners, and the whole party arrived at Purysburgh the next morning and joined the American camp. There are but few instances upon record where personal exertions, even for self-preservation from certain prospect of death, would have induced a resort to an act so desperate of execution.

After the gallant defence at Sullivan's Island, Colonel Moultrie's regiment was presented with a stand of colours by Mrs. Elliot, which she had richly embroidered with her own hands; and as a reward for Jasper's particular merit, Governor Rutledge presented him with a very handsome sword. During the assault against Savannah, as previously stated, two officers had been killed, and one wounded, endeavouring to plant these colours upon the enemy's parapet of the Spring Hill redoubt; when, just before the retreat was ordered, Jasper endeavoured to replace them upon the works, and while he was in the act, received his mortal wound and fell into the ditch. When a retreat was ordered, he recollected the honourable conditions upon which the donor presented the colours to his regiment, and among the last acts of his life, succeeded in bringing them off.

Major Horry called to see him soon after the

retreat, to whom it is said he made the following communication: "I have got my furlough. That sword was presented to me by Governor Rutledge, for my services in the defence of Fort Moultrie; give it to my father, and tell him I have worn it in honour. If the old man should weep, tell him his son died in the hope of a better life. Tell Mrs. Elliot that I lost my life supporting the colours which she presented to our regiment. Should you ever see Jones, his wife and son, tell them that Jasper is gone, but that the remembrance of that battle, which he fought for them, brought a secret joy into his heart when it was about to stop its motion for ever." He expired a few moments after closing this sentence.

Count Pulaski, who fell mortally wounded during the same assault, was a native of Poland, whose king, Stanislaus, had been raised to the throne, not by the customary voices of the people, but by the influence of the Empress of Russia.

Indignant at this innovation on the elective franchise, a number of patriotic nobles, among the foremost of whom was Pulaski, confederated together to rescue their country from foreign influence by force of arms. Pulaski, for his high character and military enterprise, was elected their general.

Finding the force and resources of the confederates unequal to the objects they had in view, Pulaski applied to France for assistance, and was secretly encouraged and supplied with money. A number of French officers also engaged as volunteers in his service; but the numbers that joined his standard were not sufficient to enable him to achieve more than partial success.

At length, the confederates determined to seize on the person of the king. A party selected for that purpose attacked and wounded him in the streets of Warsaw. They succeeded in bearing him off a prisoner; but the guard deserted, and suffered Stanislaus to escape to his palace. Shortly after this, Russia, supported by Prussia and Austria, sent troops into Poland, and under the plausible pretext of aiding Stanislaus in the recovery of his rights, stripped him of the greater part of his territories. The confederates sued for peace and pardon: Pulaski, and others of the chiefs, fled to France. The American ministers, to whom he was made known at Paris, recommended Pulaski to the consideration of Congress, from whom he received, on his arrival, the appointment of brigadier-general of cavalry.

The remainder of Pulaski's life was devoted to the service of the United States; and it may be truly said, that on all occasions when he had an opportunity to act, "he sought the post of danger, as the post of honour;" welcomed every opportunity of being engaged with the enemy, and was always foremost in the day of battle.

After being wounded in the attack on Savannah, the vessel in which he was being conveyed to Charleston having a long passage, he died at sea, and his body was launched and sunk beneath the waves. The funeral rites were performed in Charleston with military honours. The death of that gallant officer was greatly lamented by all the Americans and French who had witnessed his valour or knew how to appreciate his merits.

CHAPTER XVIII.

Sufferings of the Georgians—Mrs. McIntosh—The forged letter—Skirmish at Ogechee Ferry—Siege and surrender of Charleston—Removal of the Georgia records—Governor Howley—Defection of Brigadier-general Williamson—Murder of Colonel Dooley—Inhuman treatment of Mrs. McKay—Defeat of the loyalists by Jones—Skirmish at Wafford's Iron-works—Clarke defeats the British at Musgrove's Mill.

NOTHING could exceed the deplorable condition of Georgia after the repulse of the allied forces before Savannah. Flushed with the hope of expelling the enemy, many patriotic men, regardless of the danger to which their families would be exposed, had joined the standard of Lincoln, and were now to suffer the fearful calamities which always attend disastrous issues.

Future protection was not to be expected; and nothing remained for them but the halter and confiscation from the British, or exile for themselves, and poverty and ill-treatment, by an insolent enemy, for their wives and children, who were ordered forthwith to depart the country without the means for travelling, or any other means, but a reliance on charity for subsistence on their way.

The families of McIntosh, Twiggs, and Clarke, with numerous others, experienced hardships and distresses of the most afflicting character. That of Colonel Twiggs, while removing under the protection of a flag, was fired upon and a young man killed who was of the party.

The family of General McIntosh was reduced from affluence to extreme want. On reaching Virginia, Mrs. McIntosh was obliged to apply to Governor Jefferson for relief from absolute want. He furnished her with ten thousand dollars in continental money, but so greatly was its value depreciated, that it required seven hundred dollars to purchase a single pair of shoes.

The house of Colonel Clarke was pillaged and burned, and his family ordered to leave the state, With no other means of conveyance than a pony of little value, Mrs. Clarke and her two daughters set out for the north. Poor as it was, the horse was soon wrested from them, and the unfortunate females compelled to traverse on foot an enemy's country, thinly inhabited, and without any means of subsistence.

After Savannah had fallen into the hands of the enemy, the legislature dispersed without appointing a governor for the ensuing year. John Werreat, esquire, president of the council, acting as governor, issued on the 4th of November, 1779, a proclamation representing the necessity of convening the legislature, and fixing the second Tuesday of the same month for the election of members, who were to meet at Augusta without delay.

Fearful, however, that the British would seize upon Augusta before the authorized election could take place, a number of gentlemen, chosen from the county of Richmond alone, formed themselves into a body under the name of the general assembly; by whom William Glascock was chosen speaker, and George Walton, esquire, governor of the state.

During the session of this legislature a letter was forged in the name of William Glascock, the speaker, and sent to the President of Congress. This letter, written by some rancorous enemy of General McIntosh, falsely stated that his presence in his native state gave neither satisfaction to the militia nor the confederated patriots; and strongly urged upon Congress to select some distant field for the exercise of the abilities of that officer.

Fortunately, a copy of the letter was forwarded to General McIntosh and, instantly enclosed to Mr. Glascock, by whom, and by the body over which he presided, its contents were indignantly disavowed, and the attorney-general ordered to search out and prosecute its author.

In the mean time, the Georgians whose property had been confiscated were active in devising means for its recovery and removal to places of security. On the other hand, the loyalists were as energetic in their attempts to intercept it. Skirmishes and reprisals occurred continually, and with various success. Colonels Twiggs, Dooley, Clarke, Few, and Jones were still engaged in partisan warfare; sometimes on the frontiers against the Indians, and sometimes in attacking the detached parties of the British.

To repress these outbreaks, General Provost ordered Captain Conklin, with a force of sixty-four men, to proceed to Governor Wright's plantation and disperse the Americans who were collected, to the number of sixty, at that place.

At the Ogechee Ferry, Conklin was discovered while in the act of crossing over, but was suffered by Pickens and Twiggs to pass the river without interruption; they encouraged the advance of the enemy by exhibiting only twenty militia dragoons, under the command of Captain Inman. In the early part of the skirmish which ensued, Captain Conklin received a mortal wound. Lieutenant Roney, finding his situation critical, resorted to the bayonet, with which he made a desperate charge, and was also wounded. Ensign Supple's detachment was pressed closely by

Captain Inman's dragoons, and compelled to retreat through the swamp in a rice-field, where he knew the dragoons could not carry the pursuit. He rejoined his party, and ordered the wounded to be carried to the boats. He kept up a retreating fire until he reached the river, which he recrossed. Of the enemy, two privates were killed and seven wounded: among the latter were the first and second officers in the command.

Finding that the impressions made upon the northern states were but transitory, the British generals determined to subjugate those of the south. Accordingly, on the 1st of April, 1780, Charleston was invested by land and blockaded by sea. The siege was continued until the 12th of May, when the works being considered no longer tenable, General Lincoln surrendered the city to the British army and navy.

By the fall of Charleston, General McIntosh, with the remnant of the Georgia brigade, all the other continental troops in the southern department, several thousands of the militia, and the residue of the ordnance and military stores in the southern states, fell into the hands of the enemy.

The situation of the Governor of Georgia at Augusta being no longer safe, he retreated with part of his council, and a number of his civil officers to North Carolina, and narrowly escaped capture by the way.

Colonel Heard, president of the council, with several other members, retired to Wilkes county, where the semblance of a government was still kept up.

The records of the state had been previously removed to Charleston; they were now sent to North Carolina. Upon the passage of the British army through the latter state, the Georgia records were carried to Maryland, where they remained until the close of the war.

During the brief administration of Governor Howley, the gay and joyous temperament of that gentleman, and of his secretary of state, sustained the spirits of the fugitive council from sinking into gloom and despondency.

The value of paper money was at that time so depreciated, that the governor dealt it out by the quire for a night's lodging for his party; and if the fare was any thing extraordinary, the landlord was compensated with two quires, the governor gravely signing a draft upon the treasurer made out in due form for the delivery of the same.

Public opinion about this time was strongly agitated in reference to the eccentric movements of Brigadier-general Williamson. He was encamped with three hundred men, near Augusta, and by his continual prevarications and delays induced many influential persons to suspect that Williamson was by no means averse to being captured by the enemy.

The editor of the Royal Gazette of Georgia boldly charged Williamson not only with having the king's protection in his pocket, but that he had agreed to accept a colonel's commission from the same source. The result justified the charge. Williamson did, soon after, encourage the surrender of his brigade; infamously accepted the proffered commission of a royalist colonel, and until the close of the war, warmly advocated the re-establishment of the government of the crown. Almost simultaneous with the defection of Williamson, Colonel Brown, with a detachment of royalist forces, took military possession of Augusta.

But there were, even in these desperate times, a few noble hearted patriots who would not despair of eventually saving their country. Colonel Elijah Clarke had embodied three hundred men in Wilkes county, and Colonels Jones and Few, commanding two detachments of a similar description, as soon as they were advised of the treachery of Williamson, retreated across the country and joined their forces to those already collected by Clarke. Immediately after occupying Augusta, Colonel Brown despatched emissaries into the country, with authority to give protection and administer the oath of allegiance to the British crown. One of these parties entered the house of Colonel John Dooley at a late hour of the night, and barbarously murdered him in the presence of his wife and children. The loss of so energetic a partisan as Colonel Dooley, was severely felt among the patriots, and was one among the many causes of those terrible measures of retaliation which were afterward enforced.

Previous to the murder of Colonel Dooley, a detachment was sent by McGirth into the neighbourhood of Captain McKay, in South Carolina. In two days seventeen men were massacred on their farms, and the whole of a flourishing country of thirty miles in length, and ten in breadth, was desolated by these banditti.

Disappointed in their expectations of getting possession of McKay's person, they resorted to the torture of his wife to extort from her a knowledge of the place of his concealment. The mode of inflicting the torture was by taking a flint out of the lock of a musket, and putting her thumb in its place. The screw was applied, until the thumb was ready to burst. While under this new species of torture, which would have disgraced the most savage nation in the world, in addition to the questions put to her respecting her husband, she was required to disclose the secret deposit of his most valuable property, which they alleged had been removed and hidden in the woods. If McKay was afterward charged with inhumanity to those whom he captured, the gross outrage just narrated must be admitted as affording at least some palliation for his conduct.

It was at this bloody period of the war that the well-known incident occurred, which, though variously related, has never been so well told as in the following account by Mrs. Ellet:—

"In a portion of Wilkes—now Elbert county—called by tories, "The Hornest's Nest," on account of the number of whigs among the inhabitants, a stream named 'War-woman's Creek,' joined Broad River. It was so called on account of a zealous tory-hating heroine who lived on its banks. On the occasion of an excursion from the British camp at Augusta, into the interior for the purpose of pillage and murder, five loyalists separated from their party, and crossed the river to examine the neighbourhood and pay a visit to their old acquaintance, Nancy Hart. When they arrived at her cabin, they unceremoniously entered it, and informed her they had come to learn the truth of a story, that she had secreted a noted rebel from a party of 'king's men,' who, but for her interference, would have caught and hung him. Nancy undauntedly avowed her agency in the fugitive's escape. She had heard at first, she said, the tramp of a horse, and then saw a man on horseback approaching her cabin. As soon as she knew him to be a whig flying from pursuit, she let the down the bars in front of her cabin, and motioned him to pass through both doors and take to the swamp. She then put up the bars, entered the cabin, and closed the doors.

Presently some tories rode up to the bars, calling vociferously for her. She muffled up her head and face, and opening the door, inquired why they disturbed a sick, lone woman. They said they had traced a man they wanted to catch near to her house, and asked if any one on horseback had passed that way. She answered no, but that she saw some one on a sorrel horse turn out of the path into the woods, two or three hundred yards back. 'That must be the fellow!' said the tories; and asking her direction as to the way he took, they turned about and went off, 'well-fooled,' concluded Nancy, 'in an opposite course to that of my whig boy, when, if they had not been so lofty-minded, but had looked on the ground inside the bars, they would have seen his horse's tracks up to that door, as plain as you can see the tracks on this floor, and out of t'other door down the path to the swamp.'

"This bold story did not much please the tory party, but they contented themselves with ordering her to prepare them something to eat. She replied that she never fed traitors and king's men if she could help it—the villains having put it out of her power to feed even her own family and friends, by stealing and killing all her poultry and pigs, 'except that one old gobbler you see in the yard.' 'And *that* you shall cook for us,' said one who appeared to be a leader; and raising his musket he shot down the turkey, which another brought in and handed to Mrs. Hart to be cleaned and cooked without delay. She stormed a while, but seeming at last disposed to make a merit of necessity, began with alacrity the arrangements for cooking, assisted by her daughter, a little girl ten or twelve years old.

"The spring—of which every settlement had one near—was just at the edge of the swamp; and a short distance within the swamp was hid among the trees a high snag-topped stump, on which was placed a conch-shell. This rude trumpet was used by the family to convey information, by variations in its notes, to Hart or his neighbours, who might be at work in a field or 'clearing' at hand—to let them know that the 'Britishers' or tories were about—that the master was wanted at the cabin—or that he was to keep close, or 'make tracks' for another swamp. While cooking the turkey, Nancy sent her daughter to the spring for water, with directions to blow the conch in such a way as should inform her father there were tories in the cabin; and that he was to keep close with his three neighbours until he should again hear the signal.

"While the men, who had become merry over their jug of liquor, were feasting upon the slaughtered gobbler, Nancy waited on the table, and occasionally passed between them and their muskets. She had contrived that there should be no water in the cabin; and when it was called for, despatched Sukey a second time to the spring, with instructions to blow such a signal on the conch as should call up Hart and his neighbours immediately. Meanwhile she had managed by slipping out one of the pieces of pine which form a 'chinking' between the logs of a cabin, to open a space through which she was able to pass to the outside two of the five guns. She was detected in the act of putting out the third. The men sprang to their feet, when, quick as thought, Nancy brought the piece she held, to her shoulder, declaring she would kill the first man who approached her. The men arriving from the field, the tories were taken prisoners, and, sad to relate! received no more mercy than had some of the whigs at the hands of their enemies."

During the month of June, Colonel Clarke was actively engaged in collecting additional troops, and in concerting with the authorities of South Carolina the plan of a campaign against the enemy.

Agreeably to appointment, on the 11th of July, one hundred and forty men, well mounted and armed, reached the rendezvous at Freeman's Fort; but as the British and loyalists were in force in his front, Clarke proposed to disband his men for a time, and wait until a more favourable opportunity occurred for carrying out his designs.

This arrangement was very generally approved, but Colonel Jones, joined by some thirty-five men, determined to force their way across the state into North Carolina, and join the American army wherever it was to be found.

On the 14th, Jones surprised, by stratagem, a party of loyalists, killed one and wounded three, and took twenty-eight prisoners. The next day he joined Colonel McDonald at Earls' Ford, on Packolet River. The united forces numbered over four hundred men.

Ignorant of the approach of McDowell, Colonel Innis, commander of the British garrison at Prince's Fort, despatched Captain Dunlop with seventy dragoons, in pursuit of Jones. Dunlop pressed forward with rapidity, attacked the American encampment during the night, killed and wounded thirty-eight men, and retreated with the loss of but one man wounded.

A pursuit was immediately ordered, and after a march of fifteen miles in two hours, Dunlop was himself defeated in turn, with the loss of eight men killed at the first fire, and many others killed and wounded before he was enabled to reach the fort.

Clarke, having in the mean time, re-assembled his regiment, was joined soon after by Colonel Jones, near the line which separates North from South Carolina. His presence forming a great annoyance to Colonel Innis and his garrison, the latter determined to bring on a general action; but after a short but indecisive skirmish at Wafford's Iron-works, in which Major Burwell Smith was killed, both parties retired from the field.

The loss of Major Smith was greatly regretted by Colonel Clarke, who considered him as one of his best partisan officers.

The continued success of the American foraging parties determined Colonel Innis to increase his force, renew the attack upon Clarke's camp, and, if possible, drive him out of the country. On the night of the 17th of August, the approach of Innis—whose command consisted of three hundred and fifty men—was communicated to Colonel Clarke. Fortunately, the latter had previously been joined by Colonels Williams, Branham, and Shelby, whose forces had raised Clarke's numbers to an equality with those of the enemy. It was, therefore, determined to give battle the next morning.

About four miles from Musgrove's Mill there was a plantation, through which was a lane, and Clarke considered that the north end of it afforded him a favourable position for an attack.

He advanced with one hundred men, himself on the right, and Major McCall on the left; forming in the edge of the thick wood across the road, and extending his flanks near the fence. Williams and Branham were ordered to form close in the rear of the flanks, and Shelby to cover the centre as a reserved corps, and to throw his force wherever circumstances might require. The advance-guard of the enemy were within fifty paces before they were aware of danger. When

Clarke commenced the attack, Innis ordered his dragoons and mounted militia to charge upon the Americans, and force them from the ground they occupied, that he might have room to form his regulars. Clarke was aware that the issue of the battle depended on his holding his ground, so as to force the British regulars to form in the open field, while his own men would be covered by the fence and the woods. Williams and Branham advanced and formed upon the right and left, and Shelby to the support of the centre, when the contest became close and sanguinary. Observing this additional force, the dragoons and royal militia retreated into the lane among the British regulars, thus increasing the confusion, and flying from the field in the utmost disorder. The regulars had not room to form, and if they had done so in the open field, it would have been to great disadvantage. In this confused state, exposed to a galling fire from the American riflemen, they remained but a few minutes before seven British officers out of nine were either killed or wounded; and the men tumbled down in heaps, without the power of resistance. Among the wounded was the British commander. Captain Ker, second in command, finding that resistance would then be vain, and without hope of success, ordered a retreat; which was effected in close order for four miles, resorting to the bayonet in flank and rear. The pursuit was continued by the victors, until the enemy took refuge in Musgrove's Mill. The British loss was sixty-three killed, and one hundred and sixty wounded and prisoners. The American loss was four killed and nine wounded. Among the former was Captain Inman, and among the latter were Colonel Clarke and Captain John Clarke. The colonel received two wounds with a sabre on the back of his neck and head. His stock-buckle saved his life. He was for a few minutes a prisoner with the enemy, in charge of two men; but taking advantage of his strength and activity, he knocked one of them down, and the other fled.

Colonel Clarke, after burying his dead, returned to his former encampment near the iron-works.

CHAPTER XIX.

Cornwallis violates his pledges of protection—Indignation of the people—Clarke returns to Georgia—Siege of Augusta—Brown's desperate defence—Cruger advances to reinforce Brown—Retreat of Clarke—Cruelty of Brown toward his prisoners—Savage treatment of Mr. Alexander by Colonel Grierson—Ferguson ordered to intercept—Is pursued himself—Battle of King's Mountain—Skirmishes—Clarke wounded.

Lord Cornwallis, having, as he supposed, entirely subjugated the states of Georgia and South Carolina, now shamefully determined to violate those pledges of protection which many of the inhabitants had been compelled previously to accept.

The impression first made upon the public mind was, that persons and property were to be secured against outrage and molestation by the British troops and loyalists; and that peaceable citizens were not to take up arms against the crown of Great Britain so long as these conditions were duly regarded.

So soon, however, as Cornwallis had succeeded in restoring the government of the crown, he wrote secret orders to the commanders of his outposts, directing them to punish with the utmost rigour all who had taken part in the revolt, to imprison all who refused to take up arms on the side of the British, and to confiscate or destroy their property. The most positive instructions were also given to hang every militia-man who, after having once borne arms for the crown, had subsequently joined the patriots.

Orders of so sanguinary a character could not remain long unknown to the people. Indignant at this gross violation of the compact entered into between themselves and their brutal rulers, many immediately flew to arms; while others of a cooler temperament smothered their resentment for a time, but were not the less resolved to shake off, at the first favourable opportunity, their allegiance to a government as treacherous as it was bloodthirsty. Among the most confident of those who entertained hopes that the authorized cruelties, which ensued soon afterward, would rouse a large proportion of the population into open rebellion, were Colonel Elijah Clarke and Lieutenant-colonel McCall.

About the 1st of September, 1780, the first returned to Wilkes county in Georgia; while the other went into the western part of Ninety-Six district, with the expectation of raising a joint force of at least one thousand men. To such an army it was supposed that Augusta would submit with little or no resistance, and that Ninety-Six might soon afterward be menaced, and would probably be evacuated by the enemy. The success of this scheme would have given the Americans the whole of the western divisions of Georgia and South Carolina.

Instead of five hundred men, which McCall had confidently calculated on from Carolina, his persuasions could only induce eighty to accompany him upon the expedition. Clarke had been more successful. His numbers amounted to three hundred and fifty.

With this small band he determined to precipitate himself suddenly upon Augusta; and as soon as he was joined by McCall, he commenced his march.

The garrison of Augusta consisted, at the time of Clarke's approach, of five hundred and fifty rangers and Indians, under the command of the renegade Colonel Brown.

On the morning of the 14th of September, the Americans halted, unobserved, near the town, and separated their forces into three divisions. One of these divisions, under Major Taylor, while advancing to the attack, fell in with an Indian camp near to Hawk's Creek, and drove the savages back upon their allies. Taylor pressed on to get possession of McKay's trading-house, denominated the white house, one mile and a half west of the town. At this house the Indians joined a company of the king's rangers, commanded by Captain Johnston. The attack upon the camp gave the first intimation to Brown of the Americans' approach. He ordered Grierson to reinforce Johnston, and advanced to the scene of action in person, with the main body. The centre and right divisions completely surprised the garrisons of the forts, and took possession without resistance. Seventy prisoners, and all the Indians present, were put under charge of a guard, and Clarke marched with the residue to the assistance of Major Taylor. Brown and Grierson had joined Johnston and the Indians, and upon Clarke's approach, took shelter in the white house, and defended it. Several attempts were made to dislodge the enemy, by taking possession of some small out-houses to the eastward; but they failed, from the houses being too small and flanked by the Indians. Finding that these houses furnished little or no defence, they were abandoned. A desultory fire was continued from eleven o'clock until night, but it was found that the enemy could not be dislodged without artillery.

At the close of the day the firing ceased, and strong guards were posted to keep the enemy in check. Under cover of the night, Brown strengthened his position by throwing up some works around the house, and by filling the interstices between the weather-boarding with earth.

The next morning Clarke brought up two pieces of artillery from Grierson's Fort, which were placed in a position to bear upon the house; but owing to unskilful management, and the fall of his only artillerist, they proved of little use.

On the morning of the 16th, the Americans succeeded in driving the Indians from their shelter, and cut off the supply of water, by which the enemy, particularly the wounded, suffered greatly. Early in the engagement, Brown was shot through both thighs and suffered among the wounded, who were often heard calling for water and medical aid.

The sufferings of the wounded, the nauseous smell of animal putrefaction from the dead bodies of men and horses lying around, and the want of water, it was supposed, would induce the enemy to surrender.

Accordingly, on the 17th, Clarke sent Colonel Brown a summons, but the proposition was rejected. In the afternoon the summons was repeated; the reply of Brown expressed his determination to defend himself to the last extremity.

The only hope of the latter rested upon the messengers he had sent off early in the contest to Colonel Cruger at Ninety-Six, asking immediate reinforcements. Nor were these hopes fallacious. On the night of the 17th, Clarke's spies informed him of the approach of Cruger by forced marches, with five hundred British regulars and militia; and at ten o'clock on the morning of the 18th, the Americans raised the siege, after having held the enemy for three days almost within their grasp. The retreat itself was a bitter mortification, but the consequences which immediately followed it were horrible.

When Clarke felt himself compelled to retire before a vastly superior force of the enemy, he humanely paroled his prisoners, to the number of fifty-four officers and men, hoping that this considerate policy would operate favourably in regard to such of his own wounded as were not in a condition to be removed from the town. He had fearfully mistaken the character of his enemy. The prisoners he had released immediately violated their parole, and took up arms against him.

Captain Asby, an officer noted for his bravery and humanity, with twenty-eight others, including the wounded, fell into the hands of the enemy, and were disposed of, under the sanguinary order of Lord Cornwallis, in the following manner: Captain Asby and twelve of the wounded prisoners were hanged on the staircase of the White-house, where Brown was lying wounded, so that he might have the satisfaction of seeing the victims of his vengeance expire. Their bodies were delivered up to the Indians, who scalped and otherwise mangled them and threw them in the river. Henry Duke, John Burgamy, Scott Redden, Jordan Ricketson, —— Darling, and two youths, brothers, of seventeen and fifteen years of age, named Glass, were all hanged: the former of these youths was shot through the thigh, and could not be carried off when the retreat was ordered, and the younger brother could not be prevailed on to leave him; his tenderness and affection cost him his life. A horse was the fatal scaffold on which they were mounted, and from the gibbet they entered together on the long journey of eternity.

All this was merciful, when compared with the fate which awaited the other prisoners. They were delivered to the Indians to glut their vengeance for the loss they had sustained in the action and siege. The Indians formed a circle and placed the prisoners in the centre, and their eagerness to shed blood spared the victims from tedious torture: some were scalped before they sunk under the Indian weapons of war; others were thrown into fires and roasted to death.

Thus mournfully ended an expedition which, had it been successful, would have been lauded as highly as it was subsequently censured.

After the siege was raised the country was searched, and those whose relations were engaged in the American cause were arrested and crowded into prisons: others who were suspected of having intercourse with any of Clarke's command were hanged without the forms of trial. The venerable grandfathers of the American patriots, whose hoary heads were bending toward the grave, were crowded into filthy places of confinement for no other crimes than those of receiving visits from their descendants, after a long absence. Among the number was the father of Captains Samuel and James Alexander, in the seventy-eighth year of his age: he was arrested by a party commanded by Colonel Grierson, and by his order was ignominiously chained to a cart, and dragged like a criminal forty miles in two days; and when he attempted to rest his feeble frame by leaning upon the cart, the driver was ordered to scourge him with his whip. These old men were kept in close confinement, as hostages for the neutrality of the country; but by the inclemency of the season, the small-pox, and inhuman treatment, very few of them survived to greet their friends in freedom, upon the re-conquest of it by the American troops.

So soon as Lord Cornwallis heard of the retreat of Clarke from Augusta, he directed Major Ferguson, a partisan officer of distinguished merit, to march to the frontiers of South Carolina and intercept Clarke.

The hardy mountaineers of Virginia and North Carolina, collecting at this time from various quarters, constituted a formidable force, and advanced by a rapid movement toward Ferguson.

At the same time, Colonel Williams, from the neighbourhood of Ninety-Six, and Colonels Tracy and Banan, also of South Carolina, conducted parties of men toward the same points. Ferguson, having notice of their approach, commenced his march for Charlottesville. The several corps of militia, amounting to near three thousand men, met at Gilbert-town, lately occupied by Ferguson. About one thousand six hundred riflemen were immediately selected, and mounted on their fleetest horses, for the purpose of following the retreating army. They came up with the enemy at King's Mountain, October 7th, 1780, where Ferguson, on finding he should be overtaken, had chosen his ground, and waited for an attack.

The Americans formed themselves into three divisions, led by Colonels Campbell, Shelby, and Cleaveland, and began to ascend the mountain in three different and opposite directions. Cleaveland, with his division, was the first to gain sight of the enemy's picket, and halting his men, he addressed them in the following simple, affecting, and animating terms:—"My brave fellows, we *have* beat the *tories*, and we *can* beat them; they are all cowards. If they had the spirit of men, they would join their fellow-citizens in supporting the independence of their country. When engaged, you are not to wait for the word of command from me. *I will show you how to fight by my example.* I can undertake no more. Every man must consider himself as an officer, and act from his own judgment. Fire as quick as you can. When you can do no better, get behind trees or retreat, but I beg you not to run quite off. If we are repulsed, let us make a point to return and renew the fight; perhaps we may have better luck in the second attempt than in the first. If any of you are afraid, such have leave to retire, and they are requested *immediately to take themselves off.*"

This address, which would have done honour to the hero of Agincourt, being ended, the men rushed upon the enemy's pickets, and forced them to retire; but returning again to the charge with the bayonet, Cleaveland's men gave way in their turn. In the mean time, Colonel Shelby advanced with his division, and was in like manner driven back by the bayonets of the enemy; but there was yet another body of assailants to be received: Colonel Campbell moved up at the moment of Shelby's repulse, but was equally unable to stand against the British bayonets, and Ferguson still kept possession of his mountain. The whole of the division being separately baffled, determined to make an other effort in co-operation, and the conflict became terrible.

Ferguson still depended upon the bayonet; but this brave and undaunted officer, after gallantly sustaining the attack for nearly an hour, was killed by a musket-ball, and his troops soon after surrendered at discretion. The whole army of the enemy, consisting of over eleven hundred men, with but few exceptions, were either killed, wounded, or taken prisoners; and all their arms, ammunition, camp equipage, horses, and baggage of every description fell into the hands of the victorious Americans. The loss of the latter did not exceed twenty in killed, though the number of their wounded was very considerable.

After disposing of their families among the hospitable inhabitants of Kentucky, Clarke collected the remains of his regiment, recrossed the mountains, and formed a junction with General Sumpter, on the borders of South Carolina. While they remained in the latter state, the Georgians took an active and an honourable part in the battles of Fishdam Ford, Blackstocks, and Longcane, and subsequently, under Morgan, shared in the more important victory at the Cowpens. Colonel Clarke, however, was unable to take any part personally in the latter battle, owing to his having received a dangerous wound during the action at Longcane.

CHAPTER XX.

Skirmish at Beattie's Mill—Sickness of Clarke—Death of McCall—Georgians harass the British—Skirmish at Wiggins's Hill—Death of Rannal McKay and others—Augusta invested by Williamson—Clarke assumes command—Is reinforced by Pickens and Lee—Fort Grierson abandoned—Colonel Grierson shot—Surrender of Brown—Mrs. McKay's interview with him—Fort Ninety-Six abandoned by Cruger—Wayne advances toward Savannah—Defeats three hundred Creek Indians—Pickens marches against the Cherokees—Closing of the war—Savannah evacuated—Treaty of peace concluded at Paris.

As soon as Clarke had sufficiently recovered of his wound, he joined General Pickens in Ninety-Six district, and took part in the skirmish at Beattie's Mill on Little River. In this spirited affair, Major Dunlop, with seventy-five British dragoons, were signally defeated; Dunlop himself killed, nearly half of his entire force either killed or wounded, and the remainder made prisoners of war.

When it became known that General Greene intended to advance into South Carolina, Clarke proceeded into Georgia with his troops, accompanied by McCall and a part of his regiment from South Carolina.

About the middle of April, 1781, both these officers were seized with the small-pox. Clarke eventually recovered, but McCall returned into Carolina and died of the disease.

When the Georgians returned into their own state, they dispersed into parties of ten and twelve men each, so as to spread themselves over the settlements and harass the enemy as much as possible.

Information having been received by Colonel Brown, that Colonel Harden with a body of American militia was in the neighbourhood of Coosawhatchie, he ordered his provincials to join him at Augusta and defend it; but they shrunk from the dangerous task, and fled into the Indian country.

Brown now determined to attack Harden in person. They met at Wiggins's Hill; where, after a sharp contest, the Americans were defeated, with the loss of seven killed and eleven wounded. Several prisoners were captured after the skirmish by detached parties of the enemy. Among these was Rannal McKay, a youth of seventeen years of age. Mrs. McKay, who was a widow, hearing of the captivity of her son, repaired to Brown's camp, carrying with her some refreshments which she intended to present to him, as a means of obtaining more ready access to his person.

Brown received the refreshments, but turned a deaf ear to her entreaties, and would not permit her to have an interview with her son, whose fate she already foresaw: she was forced without the sentries. Colonel Rannal McKinnon, a Scots officer, who was a soldier of honour, and unused to murderous warfare, remonstrated with Brown against hanging the youth, and gave Mrs. McKay some assurances that her son would be safe. Brown returned that night and encamped at Wiggins's Hill, and caused a pen to be made of fence rails, about three feet high, in which he placed his prisoners, and covered it over with the same materials. Mrs. McKay had followed to the camp, but was not permitted to enter it; and Captain McKinnon, the advocate of humanity, was ordered on command.

On the ensuing morning, the prisoners, Rannal McKay, Britton Williams, George Smith, George Reed, and a Frenchman, whose name is not known, were ordered forth to the gallows; and after hanging until they were nearly dead, they were cut down and delivered to the Indians, who scalped them and otherwise abused their bodies in their accustomed savage manner.

The fate of young McKay inspired his brother, a youth of fifteen, to join his countrymen and add his strength in avenging the murder of his brother.

But the period was fast approaching when Georgia, bleeding and desolated, was to be relieved of the presence of her sanguinary oppressors.

On the 16th of April, Lieutenant-colonel Williamson, on whom the command of the Georgian militia was devolved during the illness of Colonel Clarke, assembled his detachment at the appointed rendezvous on Little River, where he was shortly afterward joined by other detachments of Georgians and Carolinians. With this force, but little superior in numbers to his adversary, he marched at once upon Augusta.

Williamson took up a position within twelve hundred yards of the town, and fortifying his camp kept Brown in a state of blockade until the 15th of May. On that day, Colonel Clarke arrived with a reinforcement of one hundred men, and assumed the command.

Clarke was unfurnished with cannon, but had picked up an old four-pounder in the field, which had been thrown away by the British: believing it might be converted to use, he had it mounted, and employed a blacksmith to form pieces of iron into the shape of balls; and commenced his approaches by constructing a battery at four hundred yards distánce from Grierson's Fort, and placed his gun upon it. Powder was so scarce, that orders were given not to use it when the sword could be substituted. He sent an express to General Pickens, stating his situation and requesting assistance.

At the time the messenger reached him, Pickens had so weakened his force by detachments against the Indians, that he was unable to comply with the request. He sent, however, a letter to General Greene, who, as soon as he was informed of the condition and prospects of Clarke, ordered a detachment under Colonel Lee to march to his relief. Almost immediately afterward, Pickens was placed in a condition to follow.

On the 23d of May, a junction was formed by Pickens, Lee, and Clarke. After reconnoitring the ground and the British works, it was determined to dislodge Grierson, who was garrisoned about half a mile west of Fort Cornwallis, and either destroy or intercept him in his retreat. The attempt was immediately made. Discovering that Grierson was in a critical situation, Brown drew out a part of his forces, and made an ineffectual attempt to relieve his subordinate.

Grierson, finding resistance would be vain, evacuated his fortress, and endeavoured, under shelter of a ravine leading to the river's bank, to unite his command with that of Brown in Fort Cornwallis.

In this hazardous retreat, he had thirty men killed, and forty-five wounded and taken prisoners. Grierson himself was shot, after he had surrendered, by one of the Georgia riflemen. A reward was offered by the American commander for the apprehension of the offender, but without effect. The death of Grierson was in retaliation for his numerous cruelties, but especially for his barbarous conduct toward the venerable Mr. Alexander a short time previous. As the company of Captain Alexander formed a part of the American force before Augusta, it may easily be conjectured by whose hand Grierson fell.

Brown, finding that he would be closely invested, applied himself to strengthen his fortress; and every part which required amendment was repaired with industry. He placed the aged Alexander, and others who had long been in captivity, in one of the bastions most exposed to the fire of the rifle batteries; one of which was manned by Captain Samuel Alexander's company: thus the father was exposed to be killed by the hand of his son; but he escaped uninjured.

These preparations on the part of the enemy could not be counteracted. The Americans had but one field-piece, and all that could be done was only to be achieved by close investure and regular approaches.

At length, Colonel Lee suggested the plan of raising a tower of square logs, some thirty feet high, proof against the enemy's artillery, and sufficiently large and strong to sustain a six-pounder.

By the 1st of June, the tower was raised sufficiently high to overlook the works of the enemy, and Brown, anticipating the fatal consequences which would result from its completion, directed his attention to the destruction of it. Finding it could not be destroyed by fair and open combat, Brown resorted to stratagem to effect his object; but in this also he was equally unsuccessful.

On the 31st of May, Brown had been summoned to surrender, but refused. On the morning of the 3d of June, another opportunity was afforded him, which he rejected.

During the day an incessant and galling fire was kept up from the rifle batteries, which were raised so high as to enable the besiegers to unman the field-pieces, and drive the enemy from the opposite bastions. The six-pounder in the tower had dismounted the enemy's artillery, and rendered it useless. They were obliged to dig vaults in the ground within the fort, to secure themselves from the fire of the American riflemen.

The morning of the 4th, at nine o'clock, was destined for the assault: as the hour approached, and columns were arrayed waiting the signal to advance, a British officer appeared with a flag, and presented a letter at the margin of the trenches, addressed to General Pickens and Colonel Lee, offering to surrender on the conditions specified in the communication. After a day's delay, the terms which the Americans offered as their ultimatum were agreed to; and, on the morning of the 5th of June, the fort and garrison were surrendered.

The British loss during the siege was fifty-two

killed, and three hundred and thirty-four, including the wounded, were made prisoners of war. The American loss was sixteen killed, and thirty-five wounded, seven of them mortally. Brown and his officers were placed under a strong guard to secure their safety. Young McKay, the brother of the youth murdered by Brown, endeavoured to kill the latter, but was prevented by the guard. Mrs. McKay was said to have armed herself for the same purpose. As the prisoners were on their way to Savannah for the purpose of being exchanged, she met the escort at Silver-bluff, and, after promising the officer in charge to do no violence to Brown, obtained leave to speak with him. As soon as she was admitted to his presence, she thus addressed him:

"Colonel Brown, in the late day of your prosperity, I visited your camp, and on my knees supplicated for the life of my son; but you were deaf to my entreaties: you hanged him, though a beardless youth, before my face. These eyes saw him scalped by the savages under your immediate command. As you are now a prisoner to the leaders of my country, I lay aside for the present all thoughts of revenge; but when you resume your sword, I will go five hundred miles to demand satisfaction at the point of it, for the murder of my son!"

Immediately after the capture of Augusta, Pickens and Lee, with a part of the Georgians, joined General Greene in his investment of Fort Ninety-Six. The approach of Lord Rawdon at the head of two thousand men compelled Greene to raise the siege and retire toward North Carolina. The situation of the British becoming every day more precarious, Ninety-Six was soon afterward abandoned by Colonel Cruger, who destroyed the works, and, retreating upon Orangeburg, formed a junction with Rawdon.

The attention of the continental officers was now turned to the reduction of Savannah; but before this could be accomplished, it was found necessary to organize an expedition against the Indian towns, to chastise the savages and loyalists, who had for some time been murdering and plundering along the frontiers. The expedition terminated favourably, and for a few months the inhabitants were left in the enjoyment of peace.

At length, the success of the American army under General Greene in South Carolina enabled him to send a force, commanded by General Wayne, to the assistance of the Georgians.

The British Brigadier-general Clarke, who at this time commanded in Savannah, on learning the advance of Wayne, called in his outposts and made preparations for a vigorous defence. He despatched expresses to the Creek and Cherokee Indians, requesting them to march to his assistance; but the defeats they had suffered from Pickens and Lee had in some measure discouraged them. They met in council in the spring of 1782, and while some agreed to join the British on the southern frontier by the middle of May, the greater part of the warriors resolved to remain neutral. In the mean time, in endeavouring to keep open the communication to the southward of Savannah for the purpose of giving free passage to his savage allies, the detachments of the British commander suffered several defeats.

On the night of the 23d of June, three hundred Creek Indians, headed by Guristersigo, reached undiscovered the vicinity of Wayne's camp, and while seeking to avoid it by surprising the pickets, fell upon the main body. After a short conflict the Indians were routed. Scattering into small parties they returned to the Creek nation, leaving seventeen men dead upon the field, and one hundred and seventeen pack-horses loaded with peltry, in the hands of the victors.

Shortly after this, an expedition was organized by Pickens and Clarke against the Cherokees, the effect of which was to bring about a treaty with that nation, by which the Cherokees ceded to Georgia all the lands south of Savannah River, and east of the Chattahoochee, as the price of peace.

Early in 1783, the chiefs repaired to Augusta, and, on the 30th of May, formally ratified the treaty entered into with General Pickens the September previous.

20

Another treaty was made soon after with the Creeks, by which the lands claimed by them east of the Oconee River were surrendered to Georgia.

The war was now rapidly drawing to a close. The defeat of Burgoyne at Saratoga, the capture of Cornwallis at Yorktown, joined to the ill-success which had attended the British arms generally, had rendered the war very unpopular in England.

After numerous debates upon the subject, General Conway, on the 29th of February, 1783, moved in the House of Commons, "That a further prosecution of hostilities against the colonies would tend to increase the mutual enmity so fatal to the interests of both Great Britain and America."

A change of ministry and policy soon succeeded. General Sir Guy Carleton was ordered to take command of the British forces in America, and, in conjunction with Admiral Digby, was appointed to negotiate a peace with the American government.

On the 2d of May, General Leplie, who commanded the British forces in the southern department, proposed to General Greene a cessation of hostilities; but the latter declined entering into any stipulation of the kind without authority from Congress. It was understood, however, that measures were in progress for withdrawing the British forces from America, and that terms of peace had been offered by Great Britain to the American commissioners at Paris.

About the 1st of July, a deputation from the merchants of Savannah visited General Wayne, for the purpose of ascertaining upon what terms British subjects might be permitted to remain in the city after it should be evacuated by the troops of the enemy.

After some preliminary difficulties had been overcome, the conduct of the negotiation on the part of Georgia was intrusted principally to Major John Habersham, and on the 11th of July, 1783, the embarkation of the British troops was commenced. The American army entered and took possession of the city the same day. Between the 12th and 25th of the same month, twelve hundred British regulars and loyalists, five hundred women and children, three hundred Indians, and five thousand negroes sailed from the port of Savannah.

The metropolis of Georgia had been three years, six months, and thirteen days, in the entire possession of the enemy; and at several times, the whole state had been under the control of the British government. The number of the disaffected to the republican government appears, by the act of confiscation and banishment, to have amounted to two hundred and eighty. A considerable number of them were afterward restored to the rights of citizenship, and some of them to the enjoyment of their property, upon paying twelve and a half per cent. upon the amount thus restored; and others upon paying eight per cent. into the public treasury.

No correct estimate can be made of the immense losses sustained by the inhabitants of Georgia during the Revolutionary war. The negroes and other property which was carried off; the houses, plantations, and produce, destroyed by fire; the loss of time, by constant military employment; the distressed condition of widows, who were left by the numerous murders committed upon the heads of families, and killed in the field of battle,—seem to bid defiance to calculation. If the inhabited part of the state, with all the property it contained, had been valued at the commencement of the war, half of the amount would probably have been a moderate estimate of the loss.

As early as the 30th of November, 1782, provisional articles of peace were entered into at Paris between the American commissioners and the commissioner on the part of Great Britain, but the definitive treaties between England, France, and America, were not finally ratified until the 3d of September, 1783.

Thus ended the terrible but glorious war of the American Revolution; terrible in the calamities which it brought upon a patriotic people, glorious in its final result. Never in the history of the world did an appeal to arms originate from purer motives, or entail more blessings upon future generations by the success which followed it.

CHAPTER XXI.

Condition of the colonies at the close of the war—Re-organization of the Federal government proposed—Delegates meet at Annapolis—Recommend a convention to meet at Philadelphia—Convention meets—Number of states represented—Washington elected chairman—Rules of proceeding—The first questions considered, ratio of representation, and rules of voting—Contest between the larger and smaller states—Vote of Georgia—The executive—A counter project—Grand committee of conference—Proposition of Franklin—Rule of appointment—Committee of detail—New difficulties—Compromises—Doubts and fears respecting the constitution—Territorial suit between Georgia and South Carolina—Georgia called upon to cede her public lands—Congress of 1790—Slavery petitions.

THE long and bloody struggle against British oppression was now closed. That independence in political action, for which the colonies had dared and suffered so much, was acknowledged and confirmed. They were henceforth, in the eyes of all Europe, free and sovereign states. But they had yet many difficulties to encounter. They were about to take upon themselves a form of government, the permanence of which all previous examples had shown to be precarious and uncertain. In addition to this cause for reasonable doubt, there were others equally calculated to operate injuriously to the free working of the new institutions.

The war was indeed over, and peace once more smiled upon the land; but the disruption of social ties during a prolonged contest, the depressed condition of trade, the interruptions which commerce had so long experienced, and above all, the heavy load of debt by which the nation was encumbered, rendered the experiment of self-government not merely hazardous in the extreme, but, in the opinion of many profound thinkers, certain to end, after the lapse of a few years, in the entire destruction of the commonwealths.

One of the first acts of the disenthralled states showed a thoughtful recognition of the future. They proposed a re-organization of the federal government with powers equal to the importance of its functions.

Delegates from six states, responding to the call of Virginia, met at Annapolis in September, 1786; but finding their number so few, and the powers of several of them very much restricted, they resolved to recommend a convention of delegates from all the states, to meet at Philadelphia the following May, to consider the articles of confederation, and to propose such changes therein as might render them adequate to the exigencies of the Union.

The proposal was transmitted to all the state legislatures, and was presently laid before Congress. At first, it was received with marked coolness; but circumstances occurring soon after that rendered some action of the kind imperatively necessary, the proposed convention was sanctioned and approved, and delegates chosen from all the states, except Rhode Island and New Hampshire.

Although the 14th of May was the day appointed for the meeting of the convention, on the 25th there were but seven states represented.

By the end of the month, however, fifty delegates from eleven states were present—men highly distinguished for talents, character, practical knowledge, and public services.

Of this convention Washington was elected President. The rules of proceeding adopted were copied chiefly from those of Congress. Each state was to have one vote; seven states were to constitute a quorum; all committees were to be appointed by ballot, and the debates to be conducted with closed doors and under the injunction of secrecy.

The first questions which were considered related to the ratio of representation and the rule of voting in the national legislature; whether it should be by state, or by the individual members. The small states desired to retain that equal vote which, under the confederation, they already possessed. The larger states, on the other hand, were firmly resolved to secure to themselves, under the new arrangement, a weight proportionate to their superior wealth and numbers. Georgia, and the two Carolinas, anticipating a speedy increase of population, voted with the larger states, and representation by population was thus carried by a majority of one only.

The election of the first branch of the national legislature by the people was strongly opposed by Roger Sherman and Elbridge Gerry; the latter of whom said:—"All the evils we experience flow from excess of democracy. The people do not want virtue, but are the dupes of pretended patriots. In Massachusetts, they are daily misled into the most baleful measures and opinions. He had been too republican heretofore, but had been taught by experience the danger of a levelling spirit."

In reply to this, Madison and others argued that no republican government could stand without popular confidence, which confidence could only be secured by giving to the people one branch of the legislature.

In this opinion the delegates from Georgia coincided, and voted for the resolution, which was successfully carried, in opposition to the neighbouring delegates from South Carolina, who thought a choice by the people impracticable in a scattered population.

The election of senators now came up, and after much debate, it was agreed that their nomination should emanate from the second branch of the state legislatures; and it was carried by a vote of six states to five, that the same ratio of representation should prevail in both branches. When the question arose, "Whether the executive should consist of one person or several?" it gave rise to considerable hesitancy among the members. At length, James Wilson, of Pennsylvania, moved that it be composed of a single person.

After an animated debate, during which C. Pinckney, of South Carolina, denounced unity in the executive officer as the "fœtus of monarchy," the motion was carried; Georgia voting in the affirmative.

The mode by which the executive should be elected was next discussed. Wilson proposed at first, doubtfully, the election by the people; and, subsequently, by a college of electors chosen by the people: Sherman proposed an election by the national legislature; and this was at length acceded to as part of the plan.

The term of office was then fixed, after considerable varying, at seven years, with ineligibility afterward. The Georgia members—who preferred three years with re-eligibility—voting with the minority.

A motion to allow the executive a modified veto was next carried; making a vote of three-fourths in both branches necessary to pass laws objected to by the executive.

Considerable excitement having arisen from the determination of the larger states not to admit an equality of representation in the second branch of the legislature, Paterson, of New Jersey, brought forward a counter scheme.

This counter project, and the plan just reported to the house, were referred to a new committee of the whole, and the entire question of a national government, or not, had again to be gone over.

The report of the committee of the whole being now taken up, each article of the plan previously passed was separately considered anew; many alterations were suggested, and several were made.

Two difficulties, however, presented themselves, in so serious an aspect, that they threatened to result in the breaking up of the convention.

The first of these arose from the determination of the smaller states to agree to no plan which did not concede an equality of representation in the second branch of the national legislature.

As a last resource, the convention appointed a grand committee of conference, consisting of one member from each state.

In this committee, the proposition of Franklin, giving to the first branch of the legislature one representative for every forty thousand persons, according to the three-fifths ratio, with the sole power to originate money-bills: and to the second branch, an equal representation by the states: was reluctantly acquiesced in by the larger states, and thus this vexatious question was settled.

The rule of apportionment was another difficulty. Paterson, of New Jersey, considered a mere reference to wealth and numbers too vague; and asked, "if negroes, being regarded in the light of property in the states to which they belong, are not represented in those states, why should they be represented in the general government?"

King contended for a compromise between the north and south, and argued that as eleven of the thirteen states had agreed to consider slaves in the apportionment of taxation, taxation and representation ought to go together.

Gouverneur Morris expressed great apprehensions of the new states to be formed in the west; and proposed to leave the future apportionment of members of the first branch to the discretion of the legislature. Edmund Randolph, supported by Mason and Wilson, objected to any such arrangement, as it would put the majority into the power of the minority. The former, therefore, proposed that future appointments should be regulated by a periodical census.

Williamson, of Maryland, moved, as a substitute, to reckon in this census the whole number of freemen, and three-fifths of all others. Butler and C. Pinckney insisted that all the slaves ought to be counted. Gerry thought three-fifths quite enough. Gouverneur Morris denounced the three-fifths clause as an encouragement to the slave-trade, and an injustice to human nature.

Wilson, while professing his ignorance of the principles upon which the admission of the blacks could be explained, acknowledged the existence of difficulties which were only to be overcome by a spirit of compromise. The voting now commenced. Butler's motion to count blacks equally with whites was rejected: Georgia voting in the affirmative.

The three-fifths clause, moved by Williamson, was also voted down. Randolph's periodical census was next rejected. The question then recurring on the report of the special committee, authorizing the legislature to regulate future apportionments on the basis of wealth and numbers, Gouverneur Morris moved a preliminary proviso, that taxation should be in proportion to representation, which, being restricted to direct taxation, was unanimously agreed to.

Davie, of North Carolina, now rose and declared, "it was time to speak out. He saw that it was meant by some gentlemen to deprive the southern states of any share of representation for their blacks. He was sure North Carolina would never confederate on any terms that did not rate them at least as three-fifths. If the eastern states meant therefore to exclude them altogether, the business was at an end."

This plain speaking brought matters to a crisis. After several ineffectual attempts to restore harmonious action in the convention, a motion was made by Randolph to adjourn till the morrow; "to devise, (as he said,) if possible, some conciliatory expedient; or, in case the small states continued to hold back, to take such measures—what he would not say—as might seem necessary." The adjournment was carried. The delegates from the larger states met in consultation, but nothing could be agreed upon. The next day the question was set at rest by a failure of the motion to reconsider, and the convention proceeded to take up the remaining articles of the report.

The provisions respecting the national legislature having thus been decided upon, the convention passed to the articles on the executive, and after two warm debates, succeeded, with some few modifications, in completing them.

In the articles relating to the judiciary, no essential change was made.

The amended report was now referred to a committee of detail, which, after an adjournment of ten days, brought in their report—a rough sketch of the constitution as it now stands.

This draft gave to the national legislature the name of Congress; the first branch to be called the House of Representatives; the second branch the Senate. The name of President was given to the executive.

In detailing the powers of Congress, some new provisions had been introduced by the committee, which were the occasion of exciting considerable feeling in the convention. Those subjects which elicited the strongest opposition were the taxes on exports, the regulation of commerce, and the importation of slaves.

The eastern ship-owning states were in favour of empowering Congress to enact navigation laws. The southern states dreaded any such laws, as likely to enhance the cost of transportation.

The prohibition of the slave-trade was no new idea. The Continental Congress had long before resolved "that no slave be imported into any of the United States."

Delaware, Virginia, and Maryland, and all the more northern states, had expressly acquiesced in the prohibition. Notwithstanding this, merchant vessels belonging to the northern states continued to carry on the traffic elsewhere, and already, since the acknowledgment of independence, some New England ships were engaged in transporting slaves from Africa into Georgia and South Carolina; and the latter expressed themselves determined to maintain, not the institution of slavery only, but the importation of slaves likewise.

In the midst of this conflict of interests, a

bargain was struck between the commercial representatives of the northern states and the delegates of South Carolina and Georgia, by which the unrestricted power of Congress to enact navigation laws was conceded to the northern merchants, and to the Carolina rice-planters, as an equivalent, twenty years' continuance of the slave-trade.

This was the third great compromise of the constitution. The other two were the concession to the smaller states of an equal representation in the senate, and to the slaveholders the counting three-fifths of the slaves in determining the ratio of representation.

After some few other amendments, offered with a view to conciliate conflicting interests, the constitution as reported received its final corrections and the sanction of the convention.

This sanction was not given by the members of the convention without a gloomy presentiment that its numerous imperfections would lead to the ruin of the confederacy.

Mason declared his belief that the proposed constitution would terminate in a monarchy, or a tyrannical aristocracy. Randolph, Mason, and Gerry, all expressed their dissatisfaction at the extended and indefinite powers conferred on Congress and the executive. Pinckney, and other southern members, on the contrary, objected to the contemptible weakness and dependence of the executive.

So opposite and inharmonious were the feelings of the members in relation to the instrument, the articles of which they had examined and passed clause by clause, that it required all the address of Franklin and other influential members, to gain for the new constitution unanimous signature.

A form was proposed which might be signed without implying personal approval of the constitution; it read thus: "Done by consent of the states present. In testimony whereof we have subscribed, &c." Hamilton, though opposed to the plan, urged the infinite misehief that might arise from refusing to sign it. Washington also addressed the convention in its favour. These appeals succeeded with some of the dissatisfied members, but Randolph, Mason, and Gerry could not be prevailed upon to subscribe their names.

The federal constitution, thus laboriously produced, was laid before Congress, then sitting at New York, with a letter from its framers recommending its reference, for approval or rejection, to state conventions, to be called by the state legislatures. Congress hesitated at first in complying with this request; but finally, on September 28th, 1787, a bill was passed, transmitting the document to the state legislatures, to be acted upon as the convention had suggested; and in the beginning of the year 1788, it was formally ratified by the state of Georgia.

During the latter part of 1787, an important territorial suit occurred between the states of Georgia and South Carolina. This suit originated in difficulties relative to their respective boundaries toward the sources of the Savannah, and especially as to the jurisdiction of the territory west of the Alatamaha, claimed by Carolina under her charter, and by Georgia under the proclamation of 1763, which annexed to Georgia the territory between the Alatamaha and the St. Mary's. It was finally arrranged by mutual consent, and on the 22d of April the settlement was announced to Congress, and the suit discontinued.

Georgia, being now loudly called upon for the cession of her western claims, offered to cede all the territory west of the Chattahoochee, and between the thirty-first and thirty-second parallels of north latitude; but demanded, in return, a guarantee of the remaining territory north of the thirty-second parallel. To this, Congress would not accede; nor would it accept the territory offered, unless so extended as to include all the district west of the Chattahoochee. After the lapse of several years, a cession was finally obtained by purchase, and on conditions very onerous to the United States.

During the session of Congress in 1790, and in the midst of the agitation as to the public debt, the house became involved in another discussion, still more exciting, in reference to slavery and the slave-trade.

Slavery still existed in every state of the Union, except Massachusetts. In the latter state it had been abolished a few years previous; while Pennsylvania, Connecticut, Rhode Island, and New Hampshire, had introduced a system of gradual emancipation. The other eight states retained their old colonial systems.

A few days after the commencement of the debate on the public debt, a petition from the yearly meeting of the Quakers of Philadelphia, seconded by another from the Quakers of New York, had been laid before the house, in which it was suggested whether, "notwithstanding seeming impediments, it was not in the power of Congress to exercise justice and mercy, which if adhered to, the petitioners did not doubt would produce the abolition of the slave-trade."

A still stronger petition was laid before the house the next day from the Pennsylvania Society for the Abolition of Slavery. It was signed by Franklin as president—one of the last public acts of his long and diversified career. He died within a few weeks afterward.

This memorial, after reasoning upon the propositions "that all mankind are formed by the same Almighty Being," and "that equal liberty was originally the portion, and is still the birthright of all men," concluded by praying Congress, "to step to the very verge of its power for discouraging every species of traffic in the persons of our fellow men."

These petitions gave rise to a most exciting series of debates. Hartley called up the Quaker memorial, and moved its commitment. Tucker and Burke opposed it on the ground of unconstitutionality; and the latter expressed himself certain that the commitment "would sound an alarm, and blow the trumpet of sedition throughout all the southern states." Scott defended its constitutionality, but acknowledged the incapacity of Congress to do more than lay a tax of ten dollars upon the head of every slave imported into the country. Jackson argued from Bible authority, that religion and slavery were not incompatible. Sherman could see no difficulty in committing the memorial, and trusted the committee would be able to bring in such a report as would satisfy both sides of the house. Baldwin regretted the introduction of petitions upon so delicate a subject. He referred to the difficulty which the members who framed the constitution had previously experienced. He reminded the house that the constitution had only been adopted by mutual concessions, and that any encroachment beyond its strict limits must tend to unsettle the public confidence. He concluded by arguing that, as the petition did in fact pray for the abolition of the slave-trade, the house had nothing more to do with it than it would have to establish an order of nobility or a national religion.

Similar ground was taken by Smith of South Carolina. He contended that the unconstitutionality of the object prayed for was a sufficient reason for not committing the memorial. He said further: "When we entered into a political connection with the other states, this property was there. It had been acquired under a former government, conformably to the laws and constitution; and every attempt to deprive us of it must be in the nature of an ex post facto law, and, as such, forbidden by our political compact."

Madison, Page, and Gerry advocated the commitment. The former suggested that, "Though Congress were restricted by the constitution from immediately abolishing the slave-trade, yet there were a variety of ways by which they might countenance the abolition of that trafic. They might, for example, respecting the introduction of slaves into the new states to be formed out of the western territory, make regulations such as were beyond their power in relation to the old settled states; an object which he thought well worthy of consideration."

The question being taken by yeas and nays, the reference was carried, forty-three to eleven Of these eleven, six were from Georgia and Caro lina, being all the members present from those two states; two were from Virginia, two from Maryland, and one from New York.

The special committee to whom the memorial was referred consisted of one member from each of the following states: New Hampshire, Massachusetts, Connecticut, New York, New Jersey, Pennsylvania, and Virginia. They reported, after a month's delay, the following resolutions:

1st. That the general government was expressly restrained until the year 1808, from prohibiting the importation of slaves.

2d. That by a fair construction of the constitution, Congress was equally restrained from interfering to emancipate slaves within the states.

3d. That Congress had no power to interfere in the internal regulation of particular states relative to the physical or moral well-being of slaves, or to the seizure, transportation, and sale of free negroes; but entertained the fullest confidence in the wisdom and humanity of the state legislatures, that, from time to time, they would revise their laws, and promote these and all other measures tending to the happiness of the slaves.

4th. That Congress had authority to levy a tax of ten dollars upon every person imported under the special permission of any of the states.

5th. That Congress had power to interdict, or to regulate the African slave-trade so far as it might be carried on by citizens of the United States for the supply of foreign countries.

6th. That Congress had a right to prohibit foreigners from fitting out vessels in the United States, to be employed in the supply of foreign countries with slaves from Africa.

The seventh, and last, expressed an intention on the part of Congress to exercise their authority to its full extent to promote the humane objects aimed at in the memorial.

Such was the report of the committee, upon which there immediately ensued a discussion of six days' duration, and of the most angry and violent character.

The final conclusions to which Congress came upon this most delicate subject are embodied in the following resolutions, which were carried by a vote of twenty-nine to twenty-five.

"That the migration or importation of such persons as any of the states now existing shall think proper to admit, cannot be prohibited by Congress prior to the year 1808.

"That Congress have no authority to interfere in the emancipation of slaves, or in the treatment of them in any of the states, it remaining with the several states alone to provide any regulations therein which humanity and true policy require.

"That Congress have authority to restrain the citizens of the United States from carrying on the African slave-trade for the purpose of supplying foreigners with slaves, and of providing by proper regulations for the humane treatment, during their passage, of slaves imported by the said citizens into the said states admitting such importation.

"That Congress have also authority to prohibit foreigners from fitting out vessels in any port of the United States for transporting persons from Africa to any foreign port."

A clear view of this remarkable discussion, together with the results arrived at by the Congress of 1790, has become of singular importance at this time from the many attempts which have been subsequently made, and are yet apparently in contemplation, in relation to this vexed question of slavery.

The whole course of the debate upon this question is instructive, and shows that the arguments which have been used in later days are by no means novel, nor have they acquired any new force beyond those which were presented at the period when the first memorial was fully and ably discussed, and the suggestions growing out of it so pointedly disposed of.

CHAPTER XXII.

Recapitulation of the various treaties made between Georgia and the Indians—Oglethorpe's treaty—Treaty of Augusta—Florida restored to the Spaniards—Frontier war commenced—Treaty of Galphinton—Treaty of Shoulderbone—Continuation of Indian hostilities—Washington appoints commissioners to treat with McGillivray—Romantic history of the latter—Conference at Rock Landing—Failure of negotiations—Colonel Willett sent on a secret mission—Interview with McGillivray—Indian council at Ositchy—Speech of the Hollowing King—McGillivray departs for New York—His reception—Treaty of New York—Its reception by Georgia—Dissatisfaction of the Creeks—Bowles the freebooter—McGillivray in Florida—Capture of Bowles.

No sooner was the independence of the United States acknowledged by Great Britain, than Georgia began to increase both in wealth and population. She had, however, many sources of disquietude, some of which were of an alarming character. To enable the reader the better to understand what follows, it will be necessary to recapitulate briefly, the previous history of the negotiations between Georgia and the Creeks and Cherokees.

The first boundaries of the province, as conceded to Oglethorpe by treaty, were confined to a narrow strip of country lying between the Savannah and Ogechee rivers. By the subsequent treaty of 1773, these boundaries were extended north of the original lines, and beyond Broad River.

By another treaty, concluded at Augusta on the 31st of May, 1783, the Cherokee delegates ceded to Georgia the country upon the western side of Tugalo, including the head waters of the Oconee. To this cession, a few Creeks subscribed their names on the 1st of November of the same year. A very large majority of the nation, who had always been adverse to the sale of their lands, denounced the act in the strongest terms, and expressed a resolution to maintain their right to the soil.

As Georgia persisted in asserting her sovereignty over the territory thus acquired, a hostile feeling was, naturally enough, engendered among the Indians of those towns whose delegates were not present at Augusta when the treaty was signed.

In addition to this fruitful source of future difficulty, by an arrangement entered into between Great Britain and Spain, in the early part of the year 1783, the former restored to the latter her old province of Florida; and by this means, Georgia was again made to suffer many annoyances at the hands of her ancient neighbour and enemy.

In 1785, the dissatisfaction between the Creeks and Georgians being fomented by the artifices of the Spaniards, a border war commenced, which the provisional government, then struggling through the last stages of the Revolutionary war, sought to close peacefully by sending commissioners to treat with the Creeks and Cherokees for the purchase of their lands. The commissioners thus appointed invited delegates from the Indian towns to meet them at Galphinton; but as only the chiefs from two towns, with fifty warriors, attended, the object of the mission was not attained, and the commissioners returned home.

They had no sooner left the appointed place of rendezvous, than three commissioners—whom Georgia, tenacious of her rights, had despatched thither to protest against any proceedings on the part of the provisional government—concluded a treaty with the Creeks then present, which confirmed not only the treaty of 1783, but extended the territorial limits of Georgia, from the junction of the Oconee and Ocmulgee to the St. Mary's River.

The treaty thus made was, like its predecessor, indignantly spurned by the chiefs of ninety-eight towns; who denied the right of any two of their country to make a cession of land which could only be valid by consent of the whole nation as joint proprietors in common.

Numerous collisions between the Georgians and the Indians succeeded. At length, a meeting for the purpose of settling existing differences was agreed upon, and in October, 1786, commissioners on the part of Georgia met a delegation of Creek chiefs and warriors, at a place called Shoulderbone, on the Oconee.

Here another treaty was entered into, which the Creeks subsequently asserted was wrung from them by the unexpected presence of a large body of armed men professing hostile intentions.

This charge the authorities of Georgia most emphatically denied. They contended that all the grants were procured fairly and honourably, and without either force or coercion; that the upper Creeks, who never occupied the Oconee lands, had no right to a voice in the matter. They admitted that armed troops were present at the treaty of Shoulderbone,—not, however, to provoke hostilities, but to suppress them if they arose.

Incursions and retaliations of course continued. Congress several times sought to interpose, but the Creeks would listen to no overtures until the Georgians were first removed from the Oconee lands.

In an earnest endeavour to put an end to this state of things, General Washington—who was now president—appointed four commissioners to treat with the celebrated Creek chief, Alexander McGillivray. This extraordinary man was the son of Lachlan McGillivray, an enterprising Scotsman of good family, trading among the Indians, and of Sehoy Marchand, a beautiful half-breed Creek girl, whose mother was of the tribe of the Wind, the most powerful and influential family in the Creek nation. The advantages in the way of commercial facilities which this marriage gave to the elder McGillivray, enabled him to rapidly accumulate a large fortune. Besides plantations and negroes upon the Savannah River, Lachlan McGillivray soon became the owner of stores filled with Indian merchandise, in the towns of Savannah and Augusta.

When his son Alexander had reached the age of fourteen years, he withdrew him, with the consent of his mother, from the Creek nation, in the midst of which he had hitherto resided, and placed him in a school at Charleston; from whence, on the completion of his studies, he was transferred to a counting-room in Savannah. But a mercantile life was soon discovered to be unfitted for a youth of Alexander McGillivray's studious and retiring disposition; and he was sent back to Charleston, to acquire, under the teaching of a clergyman of that city, a knowledge of the Greek and Latin languages.

As he grew up to manhood, the remembrance of his youthful forest haunts; the sports and games of the tribe to which he was allied by blood; the faces of the dusky warriors, who regarded him as their future chief; and the mother and sister who still resided on the banks of the Coosa, proved stronger than the ties which civilized society had thrown around him. With the old wild-woods feeling stirring his heart, he turned his back upon the settlements of the whites, and rejoined the warriors who had cherished his childish years in the midst of their sylvan recesses.

His return was warmly welcomed. Crafty, sagácious, enterprising, and well educated, he was gradually enabled so to extend his influence over the Creek and Cherokee nations, that in a few years he was invested with the supreme authority, to which he was entitled by his birth, according to the Indian custom.

When the Revolutionary war broke out, Alexander McGillivray received the rank and pay of a colonel in the British service, and during the whole of that eventful period remained, like his father, a firm and devoted loyalist; often acting in concert with McGirth and his Florida rangers, in harassing the frontiers of Georgia.

As the war drew to a close, the British were compelled to evacuate Savannah, taking with them many active and influential loyalists, among whom was Lachlan McGillivray. Having succeeded in getting together a considerable portion of his wealth, the elder McGillivray returned to his own country, entertaining the hope that in his absence his wife and family, then living in the Creek nation, might be suffered to take peaceable possession of the plantations and negroes he had abandoned. The confiscation of the property of fugitive loyalists soon after, not only frustrated the hopes of McGillivray, but compelled his wife and daughters to remain at their old home on the Coosa.

Colonel McGillivray, the son,—who had some time before this become the principal chief of the Creek and Cherokee nations,—finding himself thus deprived, at one blow, of British protection and the estates previously owned by his father, threw himself into the arms of Spain, with whose authorities in Florida he formed, on behalf of his nation, a treaty of alliance.

The chief reasons which induced him to court this alliance arose from his apprehensions of the Americans, who, as he contended, had confiscated his estates, banished his father, threatened him with death, and were constantly encroaching upon the Creek soil. The Spaniards wanted no lands, desired only his friendship, and had not encroached upon him or his people. Besides, they were the first to offer him promotion and commercial advantages. When he had signed the treaty, they made him a Spanish commissary, with the rank and pay of a colonel.

The commissioners appointed by Washington, reached Rock Landing on the Oconee about the middle of September, 1789, where they found McGillivray, who, at the head of two thousand warriors, had been encamped on the eastern bank of the river for more than a week. The commissioners pitched their camp on the western bank.

For several days the prospect of attaining the object the commissioners had in view seemed peculiarly favourable. They had several private conferences with McGillivray, by whom they were received with great courtesy and politeness. The chiefs, also, whom they visited previous to opening more formal negotiations, appeared to be animated with the most friendly spirit. All the indications promised to result in a treaty satisfactory to both parties.

On the 24th, negotiations were commenced, and a copy of the proposed treaty read to the Indians. It stipulated that the boundaries defined by the former treaties entered into between the Creeks and Georgians should remain unchanged; that the United States would guarantee the territory west of those boundaries to the Creeks for ever; that a free trade should be established with the Indians from ports upon the Alatamaha, through which they could import and export, upon the same terms as the citizens of the United States; and that all negroes, horses, goods, and American citizens taken by the Indians, should be restored.

It is a matter of surprise to this day, how intelligent commissioners could have supposed that a treaty, which took so much from the Indians, and granted so little in return, would be acceptable either to McGillivray or to the chieftains under his control.

Andrew Pickens did indeed remonstrate. He well knew that the lands on the Oconee, which the Georgians were already cultivating, would never be suffered to remain peaceably in the possession of the latter, unless some compensation was made to the Indians.

The result justified his sagacity. After the commissioners had recrossed the river to their own camp, McGillivray and his chiefs met in grand council. The next morning the commissioners were informed by a letter from McGillivray, that the terms which had been proposed were unsatisfactory, and that the Indians had resolved to break up their camp and return home.

The commissioners, startled by so abrupt a conclusion to their negotiations, now saw at once the whole folly of their course. They sought every means to induce McGillivray to remain, and begged him to state his grounds of objection to the draft of the treaty. But he broke up his encampment, and falling back upon the Ockmulgee, wrote from thence a letter to the commissioners, in which he stated that finding a restitution of territory and hunting-grounds was not to be the basis of a treaty between them, he had resolved to return to the nation and defer all further treaty until the next spring.

The commissioners, thus baffled, returned to

Augusta, and obtained from Governor Walton a statement of the various negotiations between the Georgians and the Creeks, together with a list of the citizens who had been killed, and of the property stolen during the recent hostilities.

The answers of Governor Walton placed matters in so very different a light, both as regarded the fair and open manner in which the treaties with the Indians had been made, and the great injuries sustained by their pitiless depredations, that, basing their report upon the evidence laid before them, the commissioners expressed an opinion favourable to the three treaties made by Georgia, and Washington, urged by the demands of the Georgia delegation in Congress, was at first inclined to embark in a war against the Indian confederacy.

More prudent counsels, however, prevailed. It was found that the expenses of such a war as would be necessary to bring the Creeks to terms would not be less than fifteen millions of dollars; and it was reasonably feared that the general government would not be able to sustain so large an outlay while it was struggling with difficulty under the debts incurred during the war of the Revolution.

At length a secret negotiation was determined on. Colonel Willett was selected by Washington as the agent to visit the Creek nation by a circuitous route, and endeavour to persuade McGillivray to return with him to New York, which yet remained the seat of the federal government.

In this mission Willett was eminently successful. On the 13th of April, 1790, he reached the residence of General Pickens, on the Seneca River. Having explained to the latter the object of his journey, he was immediately furnished with letters to various chiefs and traders within the nation, by whom he was received and entertained with a generous warmth and hospitality, which contrasted strangely with the consciousness that the country through which he was passing was the constant scene of murder and robbery. After a journey of ten days through the Cherokee country, Colonel Willett arrived at the house of a wealthy trader, by the name of Scott. This place was the first Creek settlement to which he had penetrated. Learning that McGillivray was then on a visit to Ocfuske, on the Tallapoosa River, Colonel Willett resolved to continue his journey, and at length came up with the Creek chief, at the house of Mr. Graison, in the Hillabees.

When the letter from General Washington had been received and read by McGillivray, he detained Willett at Graison's for two days, during which time various conversations passed between the agent and McGillivray, which, without doubt, influenced the subsequent action of the latter.

Leaving Graison's, the party, accompanied by

McGillivray and his servant, arrived on the 4th of May at the Hickory ground—a portion of the Creek territory, which the Indians considered holy—where there was a large town, and in it one of the residences of the chief.

From this place McGillivray issued his summons to the chiefs of the lower towns, to meet him at Ositchey on the 17th of May, for the purpose of consulting on public business.

The assembly met at the place appointed, and when Colonel Willett had delivered an address inviting them to the council-house at New York, where General Washington desired with his own hand to sign with Colonel McGillivray a treaty of peace and alliance, and offering many other inducements for the chiefs present to embrace the opportunity, he retired, leaving them to deliberate upon his overtures.

In about an hour after, Colonel Willett was again called in, when the Hollowing King addressed him in the following speech:

"We are glad to see you. You have come a great way, and as soon as we fixed our eyes upon you we were made glad. We are poor, and have not the knowledge of the white people. We were invited to the treaty at the Rock Landing. We went there. Nothing was done. We were disappointed, and came back with sorrow. The road to your great council-house is long, and the weather is hot; but our beloved chief shall go with you, and such others as we may appoint. We will agree to all things which our beloved chief shall do. We will count the time he is away, and when he comes back, we shall all be glad to see him with a treaty that shall be as strong as the hills and lasting as the rivers. May you be preserved from every evil."

The voice of the upper Creeks expressing sentiments similar to those of the lower, no time was lost in arranging for the departure of the deputation.

On the 1st of June, Colonel McGillivray, with his nephew and two servants, accompanied by Colonel Willett, set out from Little Tallasse for New York. They were all mounted on horseback, and attended by pack-horses. At the Stone Mountain, the Coweta and Cusseta chiefs joined them; and at the house of General Pickens, they were met by the Tallasse King, Chinnobe, the "great Natchez warrior," and several other chiefs. The deputation being complete, twenty-six warriors started for New York in three wagons, and four others on horseback. Colonel McGillivray and his suite were mounted, the agent riding in a sulky.

Taking the route by way of Guildford, North Carolina, the party passed through Richmond and Fredericksburg, and arrived at Philadelphia on the 17th of July; having been received everywhere on their journey with marked kindness and attention.

Sailing thence to New York, the chiefs were recived by the Tammany Society of that city in the full Indian dress of their order, were marched in full procession up Wall street, past the Federal Hall, where Congress was then in session, and from thence to the house of General Washington, to whom they were introduced with much pomp and ceremony.

The St. Tammany Society next entertained the chiefs at a public dinner. As being the son of a Scotsman, McGillivray was chosen an honorary member of the St. Andrew's Society.

Spain now began to feel uneasy. The authorities in Florida and Louisiana no sooner learned that McGillivray had departed for New York, than the governor-general at Havana was notified of the circumstance. After some correspondence upon the subject, an agent was sent from East Florida with a large sum of money, ostensibly to purchase flour, but in reality to embarrass the negotiations with the Creeks. Washington, apprized of the presence of this officer, had his movements so closely watched that the object of his mission was defeated.

Having first advised with the senate as to the terms of an arrangement, Washington appointed Henry Knox to negotiate with McGillivray and the chiefs, and a treaty having been concluded, it was solemnly ratified the day after the adjournment of Congress.

By this treaty, all the lands south and west of the Oconee,—including the tract recently claimed and partly occupied by Georgia,—were solemnly guaranteed to the Creeks; the latter resigning all pretensions to any lands north and east of that river, and acknowledging themselves to be under the sole protection of the United States.

As an inducement to the Indians to come into this arrangement, and to secure their fidelity, it was provided that the sum of fifteen hundred dollars should be paid annually to the Creek nation; while by a secret article agreed upon between McGillivray and Washington, annuities of one hundred dollars were to be paid to each of the principal chiefs, and to McGillivray, as agent of the United States, the sum of twelve hundred dollars per annum, with the rank of Brigadier-general.

That provision in the treaty of New York, by which the United States guaranteed to the Indians the possession of the Oconee lands, created an intense excitement in Georgia. An association was formed for settling the lands in defiance of the treaty; but the fire of resistance gradually burned itself out. The legislature of the state severely criticised the articles of the treaty, but recognised its validity, and pledged the faith of the state to support it.

On the other hand, the Creeks themselves were far from satisfied, and instigated by one Bowles, a noted freebooter, who aspired to rival McGillivray in the affections of the Indians, the influence of the great chief appeared for some time to be gradually on the wane.

McGillivray, however, was not idle. Knowing that his treaty with the United States could not be otherwise than most distasteful to the Spanish authorities in Louisiana and Florida, he quitted the nation and descended to New Orleans, leaving Bowles and his emissaries to exult in the belief that he would never dare to show his face upon the Coosa again. But the rejoicing of the freebooter did not last long. His piratical seizure of vessels trading under the protection of the Spanish flag soon brought him under the notice of that nation, which only waited a favourable opportunity for his capture.

In the mean time, McGillivray, who was visiting Pensacola, Mobile, and New Orleans, succeeded in establishing himself in as great favour as ever with the Spanish authorities. Here he arranged for the capture of Bowles, who was shortly afterward brought to New Orleans in chains, and sent from thence a prisoner to Spain; while McGillivray, returning to the banks of the Coosa, was speedily restored to the affections of his nation, and the full exercise of his former power.

CHAPTER XXIII.

New Constitution adopted—Synopsis—Indian territory—Speculations in wild land—Combined Society—Yazoo companies—Sale of Yazoo lands—Sale annulled—Seat of government removed to Louisville—Education—University of Georgia—Congress passes the fugitive slave law—Liability of states to individuals—Land speculations—Fraudulent sale by the legislature of Yazoo lands—Sale ratified by Congress—Great excitement in Georgia—Yazoo land sales repudiated—Records burned—Difficulties in relation to the Yazoo sales—Congress appoints commissioners to negotiate for the public territory of Georgia—Compact entered into—Report of commissioners concerning the Yazoo claims—Randolph's resolutions.

THE old constitution of Georgia being neither suited to the wants of the people nor the progressive spirit of the age, a convention was called for the purpose of framing a constitution better calculated to promote the interests of an independent state.

This convention met in 1789, and was in session simultaneously with the first session of Congress. Taking the Federal Constitution in some respects as a model, the legislative power, instead of being vested, as before, in a single assembly, was under the new instrument to be exercised jointly by a senate and house of representatives: the senators to be chosen for three years, one by each of the eleven counties. They were required to be twenty-eight years of age, and to be qualified, like the representatives under the first constitution, by the possession of two hundred and fifty acres of land, or other property to the value of twelve hundred dollars. The qualification of members of the house, which body was to consist of thirty-five members, was the possession of two hundred acres of land, or other property to the value of seven hundred dollars.

No clergyman could be a member of either house. The test of Protestantism, required by the first constitution, was dispensed with. The elective franchise was extended to all male tax-paying freemen, the former property qualification being dropped.

The governor was to be chosen biennially; the house to nominate three persons as candidates, one of whom the senate was to select; the candidates to be thirty years of age, the owners of five hundred acres of land within the state, and of other property to the value of four thousand four hundred and forty-four dollars and forty-four cents.

The powers of the governor were considerably enlarged. He was to have the pardoning power, except in cases of treason; the appointment of all militia officers, and a veto on all laws not repassed by a two-thirds vote.

The judges and other civil officers were to be chosen by the assembly in the same way with the governor; the judges for three years. The same system of county courts was continued as before, to be held by the chief-justice of the state, assisted by three local judges for each county; but the assembly was authorized to constitute out of these judges a court of errors and appeals, empowered to grant new trials.

This constitution, like the old one, prohibited entails, and provided, when there was no will, for an equal distribution of all estates, landed as well as personal, among all the children.

All persons were to enjoy the free exercise of religion, without being obliged to contribute to the support of any religious profession but their own.

Georgia was rapidly increasing in population, and as further constitutional changes might soon become necessary, it was provided that a convention of three persons from each county should meet for that purpose at the end of five years.

The part of Georgia to which, at this time, the Indian title had been extinguished, and which had begun to be occupied by settlers, was limited to a tract along the Savannah a considerable distance above Augusta, and extending westward to the Alatamaha, and its eastern branch the Oconee.

The Indians had also ceded the sea-coast between the Alatamaha and the St. Mary's, but this tract was almost destitute of inhabitants. By far the larger part of what now constitutes the state was in possession of the Creeks and

Cherokees. The Georgians, however, claimed in sovereignty, with exclusive right of pre-emption from the Indians, not only the whole of the present state, but also the district west of the Chattahoochee, out of which the two states of Alabama and Mississippi have since been formed.

The closing of the Revolutionary war involving the older states in great pecuniary embarrassments, led many persons, who desired to avoid the heavy taxation which was the consequence, to migrate in search of new lands. An extraordinary spirit of land speculation was the natural result.

Some ambitious spirits, looking to the western and southwestern territory, as offering an opportunity for acquiring immense wealth and noble domains, formed an association under the name of the "Combined Society," and exacted from every individual connected with it an oath of secrecy as to their plans and movements.

This society was composed of many persons occupying high stations in civil life, who were influenced by the love of personal aggrandizement rather than by sentiments of pure patriotism, and of soldiers connected with the war of the Revolution, who had fought against the British arms more from a desire for an oligarchy in America, than to throw off a foreign yoke. The secrets, however, of this dangerous combination becoming known, and the intentions of the members deservedly stigmatized, the society was disbanded.

In the year 1789, a notorious swindler, calling himself Thomas Washington, but whose real name was Walsh, set on foot a speculation in public lands, which was subsequently known as the Yazoo fraud.

This man associated himself with others, and, instigated by the descriptions of one Sullivan, formerly a captain in the Revolutionary army, and who had been compelled to fly to the Mississippi for his life, persuaded the Virginia Yazoo Company to apply to the new legislature of Georgia for permission to purchase an extensive tract of wild land beyond the Chattahoochee. The South Carolina and the Tennessee Yazoo Companies made application at the same time, and for the same purpose. All three of the applicants were successful. The legislature agreed to sell out the pre-emption right of seven millions of acres to the Virginia Yazoo Company, for ninety-three thousand seven hundred and forty-two dollars; five millions of acres to the Carolina Yazoo Company, for sixty-six thousand nine hundred and sixty-four dollars; and three and a half millions of acres to the Tennessee Yazoo Company, for forty-six thousand eight hundred and seventy-five dollars.

It was one of the conditions of sale that the money should be paid within two years; but as the companies insisted upon paying, not in cash, but in depreciated Georgia paper, a succeeding legislature took advantage of that circumstance to declare the bargain at an end. All the purchasers did not assent to this view; but the controversy on this subject was soon overshadowed by another, which sprang up a few years later, growing out of another sale of these same lands to other companies.

The new legislature fixed the seat of government at Louisville, a new town west of Augusta, and pretty nearly a central point to the then inhabited territory.

As early as the year 1784, an attempt was made to promote the cause of education, by Abraham Baldwin, a graduate of Yale, and one of the best classical scholars of his time. Though he had not been long settled in Georgia, his popularity was already so great as to obtain for him a seat in the assembly. During the session, he originated the plan of the University of Georgia, and obtained from the legislature a grant of forty thousand acres of wild land toward its endowment. A board of trustees was organized the following year, but the land being situated on the northwestern frontier, the danger of Indian hostilities, joined to the difficulty of finding purchasers, kept the fund for many years unavailable. The country was new, land abundant and cheap; much even of a good quality could be obtained by merely surveying it, and paying the fees for granting. The lands, therefore, of the university could not be made available for any valuable purpose, and the trustees were unable to commence the institution. By the treaty of Beaufort, five thousand acres were lost by falling into the state of South Carolina. None of the lands belonging to the university were sold until 1803, and then only a small portion, and at a low price. Most of them remained unsold and unproductive till 1816, when they found purchasers, and one hundred thousand dollars were vested in bank, as a permanent fund for the support of the institution.

In connection with this subject, it may not be improper in this place to show what Georgia has done to promote the cause of education throughout the state. On the 31st of July, 1783, the legislature appropriated one hundred acres of land to each county for the support of free schools. In 1792, an act was passed appropriating one thousand pounds sterling for the endowment of an academy in each county.

In 1817, two hundred and fifty thousand dollars were appropriated to the support of poor schools. The following year, every tenth and one hundredth lot of land in seven new counties were set apart for educational purposes; and in 1821, two hundred and fifty thousand dollars were devoted to the support of county academies.

But although the appropriations by the legislature have been so liberal, and private subscriptions to the amount of six hundred thousand dollars have aided in advancing so wise and humane an object, education has never been more than partial, owing to an apathetic indifference on the part of the great mass of the population.

During the session of 1793, the Congress of the United States passed an act which, although it attracted but little attention at the time, has since acquired peculiar importance from its becoming, in its revised and more stringent form, the test of harmonious action between the North and South. It was an act regulating the surrender of fugitives from justice, and the restoration of fugitives from service, as provided for in the constitution.

Fugitives from justice, on the demand of the executive of the state whence they had fled upon the executive of any state in which they might be found, accompanied with an indictment or affidavit charging crime upon them, were to be delivered up, and carried back for trial.

In case of the escape out of any state or territory of any person held to service or labour under the laws thereof, the person to whom such labour was due, his agent, or attorney, might seize the fugitive and carry him before any United States judge, or before any magistrate of the city, town, or county in which the arrest was made; and such judge or magistrate, on proof to his satisfaction, either oral or by affidavit before any other magistrate, that the person seized was really a fugitive, and did owe labour as alleged, was to grant a certificate to that effect to the claimant, this certificate to serve as a sufficient warrant for the removal of the fugitive to the state whence he had fled.

Any person obstructing in any way such seizure or removal, or harbouring or concealing any fugitive after notice, was liable to a penalty of five hundred dollars, to be recovered by the claimant.

Shortly before the termination of the session, the Supreme Court of the United States decided the first great constitutional question brought before it. One Chisholm, being a citizen of another state, had brought an action against the State of Georgia, to recover a sum of money alleged to be due him by that state. This raised the question whether the states were liable to be sued by individual citizens of other states. Judge Iredell, who seemed to lean against the jurisdiction, wished to escape a decision on an objection to the form of the action. The other judges overruled the objection, and held that, as the United States constituted one nation, the alleged sovereignty of the separate states must be considered to be so far modified thereby as to subject them, under the terms of the Constitution, to suits in the national courts.

The day after this decision was pronounced, Sedgwick offered a resolution in the house of representatives for an amendment to the Constitution, protecting the states against suits by individuals. No action was had on the motion at this time, but, subsequently, such an amendment prevailed.

The speculations in wild lands still continued. Between the years 1791 and 1795, most of the public domain, which had passed into the hands of particular states, had become exhausted. All the most valuable tracts held by Massachusetts had become individual property. Out of seven millions of acres owned by New York, five and a half millions had been disposed of at a single sale. Almost the whole of the large tracts which, upon the confiscation of the proprietary estates, had come into the possession of Pennsylvania, had been bought up by speculators.

The latter now turned their attention to the lands claimed by Georgia west of the Chattahoochee, and between that river and the Mississippi. In 1794 and 1795, the general assembly passed an act conveying to four associations, called by the respective names of the Georgia, the Georgia Mississippi, the Upper Mississippi, and the Tennessee Companies, thirty-five millions of acres of land, for five hundred thousand dollars, lying between the Mississippi, Tennessee, Coosa, Alabama, and Mobile Rivers. The bill authorizing the sale was contested in both houses of Congress. It was passed by a majority of ten in the house of representatives and two in the senate. The sale of this land, and its ratification by Congress, produced great excitement throughout Georgia, where it was known that all in the state legislature who voted for the bill, with one or two exceptions, were directly or indirectly bribed.

From the very beginning of this fraudulent scheme, General James Jackson, of Georgia, who was then in the senate of the United States, used all his influence in opposition to its consummation. The defeat of the Yazoo act was the absorbing subject of his thoughts. In 1795, yielding to the wishes of many of his fellow-citizens, he resigned his seat in the senate, and, returning home, was elected a member of the legislature, by which he was appointed a member of the committee authorized to investigate the conduct of their predecessors. The whole corruption was exposed and overturned; the odious act was repealed, and it was determined to obliterate the remembrance of it from history by committing the records to the flames. The burning was executed with great formality. The two houses, moving in procession for that purpose, were preceded by a committee bearing the obnoxious parchments. A fire having been kindled in front of the state-house, the committee handed the documents to the president of the senate, he to the speaker of the house, he to the clerk, and the clerk to the doorkeeper; who, while thrusting them into the flames, cried out with a loud and decisive voice: "God save the state, and long preserve her rights, and may every attempt to injure them perish, as these wicked and corrupt acts now do!"

Unfortunately, this solemn repudiation of the sale by no means tended to settle the question. The original purchasers had already transferred their rights to others at a large advance on the original purchase-money. These new purchasers were not at all disposed to concede the right of the legislature of Georgia to nullify the acts of their predecessors, especially in a case like the present, where the interest of third parties were concerned.

When, therefore, these same lands were subsequently sold by Georgia to the United States, Congress was loudly called upon for an indemnity to the claimants under the Georgia grant. Nearly twenty years elapsed before the matter was brought to a final settlement.

By an act of Congress in the year 1800, Madison, Gallatin, and Lincoln, who had been appointed commissioners for adjusting with Georgia her claims to the territory of Mississippi, were vested with full powers to arrange the whole matter; with the restriction, however, that no money was to be paid to Georgia except out of the proceeds of the land.

The agreement thus entered into was not communicated to Congress until late in the session of 1802. By the terms of the compact, Georgia ceded to the United States all her claims to the territory west of what now constitutes her western boundary, on condition of receiving out of the first net proceeds of the lands sold, the sum of one million two hundred and fifty thousand dollars, the United States undertaking to extinguish, at the expense of the federal treasury, the Indian title to the lands reserved by Georgia as early as the same could be peaceably obtained on reasonable terms; especially the Indian title to that tract between the Oconee and Ockmulgee. It was also provided by the terms of the compact, that whenever the population of the territory thus ceded should amount to sixty thousand, or earlier at the option of Congress, the ceded territory was to be erected into a state, on the same terms and conditions contained in the ordinance of 1787 for the government of the territory northwest of the Ohio, "that article only excepted which prohibits slavery."

The Yazoo claims never having as yet been satisfactorily adjusted, the same commissioners who had negotiated with Georgia the cession of the Mississippi country, having been authorized to inquire as to the various land claims in that territory, reported, concerning the grants of 1795, that, whatever grounds of invalidity there might be, as between Georgia and the original grantees, and even though the contract might not be legally binding, as between Georgia and the present holders, yet, as those holders claimed to stand, and to a certain extent did stand, in the position of innocent purchasers without notice, theirs seemed a proper case for compromise. Taking this view of the matter, the commissioners suggested the propriety of offering to the claimants certificates bearing interest to the amount of two millions and a half of dollars, or certificates without interest for five millions, payable out of the earliest receipts for Mississippi lands, after the stipulation to Georgia should be satisfied.

Upon this report was founded an act appropriating whatever might remain of the five millions of acres reserved by the compact, after certain specified deductions had been made, to the quieting of such unconfirmed claims as might be exhibited and recorded in the office of the Secretary of State before the close of the year, and for which Congress might see fit to make a provision.

To this act, Randolph during the next session of Congress objected, and moved a series of resolutions excluding from any compensation whatever the claimants under the Yazoo grants of 1795.

Almost all the southern, and a few of the northern members supported the resolutions; but after a fierce struggle, they were voted down by a majority of five. Thus ended the contest.

CHAPTER XXIV.

Ellicott appointed to run the line between the Creeks and Georgians—Obstacles—Assertion of Spanish claims to the Indian territory—Intrigues of McGillivray—Appointed Superintendent-general of Spain in the Creek nation—Irritation of the Georgians—Their determined stand—Sickness of McGillivray—His death—Frontier excesses—Georgia arms against the Indians—Failure of the invasion—Seagrove attends a council of the Creek chiefs—Friendly disposition of the Indians—Seagrove attacked in his house and plundered—Arrival of Genet—His extraordinary course—Fits out privateers—Organizes expeditions from Kentucky and Georgia against New Orleans and Florida—The Spanish governor remonstrates—Course of Governors Shelby and Matthews—Genet recalled—Projects of Clarke—Settles the Oconee lands—Ordered off—Refuses—Is driven off by the militia of Georgia.

In order to carry out in the clearest manner the provisions of the treaty of New York, early in the year 1791, Andrew Ellicott, a citizen of Pennsylvania, was appointed by the federal government to run the line between the Creeks and Georgians. He reached Rock Landing upon the Oconee in May, accompanied by James Seagrove, an Irishman, who had been appointed superintendent of the Creek nation. At this place the government erected a strong fort, and threw into it a large garrison.

From this point, McGillivray was urged to obtain the consent of the Indians to the running of the boundary line, and their assistance to its execution.

Many obstacles as usual occurred. The Spanish government, alarmed by the treaty of New York, now asserted her claims to a considerable portion of the territory in question. McGillivray attributed the moodiness and discontent of the Indians to the machinations of his rival Bowles, and, after expressing his inability to control the disaffected, retired, as we have already mentioned, to Florida, where he remained during the following winter.

His return to the Coosa, which took place in 1792, only served to complicate matters which were already sufficiently entangled. The ease with which he rid himself of the presence of Bowles, as soon as he found it his interest to do so, showed very clearly, that the reluctance of the Creeks to submit to the survey did not emanate in any great degree from the influence of the freebooter. The intrigues of McGillivray with the Spanish authorities were the real cause. He had scarcely returned from Florida before a Spanish agent made his appearance in the nation, and took up his abode at the Hickory Ground upon the Coosa. The unexpected presence of this agent, Captain Don Pedro Oliver, and his familiarity with McGillivray, awakened the suspicions of Ellicott and Seagrove, who inferred, naturally enough, that McGillivray was not acting in good faith with the federal government. The supposition, though incapable of proof at the time, has since been most abundantly verified.

Through the remonstrances of William Panton, a wealthy merchant of Pensacola, whose partner in the Indian trade McGillivray had become, the Spanish government appointed the latter superintendent-general of the Creek nation, with an annual salary of two thousand dollars, which, in July of the same year, was increased to three thousand five hundred.

As McGillivray was thus an agent of Spain, with an annual salary of thirty-five hundred dollars, the copartner of Panton, trading from a Spanish port, and the agent of the United States with a salary of twelve hundred dollars, it may easily be inferred, though paid by both, toward which nation his inclinations leaned.

The ignorance of Spain in relation to the secret article in the treaty of New York, and the equal ignorance on the part of the United States of the large sum paid yearly to McGillivray by Spain, puzzled both parties greatly to account for the wavering and uncertain policy of McGillivray, which subsequent developments have so clearly explained.

In the mean while, the people of Georgia, worried alike by the Spaniards and the Indians, were chafing impatiently at the numerous impediments and delays which rendered their frontier possessions so constantly insecure.

Disgusted at length with the progress of negotiations which presented no prospect of a termination, they resolved, that if the United States delayed much longer in driving the Spaniards from their territory, to undertake it themselves.

The opposition of Spain to the survey undertaken by the agents of the federal government, her refusal to admit of American settlements on the Mississippi, joined to her express determination to protect the Creeks from any encroachments on the part of Georgia, tended still more to exasperate the latter, and embarrass the action of the government.

Friendly relations existing between McGillivray and Governor Carondelet, he continued his visits to New Orleans, giving up one of his houses to Captain Oliver, whom he had established in the affections of his people. In returning from New Orleans late in the summer of 1792, a violent fever detained him long in Mobile. He finally recovered from the attack, and reached Little Tallasse, from which place he wrote to Seagrove, the Indian agent, deploring the unhappy disturbances which existed, and attributing them to Spanish interference. This was a mere excuse, since the influence which the latter had obtained in the nation had been fostered and encouraged by McGillivray himself.

It is very evident that the great chief never cordially allied himself either to the federal government or to Georgia. The latter he could not help regarding as the natural enemy of his people; a feeling in some measure justified by that tenacious and constantly enlarging grasp with which the Georgians laid hold of the Creek territory.

But the career of this remarkable man was fast drawing to a close. He was always of a delicate constitution, and had long suffered from a complication of disorders. He was taken ill on the path coming from his Cowpen plantation, on Little River, and only retained sufficient strength to reach the house of his partner, Mr. Panton, at Pensacola, where he died eight days after his arrival, and was buried in the garden of that merchant, whose magnificent fortune he had so largely aided in building up.

No sooner were the politic restraints, with which McGillivray had undoubtedly curbed the more blood-thirsty of his people, cast loose by the death of their beloved man, than the horrors of frontier war broke out fiercer than ever. Murders were committed in various quarters: on the St. Mary's, in the new counties of Camden and Glynn, and at the Skull shoals of the Oconee.

These excesses roused the Georgians to take

the law into their own hands. Governor Telfair directed a large force to be raised for the invasion of the Creek country. At the solicitation of the Georgia delegation in Congress, Washington sent to Augusta a large stand of arms and ammunition, and authorized Governor Telfair to enlist a few companies for the protection of the frontiers, but remonstrated against the invasion. Telfair refused to accept the troops, and paid no heed to the remonstrance. He placed General Twiggs at the head of seven hundred mounted men, and ordered him into the Indian country.

The army of invasion marched as far as the Ockmulgee River, and then, weakened by the want of provisions, and rendered perfectly inefficient by insubordination, retreated.

This unfortunate failure incited the Creeks to commit still greater excesses. Telfair called out a mounted force of militia, which scoured constantly the country between the Oconee and Ockmulgee. Washington again remonstrated; when some of the malcontents, forgetful of the respect that was due to the President of the Republic, vented their indignation by placing his effigies upon pine trees and firing at them. Seagrove, the accredited agent of the federal government, still remained near the Indians, communicating with them occasionally through

Timothy Barnard, a trustworthy man who resided within the nation.

In March, 1793, a council of the chiefs, consisting of delegates from the upper and lower towns, invited Seagrove to a personal conference. To this mission Governor Telfair objected, on the ground that it would interfere with his military operations; and stating further, that Georgia would submit to no treaty made with the Creeks, where her agents were not permitted to participate.

Seagrove, however, accepted the invitation, and after some delay set out from Fort Fidius, escorted by a military guard. When he reached the Ockmulgee the guard was dismissed, and one hundred and thirty warriors accompanied him from thence to Cusseta upon the Chattahoochee. After being saluted at this place with the beating of drums and the fire of artillery, he proceeded to the Tallapoosa River, on the west bank of which stood Tookabatcha, the capital of the nation.

On the 23d of November, 1793, he addressed a vast assembly of the Indians convened for that purpose, and in a speech of unusual force and vigour, commented upon the character of their repeated aggressions and their faithlessness in not assisting to carry out the provisions of the treaty of New York.

A deliberation among the chiefs themselves

followed, the result of which was, that they agreed to deliver into the hands of the agent, the negroes, horses, cattle, and other property taken from the Georgians during the twelve months preceding; and to put to death several of the principals engaged in the late murders upon the frontiers.

But while Seagrove was congratulating himself upon the success of his mission, a party of Creeks who preferred treating with commissioners from Georgia, and were opposed to any interference on the part of the United States, combined secretly to attack him. Led by the Tallasse king, they entered one night the house at which Seagrove was staying, plundered him of his property, and forced him to fly for his life and hide himself in a deep pond screened by trees and bushes.

In the morning, however, by the interposition of friendly chiefs, peace was restored, the agent withdrawn from his hiding-place, and subsequently escorted in safety back to the frontiers.

In addition to that fruitful source of annoyance, her Indian claims, Georgia had been profoundly agitated during this year by an event which had its origin in the French Revolution. This was no other than the arrival at Charleston of Citizen Genet, appointed to supersede Ternant as ambassador from France. Genet brought with him news of the French declaration of war against Great Britain. The people of Charleston received him with enthusiasm. Being provided with blank commissions, both naval and military, he caused to be fitted out two privateers, manned mostly with Americans, which put to sea under the French flag, and, cruising along the coast, soon made numerous captures of homeward-bound vessels. He also assumed, under a decree of the convention, the extraordinary power of authorizing the French consuls throughout the United States to erect themselves into courts of admiralty for trying and condemning such prizes as the French cruisers might bring into American ports.

The federal government, listening to the complaints made by the British minister, declared that the privateering commissions issued by Genet, as well as the condemnation of prizes by the French consuls, were unauthorized by treaty, irregular, and void.

Against this decision Genet most vehemently protested. Washington remained firm; but for a considerable period it was doubtful whether Genet, supported by the fiery enthusiasm of a considerable portion of the American people, would not be able to place himself beyond the control of the federal government.

France had now also declared war against Spain. This rendered the mission of Genet most welcome to many of the Georgians, who desired nothing more earnestly than to crush, by any means whatever, the power of her troublesome neighbour.

Four French agents were sent by Genet to Kentucky, with orders to enlist in that state an army of two thousand men; to engage the services of a distinguished American officer, as commander-in-chief, and, descending the Ohio and Mississippi in boats, attack the Spanish settlements at the mouth of the Mississippi, and bring the whole of that country under the dominion of the French republic. The command of this force was confided to General George Rogers Clarke, who accepted the commission of major-general in the service of France, with an annual salary of ten thousand dollars.

Emissaries were also busily engaged at the same time in issuing commissions and collecting a military force in South Carolina and Georgia. The expedition from Kentucky was destined for New Orleans; that which had its appointed rendezvous in Georgia was intended for the invasion of Florida. General Elijah Clarke accepted command of the latter, under a commission and salary similar to that of General Clarke of Kentucky. A considerable body of Creeks and Cherokees had likewise been enlisted in the service of the French republic. An agent was furnished with ten thousand dollars, to purchase supplies for the Georgia army, which was to assemble at St. Mary's.

Alarmed at these preparations, the Governor of East Florida remonstrated with the Governors of Kentucky and Georgia.

Governor Shelby, of the former state, in conjunction with a considerable portion of the citizens of Kentucky, who desired a free navigation of the Mississippi, was strongly inclined to favour the projects of Genet. Governor Matthews, whatever might have been his private feelings in the matter, immediately issued a proclamation forbidding the people of Georgia to engage in the enterprise.

Washington also publicly denounced the whole project, and authorized the governors of the various states within whose limits such expeditions were forming, to employ the United States troops in putting down the contemplated invasion.

Kentucky still resisted. Democratic societies were established, in imitation of the Jacobin clubs of Paris. Inflammatory harangues were made, expressive of a determination to force the navigation of the Mississippi, untrammelled by any foreign authority. The East was charged with jealousy of the West and South, and an exasperated state of feeling produced, which threatened at one time to seriously endanger the integrity of the confederation.

To their honour be it said, Georgia and South Carolina supported Washington in this hour of difficulty. The schemes of Genet were frustrated, his agents arrested, and his projects disavowed by the new administrators of the French government, who, yielding to the request of Washington, consented to recall their obnoxious ambassador. Genet, however, being perhaps apprehensive of the fate which might befall him, did not choose to risk the danger of returning to France. He married a daughter of Governor Clinton of New York, became a resident of that state, and, ceasing to exercise the functions of a French minister, soon sunk into almost total obscurity.

This concert of action between the general and state governments was by no means pleasing to many of the restless spirits who had entered so ardently into the schemes of Genet. There were at that time large numbers of persons, who, having been actively engaged throughout the whole war of the Revolution, had acquired that thirst for excitement and those roving habits which a war of any continuance is so apt to engender. These men found it difficult to settle themselves down to any calm and peaceful avocations; and even such as had occupied high stations in the army felt it difficult to conform to the new state of things.

Some of this unquiet class of men no sooner

found themselves deprived of the prospects of a campaign in Florida, than they turned their attention to the possession of the long-disputed lands between the Oconee and Ockmulgee. General Elijah Clarke, the brave old Revolutionary veteran, placed himself at the head of this movement. Accompanied by a large party of Georgians, he began a settlement opposite Fort Fidius, on the west side of the Oconee, and upon the lands guarantied by the federal government to the Indians.

General Irwin, on the part of the state, ordered him to remove, which he refused to do. Governor Matthews forbade by proclamation the contemplated settlement, and accused Clarke of an attempt to form a separate and independent government. The latter appeared before the superior court of Wilkes county, and surrendered himself for trial. The proceedings partook of the nature of a farce. He was found not guilty, and discharged.

Many persons now flocked to his standard. His settlements were pushed with vigour; a town was laid off, and Forts Advance and Defiance were erected and garrisoned.

Washington called the attention of the state government to this illegal occupation of the Indian territory, and offered the services of troops to assist in driving off the settlers. Governor Matthews directed Generals Twiggs and Irwin to break up the settlements begun by Clarke. This duty was performed by the Georgia militia, firmly, yet without undue harshness. On the 25th of September, 1794, General Clarke, finding himself abandoned by all but twenty of his men, surrendered upon condition that his property and the property of the colonists should be returned to them. The forts and houses were destroyed by fire, and the affair ended happily without the shedding of blood.

CHAPTER XXV.

Council of Coleraine—Treaty of New York formally renewed and ratified—Discontent of Georgia—Treaty with Spain—Settlement of boundaries—Ellicott appointed commissioner to run the boundary between Spain and the United States—Intrigues of Carondelet—His reluctance to carry out the conditions of the treaty—Sends an emissary to Kentucky—Fort Panmure summoned by the Americans—Increase of American force—Gayoso evacuates Fort Panmure—Survey commenced—Interruptions feared from the Creeks—Council at Miller's Bluff—Governor Folch, of Pensacola, instigates the Creeks to break up the survey—Ellicott proceeds to St. Marks—Joins the surveyors on the St. Mary's—Bowles the freebooter—Refuses to enter the Spanish service—Sent to Manilla—Escapes—Reaches Florida—Is captured—Sent to Havana—Dies in Moro Castle.

The sale of the public lands, entered into by the legislature of Georgia in the early part of February, 1795, and stigmatized as the Yazoo fraud, has been already mentioned in a previous chapter.

In May, 1796, commissioners on the part of the United States and Georgia met the Indians in council at Coleraine upon the St. Mary's River. The object for which the conference was called was the formation of a treaty of peace with the Creeks, and the cession of the long-contested lands between the Oconee and Ockmulgee.

A full delegation of Indians were present, consisting of twenty kings, seventy-five chiefs, and three hundred and forty warriors. At the suggestion of Seagrove, the Indian agent, the council was removed from Coleraine to Muskogee, a short distance off. Here a considerable time was spent in listening to the speeches of the commissioners, and in subsequent deliberations.

At length, on the 29th of June, the chiefs of the whole Creek nation concluded a treaty with the federal commissioners, by which the treaty of New York was formally renewed and ratified; the Indians pledging themselves to carry out its provisions, and to assist Spain and the United States to run their line; but they positively refused to cede any portion of the Oconee and Ockmulgee territory to Georgia.

This renewal of the previous treaty failed to satisfy the Georgians, as no new cessions of land were obtained; but it put an end to the mutual depredations which had prevailed on that frontier, and provided for the restoration of prisoners and property taken by the Indians.

Previous to this, Washington had despatched Thomas Pinckney on a special mission to Spain, which ended in settling at last the long-disputed questions of the Spanish boundary, and the navigation of the Mississippi River. By this treaty, which was made on the 20th of October, 1795, the Florida boundary was stipulated to be the thirty-first degree of north latitude, between the Mississippi and Appalachicola; and east of the Appalachicola a line from the junction of the Flint to the head of the St. Mary's; and thence by that river to the sea. It was further stipulated, that Spain should not hereafter form treaties of alliance with Indians living upon American soil, nor the federal government with Indians living upon Spanish territory; and that Spanish and American commissioners should mark the boundary before the expiration of six months after the ratification of the treaty.

In order to carry out the latter clause of the treaty as speedily as possible, Andrew Ellicott, who had waited on the frontiers of the Indian territory so long for an opportunity to survey the line of the Oconee lands, was appointed a commissioner on the part of the federal government to run the boundary between Spain and the United States. He reached Natchez, on the Mississippi, in the latter part of February, 1797, and immediately commenced negotiations with Don Manuel de Lemas, commandant at Fort Panmure, governor of the Natchez dependencies, and commissioner on the part of Spain.

But Baron Carondelet, the Spanish governor of Louisiana, having determined not to comply with the treaty, sought by various obstacles to oppose the survey of the boundary. He refused to deliver up the posts north of the thirty-first degree of north latitude, under the pretext that he apprehended a British invasion from Canada, against which the possession of these posts was necessary to an effectual resistance. Another reason alleged by him for still retaining them, was the uncertainty he entertained whether, under the treaty stipulations, the fortifications were to be destroyed or left standing. His reluctance to acknowledge the validity of the treaty led him to violate it still more flagrantly. He sent one Thomas Powers as a secret agent to Kentucky, to intrigue with the old Spanish partisans in that region for the dismemberment of the Union, and its erection into an independent state, in close alliance with Spain. Many influential men in the west entered zealously into the project. Others who were applied to for the same purpose coldly declined to take any part in the enterprise, but kept the intrigue concealed from the federal government.

Meanwhile, Lieutenant McLeary, with an

American force, unfurled the American flag on the heights of Natchez, and marching soon afterward to Fort Panmure, demanded its surrender. But as the latter, in anticipation of such a summons, had been repaired and strengthened with men and artillery, Gayozo, the commandant, declined to evacuate it, and McLeary had not the means of capturing it, either by siege or storm.

Ellicott warmly remonstrated against this breach of the treaty, and an angry correspondence followed. About this time, Lieutenant Pope arrived at Natchez with forty men, which were added to the American force. Gayozo now began to grow alarmed; but still invented excuses for not complying with the demands of the commissioner. The Natchez population, increasing rapidly, desired the expulsion of the Spaniards. Ellicott insisted that Gayozo should appoint a day upon which he would meet him and commence the survey. The latter answered by evasions. Finding the people indisposed to wait much longer, he issued a proclamation, announcing that the treaty would ultimately be complied with, but refrained from saying when. The imprisonment of an American citizen by Gayozo added to an excitement already sufficiently fierce. Public meetings were called, and violent measures advocated. Gayozo sought to temporize, but was answered by indignant threats. The personal influence of Ellicott alone prevented the people from committing acts of violence.

In this way nearly a whole year was passed. Perceiving, from the continual influx of Americans, that his position was becoming every day one of greater danger, Gayozo concluded at length to evacuate the fort, and sail with his troops lower down the river. This was done on the 29th of March, 1798, and immediately afterward Ellicott proceeded to Tunica Bayou, and commenced his survey in a dense swamp, on the eastern bank of the Mississippi, where the line of thirty degrees strikes it.

The work had scarcely been commenced before the commissioners appointed by Spain joined Ellicott. The progress of the survey was, however, very slow. It was not until the middle of March, 1799, that the line was completed to Mobile River. The Choctaw nation had offered no resistance to the progress of the party through their territory; the Creeks, however, appeared more disposed to interfere. It was decided to meet the latter in council upon the Conecuh. The Spanish governor of Pensacola suggested that the proposed council should be held at Pensacola; but as the American commissioners suspected that Governor Folch designed to interrupt the survey by fresh intrigues with the Indians, they adhered to their former resolution. A conference was accordingly held at Miller's Bluff, in the presence of the commissioners of both nations and several Spanish officers. The proceedings were characterized by great unanimity. The Indians appeared satisfied with the explanations they received, and consented to assist in running the line.

Baffled by the manly and straight-forward course taken by the respective commissioners, Governor Folch secretly instigated a large number of the Creeks to interrupt the survey by hostile demonstrations.

With large bodies of insolent Indian marauders hanging upon his rear, and plundering the effects of his party, Ellicott pushed the survey to the Chattahoochee, where he fortified himself.

Notwithstanding the resolute conduct of Colonel Hawkins, who, with a small party of military, succeeded in restraining the Indians from plundering the camp, the commissioners found it impossible to proceed any further. The surveyors, attended by the military escort, set out for St. Mary's, while Ellicott, embarking in his schooner, the rigging of which had been cut to pieces by the Indians, propelled her in the best way he could down the Appalachicola to St. Marks, where he remained at the house of the Spanish commandant, Captain Portell, until the schooner was repaired. He then sailed around the peninsula, and went up the St. Mary's to the camp of the surveyors, where, in conjunction with Captain

Mina, the surveyor on the part of Spain, he determined, on the 20th of February, 1800, the point of the line of thirty-one degrees, and to indicate it erected on the spot a large mound. Thus ended a difficult and dangerous survey, which, through the treachery and duplicity of Spain, had been protracted over a space of three years.

While Ellicott was on his way to St. Marks, a singular adventure befell him which deserves something more than a passing notice. At Fox-point he found a British schooner wrecked, and among the crew the notorious freebooter Bowles, he who had been handed over to the Spanish governor by McGillivray, and sent in chains to Madrid. Knowing that this man was possessed of considerable influence among a certain portion of the Indian tribes, the Spanish government had sought to win him over to its interest, by the offer of a military commission and an annual salary. Finding these would not tempt him to desert his loose allegiance to England, the court of Madrid then removed him from his prison to handsome quarters, and hoped to win upon his gratitude by supplying him with obsequious attendants, and feasting him with costly wines, and viands of the richest and most delicate kinds. But Bowles remained intractable, and, irritated at length by his obstinacy, he was again placed in irons and sent a prisoner to Manilla, on the Pacific. Here he remained until 1791, when he was again sent to Spain. At the island of Ascension, while on the voyage, Bowles managed to make his escape, and from thence, in some manner, reached Sierra Leone, where he obtained a passage to London. He had returned to the coast of Florida in the schooner, the wreck of which had been discovered by Ellicott, and taking advantage of the war between Spain and England—whose subject he professed to be—had carried on for some time a sort of predatory warfare upon the coasting vessels and property of Spanish subjects.

In his conversations with Ellicott, he declared his bitter hatred of the latter power, whose posts in Florida he avowed his intention of harassing by incessant attacks, at the head of the Creeks, whom he designated as "my people."

Soon after this, Bowles succeeded in quitting the point where Ellicott had discovered him, and, entering the Creek nation, was soon enabled to acquire a considerable portion of his former power.

For the next three years he kept up a succession of forays into the Spanish territory, and bringing back into the Indian country the plunder he took, shared it among his adherents.

The alarm with which his name now inspired the Spanish population, and the prosperous issue of his incursions, gradually increased his daring. At the head of his swarthy followers, he penetrated the Spanish territory as far as St. Marks, captured the fort, and came off with the booty unmolested.

These repeated outrages finally aroused the Spanish authorities, and the federal agent, Colonel Hawkins. A large reward was secretly offered for the capture of the freebooter, and a plot arranged for carrying it into effect. It was accomplished. Bowles while at a great feast was suddenly seized by concealed Indians, who sprang upon him, bound him, and carried him down the river in a canoe filled with armed warriors.

While the canoe was fastened to the bank of the river for the night, Bowles succeeded in making his escape from the guards, by gnawing asunder the cords that bound him. Crossing the river, he entered a dense cane-swamp and fled; but was eventually recaptured, and taken to Mobile. From thence he was sent to Havana, where, after a few years, he ended his romantic but turbulent life in the dungeons of Moro Castle.

CHAPTER XXVI.

Revision of the constitution of 1789—Cession of Louisiana to France — Jefferson's letter to Livingston — Negotiations—Louisiana purchased by the United States—Claiborne appointed governor—Takes possession of New Orleans—Flourishing condition of Georgia—Milledgeville laid off—Becomes the seat of government—Foreign relations of the United States—Disputes with England—Embargo laid on French ports—Berlin and Milan decrees of Napoleon—Injuries sustained by American commerce—Declaration of war against England—Dissatisfaction among the Indians—Tecumseh—Confers with the British agents at Detroit—Departs for the south—Stimulates the Seminoles to hostilities—Enters the Creek nation—Gains many proselytes—Returns to his nation—Outrages on the frontiers—Civil war among the Indians—Creek war—War with Great Britain—Peace proclaimed—Difficulties between Georgia and the general government.

UNDER the provision to that effect in the state constitution of 1789, that instrument was revised in 1798. The pecuniary qualifications of governor and members of the legislature were slightly diminished, but new qualifications of citizenship and of residence in the state were added: six years residence and twelve years citizenship were required to render a candidate eligible to the office of governor; in case of members of the legislature, three years residence; nine years citizenship for senators, and seven years for representatives.

Representation in the house was henceforth to

be regulated by a compound basis of territory and population, including in the count three-fifths of the people of colour.

Three thousand inhabitants, according to the ratio, were to entitle a county to two members; seven thousand, to three members; and twelve thousand, to four members; but no county was to have less than one member nor more than four.

Each house was expressly vested with power to expel, censure, fine, or imprison its own members for disorderly conduct, to preserve its own dignity from disorderly conduct on the part of any persons not members, and to punish threats or assaults upon any member for any thing said or done in the assembly.

The further importation of slaves from Africa or any foreign place was expressly prohibited.

By a clause copied from the constitution of Kentucky, the legislature of Georgia were not permitted to pass laws for the emancipation of slaves, except with the previous consent of individual owners; nor were they to prohibit immigrants from bringing with them "such persons as may be deemed slaves by the law of any one of the United States."

By a further provision, any person found guilty of maliciously killing or dismembering a slave was to suffer the same punishment as if the acts had been committed on a free white person, except in cases of insurrection, or "unless death should happen by accident, in giving the slave moderate correction."

A subsequent clause claimed, as the property of the state, the whole territory as far west as the Mississippi, between the thirty-first degree of north latitude and a due west continuation of the northern line of Georgia. Other clauses followed, regulating the manner by which such territory might be sold, and enjoining that means should be provided for refunding such sums as had been received by the state under the fraudulent Yazoo contracts.

Provision was made for amending the constitution in future by bills for that purpose, to be passed by a two-thirds vote in both houses of two successive legislatures, with an intervening publication for at least six months prior to the election of the members of the second legislature.

During the years 1801–2, many rumours had reached the government which led to a suspicion that France intended to obtain from Spain the retrocession of Louisiana, and perhaps with the addition of Florida also.

These rumours increasing, instructions were sent to the American ministers at Paris, Madrid, and London, to endeavour to defeat the cession. The surrender of the province of Louisiana, however, had already been made by a secret treaty, dated October 1st, 1800; but the treaty was not to take effect until six months after certain stipulations made therein, in favour of Spain, were complied with.

The possession of the mouth of the Mississippi by a friendly but enterprising nation like France was a matter well calculated to arouse the fears of the federal government.

"This state of things," wrote Jefferson to Livingston, then in Paris, "completely reverses all the political relations of the United States, and will form a new epoch in our political course. We have always looked to France as our natural friend—one with whom we could never have an occasion of difference; but there is one spot on the globe the possessor of which is our natural and habitual enemy. That spot is New Orleans. France placing herself in that door assumes to us an attitude of defiance. The day that France takes possession seals the union of two nations, who, in conjunction, can maintain exclusive possession of the ocean. From that moment we must marry ourselves to the British fleet and nation." Much more was added, and reasons given why the French government should consent to the transfer of Louisiana to the United States; or if not the whole province, at least the island of Orleans; suggestions, which Mr. Livingston was instructed to make in a way not to give offence.

Sentiments so strong doubtless had their effect in pressing to a final issue the negotiations which succeeded. The difficulty under which Livingston laboured, however, was the want of authority to offer any particular sum for the territory, so absolutely required for the safety of the United States, and the facilities of its western commerce.

Livingston's personal application to Bonaparte met with no favourable response until the apprehension of the latter was quickened by the approach of a new European war. On the 11th of April, 1803, and shortly before Monroe's arrival at Paris, Livingston was requested by Talleyrand to make an offer for the whole province of Louisiana.

The government of the United States had contemplated the purchase, not of Louisiana alone, but of Florida also, and had instructed both Monroe and Livingston to that effect; the supposition at the time being, that Spain either had included or would include both provinces in her cession to France.

The highest amount authorized to be paid for the whole was ten millions of dollars. If France refused to entertain negotiations at all, the ministers were instructed to open a correspondence with Great Britain, with the view of preventing the French from taking possession of Louisiana, and of ultimately securing it to the United States.

The price asked by Bonaparte for Louisiana was twenty millions of dollars, with the addition of the payment, by the United States, of the claims of American merchants recognised by a previous convention.

The price was finally agreed upon at twelve millions of dollars, and the discharge by the home government of American claims upon France to the extent of four millions more, if they should amount to so much.

The news of this arrangement was received with great satisfaction by the president and his cabinet, and met with the hearty concurrence of the American people. Governor Claiborne was soon after appointed governor of Louisiana territory, and, sailing from Natchez down the Mississippi, with a military force under General Wilkinson, and a large body of emigrants, took formal possession of the city of New Orleans on the 20th of December, 1803.

No longer suffering to any extent from the incursions of the Indians, nor annoyed by the Spaniards of Louisiana, Georgia continued to extend her population—which had doubled its numbers between 1790 and 1800—over portions of the state hitherto uninhabited. Counties were laid off, and steadily but quietly settled. Towns and villages sprang up in the wilderness. Out of a part of the long-coveted Oconee lands the county of Baldwin was laid off in 1803, and a site for the town of Milledgeville selected by commissioners appointed by the legislature, with the view of making it the capital of the state, as soon as the proper buildings could be erected for that purpose. This took place in 1807, in which year Milledgeville became the seat of government.

Nothing material interfered to disturb the domestic condition of Georgia for several years. Her citizens had indeed suffered under pecuniary difficulties, arising from excessive speculation in public lands; but this condition of things did not attach to Georgia alone; other states had also suffered from the same cause. The operation of what were termed alleviating laws served in some measure to correct the temporary embarrassments, and the recuperative energies of an industrious people gradually overcame the difficulty entirely. But if the local government was working smoothly and with but comparatively few checks or annoyances, such was not the case with the federal government.

The foreign relations began every day to grow more critical. A gallant and spirited resistance to the aggressions of the Bashaw of Tripoli had ended in a manner honourable to the American character.

The oppressive acts of Great Britain, partly brought on by the war between that nation and France, and partly arising from her own imperious determination to exercise the right she claimed of searching any vessels upon the high seas for deserters who might be suspected of being English subjects, became the source of fierce discussion among all classes of the American people.

Many English seamen, tempted by the high rate of wages offered by American merchants, were employed in our commercial marine. The enormous navy maintained by England required to be supported by constant impressment; and, under colour of seizing her own citizens, she was in the habit of constantly stopping American merchantmen, and selecting from the crews such men as her subordinate officers chose to consider subjects of Great Britain, but who were frequently found, subsequently, to be native American citizens. For this high-handed conduct, redress could very rarely be obtained. The grievance had been the subject of repeated remonstrances from the period of the administration of Washington to the opening of the war; but Great Britain as constantly refused to abandon the exercise of a power which she had always heretofore claimed as a right.

As if this cause of complaint was not enough to revive old national animosities—for the bitter hatred engendered by the war of the Revolution had not yet wholly subsided—England issued, in 1806 and 1807, a series of paper-blockades, by which most of the French ports were laid under embargo, and American vessels bearing French products were declared lawful prize. France retaliated by the famous Berlin decrees, which declared the British Islands in a state of blockade, and all neutral vessels trading thither lawful prize.

Both decrees were equally hostile to American commerce. But the English had set the first example, and the practical operation of their orders in council was far more destructive than the Berlin and Milan decrees of Napoleon.

One thousand American vessels, richly laden, became the prize of the British cruisers; irritating causes of impressment were of constant occurrence; the attack of the English frigate Leopard upon the Chesapeake inflamed to the highest degree the national mind; the language of American diplomacy became daily more angry and impatient, that of England daily more cold and haughty. At length, endurance was worn out, and on the 18th of June, 1812, the American Congress declared war.

The unhappy differences so long existing between England and the United States could not fail to have a marked effect upon the Indian tribes whose lands were bounded by the British possessions in Canada. The turbulent spirit of the northwestern Indians soon communicated itself to those of the south.

Tecumseh, the celebrated Shawnee chief, whose own wild and lofty eloquence was sustained by the mysterious power acquired by his brother the prophet, stimulated the Indian tribes to unite into one vast confederacy, and, as allies of England, revenge upon the people of the United States their long-continued encroachments upon Indian soil.

Already renowned as a warrior, famous for his wonderful powers as an orator, and distinguished above all others by his relentless hatred of the Americans, his presence among the various tribes was the sure precursor of secret preparations for hostilities.

After having held repeated conferences with the British at Detroit in the spring of 1812, Tecumseh, attended by a chosen band of thirty warriors, left the territory of the northwest, and, moving rapidly southward, penetrated the country as far down as Florida, where he succeeded in inducing the Seminoles to join his standard. Returning thence, he entered the Creek country in the month of October, and immediately commenced his intrigues with the chiefs. By the time he reached Coosawda, he had gained many followers. Colonel Hawkins, the federal agent, was at this period holding a grand council at Tookabatcha, at which five thousand warriors were assembled. Tecumseh boldly repaired to that place, and marched into the square at the head of his party, hideously painted and adorned.

While Hawkins remained, Tecumseh declined addressing the Indians on the subject of his mission; but the agent had no sooner departed for his residence upon the Flint, than a grand council was held in the great round-house.

Here Tecumseh poured forth his passionate and heart-stirring appeal. Deriving his powers from his brother the Prophet, whose extraordinary commission and endowments were well understood, his authority was regarded with the highest veneration. He earnestly entreated them to refuse all intercourse with the whites, to throw aside the implements and clothing obtained from so hateful a source, and, abandoning agriculture, to return again to their primitive condition of hunters and warriors. After seeking by bursts of fiery eloquence to rouse their animosity against the Americans, he gave additional weight to his designs by assuring them of aid and support from the King of England, their ancient friend and ally, whose wealth and power he represented as without limits, and quite sufficient for the subjugation of the United States.

A prophet who accompanied Tecumseh next spoke. He eulogized the mission of the latter, and assured all those who were willing to join the war party that no harm should befall them, even in battle; that the Great Spirit would protect them, and bring confusion upon the Americans; and that every Georgian would be expelled from the soil as far as the Savannah.

So extraordinary an influence did these daring and eloquent discourses exert over the minds of many, that it was with difficulty the most turbulent of them could be restrained from taking up arms at once, and committing depredations on the exposed frontiers.

This hasty measure, however, Tecumseh represented as calculated to defeat the great plan of operations which he was labouring to concert; and enjoined the utmost secrecy and quietness until the moment should arrive, when, all their preparations being ready, they might be able to strike a decisive blow. In the mean time, they were to be industriously employed in collecting arms and ammunition, and other necessaries of war.

In this manner Tecumseh with his wild followers held conferences in the numerous towns of the Creek territory, gaining many proselytes, and meeting with but occasional opposition from those chiefs who either feared the consequences of an outbreak, or were stipendiaries of the federal government.

Having ordained Josiah Francis, a half-breed, chief prophet of the whole Creek nation, whose word was to be regarded as infallible, and whose directions were to be implicitly followed, Tecumseh next established a regular gradation of subordinate prophets to disseminate his doctrines through the different parts of the nation, and then, attended by a few of his proselytes, set out for his own tribe.

From this time a regular communication was kept up between the Creeks and the northern tribes in relation to the great enterprise which they were concerting together; while the parties carrying it on, growing daily more insolent and unmanageable, committed frequent depredations and murders upon the frontier settlements.

These outrages became at length so numerous as to attract the attention of the federal government. Colonel Hawkins, the Indian agent, demanded the punishment of the murderers; and some of the chiefs who were desirous of preserving their friendly relations with the United States, despatched a party of warriors to put the criminals to death. No sooner was this done, than the spirit of the greater part of the nation, which from motives of policy had hitherto been in a great measure suppressed, suddenly burst through all restraint, and arrayed the peaceful and the hostile Indians against each other in a civil war.

It is not difficult to conceive in what manner hostilities thus provoked were gradually extended beyond the limits of the Indian territory, and, as a measure of retaliation, fell upon the white population of the frontiers.

The war with Great Britain was also at this period at its height; and Georgia was not found wanting, either in patriotism toward the country at large, or in defence of her own population.

Volunteers flocked from all quarters, many of whom attached themselves to the army of General Floyd, and assisted to gain that splendid series of victories over the Indians by which General Andrew Jackson has rendered his name distinguished in history.

The early successes of the British arms in Canada were more than counterbalanced by the naval triumphs achieved upon Lake Erie and upon the ocean; by the rout of the combined British and Indian forces at the battle of the Thames, where the fierce Tecumseh fell; by the repulse of the British before Baltimore, which atoned for the disastrous retreat of the militia at Bladensburg, and the occupation of the capital; by the successes of Jackson against the southern Indians, and by the crowning glory of the war, the battle of New Orleans.

Happily for both countries, the war was not of long duration. It was closed by the treaty of peace signed at Ghent, on the 26th of December, 1814, and formally ratified by the United States on the 17th of February, 1815.

Nothing of peculiar importance arrested the progress of Georgia for the next seven years. The delays and impediments which had constantly arisen in relation to the entire extinguishment of the Indian title to lands as guarantied to Georgia in 1802 by her compact with the federal government, induced the legislature of 1823 to require of Governor Troupe to use his exertions to bring the matter to a speedy termination.

He accordingly opened a correspondence with the secretary of war, which resulted in a commission to Duncan G. Campbell and James Meriwether, two distinguished Georgians, to treat with the Creek Indians. A council was accordingly held in December, 1824, at Broken Arrow, on the Chattahoochee; but the negotiation failed, owing, it was alleged, to the adverse influence exerted by the agents of the United States.

Early in February, 1825, the commissioners again met the Indians in council at the Indian Springs, and on the 12th of that month succeeded in concluding a treaty with the chiefs then present, which was subsequently transmitted by President Monroe to the senate, and by that body solemnly ratified, notwithstanding a strong protest against it by Crowell, the Indian agent.

In May, 1825, an extra session of the legislature was called by Governor Troupe, for the purpose of providing for the immediate survey of the land acquired by the late treaty. An act was passed accordingly, and in connection with it, a strong resolution was adopted calling upon the president to remove Crowell, the Indian agent, from office, as the enemy of Georgia, and as faithless to his government.

John Quincy Adams had in the mean time succeeded Mr. Monroe as President of the United

States. He declined removing the agent, but instituted an inquiry into his conduct. He appointed a clerk of bureau for that purpose, and at the same time commissioned Major-general Gaines to repair to Georgia, suppress the disorders already arisen in the Indian nation, and compose its dissensions.

The presence of these high functionaries by no means tended to smooth the asperities of Georgia. A bitter feud then existing between two great parties in the state—though mainly on personal grounds—increased the agitation of the public mind. General Gaines allied himself with the party in opposition to Governor Troupe, and, in conjunction with the clerk of bureau, reported against the treaty, the merits of which neither of them had been instructed to inquire into. A very exciting correspondence now ensued between the executive of Georgia and the federal government. A survey was determined on by the former, and prohibited by President Adams. Troupe demanded the recall and court-martial of General Gaines, as the legislature had previously requested the removal of Crowell. The president retained both in their respective offices. All Georgia was now in a ferment. A new election for governor took place soon after, and the course of Troupe was sustained by the votes of the people. Even the legislature, although opposed to the governor in both branches on mere party politics, resolved, that "full faith ought to be placed in the treaty; that the title of Georgia under it was vested and absolute; and that the right of entry immediately on the expiration of the time limited by it should be insisted on and carried into effect." They again required the removal of the federal agent, which was again rejected.

Affairs between the state and general government were now speedily approaching a serious issue. In January, 1826, Governor Troupe issued his orders for the militia to be divided into three classes, and expressed his belief that the general officers could not find themselves indifferent to the crisis in which the country was placed. The federal government had already assembled on the Chattahoochee and Flint a force of four hundred regulars, and the peace of the union seemed every day in danger of being disturbed by that most deplorable of all evils—a civil war.

In this emergency, a new treaty was made with certain Creek chiefs at Washington on the 24th of January, 1826, which, while it annulled the treaty of 1825, ceded to Georgia nearly all the land covered by the old treaty, and extended the time of surrender to the 1st of January, 1827.

But Georgia would accept nothing less than the conditions of the previous treaty. In July, 1826, commissioners were appointed to run the line as laid down by the contract of 1802. As soon as this was accomplished the survey was commenced, and met with no resistance from the federal government until February, 1827, when the president ordered those surveyors to be arrested who should overstep the boundary laid down in the late treaty at Washington. Governor Troupe immediately retaliated by directing the proper legal officers of Georgia to bring to justice, by indictment or otherwise, all the parties who might be concerned in arresting the surveyors; and sent orders to the major-generals of the sixth and seventh divisions of militia, to hold their commands in readiness to repel any hostile invasion of the state.

This energetic opposition had its effect. The surveyors were not arrested; the surveys were completed; and the entire domain covered by the old treaty was organized and disposed of by lottery in 1827.

CHAPTER XXVII.

The soil of Georgia—Tide-swamp lands—Sea Islands—Swamp lands of the Savannah, Alatamaha, Ogechee, and the Great St. Illa—Character of the soils in the middle regions of the state—Lands in south-western Georgia—Cherokee Georgia —The gold region—Railroads—Cotton manufactories—Fidelity of Georgia to the Union—Sends volunteers to Florida —Mexico—Conclusion.

The natural quality of the soil in Georgia is very variable. The general poverty of the pine lands gave rise at an early day to an impression that a great proportion of the land in the province was infertile. As population increased, it was found that the tide-swamp lands on the southern frontier of the state would yield, with fair cultivation, immense quantities of rice, which constituted then, as it does now, one of the staple productions of Georgia. For the finer descriptions of cotton, the Sea Islands have long been famous, both at home and abroad. The tide-swamp lands of the Savannah, the Alatamaha, the Ogechee, and the great St. Illa, are now considered as among the most valuable soils in the state. The inland swamps are also very productive, but they labour under the disadvantage of a greater uncertainty in regard to their crops.

In the middle region of the state, the soil is of

a rich red loamy character, producing cotton, tobacco, and all the grains. A careless system of husbandry has done much to impoverish this healthy and beautiful region, but with increase of intelligence, new and better modes of cultivation are being introduced, and the prospects are favourable to a restoration of these choice lands to their original fertility.

In the southwestern portions of the state, there are large bodies of very superior land. In the counties of Randolph, Decatur, and Early, and in other sections between the Chattahoochee and the Flint, lands are to be found of inexhaustible fertility, producing every thing which the comfort or necessity of man requires. In Cherokee Georgia there are also large bodies of fertile land. The valleys of Chattooga, Cass, Floyd, and Murray, are exceedingly rich, producing wheat, corn, potatoes, and other vegetables; but are not so well adapted to the purposes of the cotton planter as the soils of the middle region. In Oglethorpe county there are bodies of land which have been cultivated for more than half a century, and which still produce seven and eight hundred pounds of cotton to the acre.

The northwestern part of the state is the gold region of Georgia, which, from its richness and extent, is the most remarkable feature of the primary rock formation. Its western boundary is the western base of the Blue Ridge. "The richest deposits are found occupying a belt along the eastern slope of that range of mountains, varying in width from fifteen to twenty miles; but gold has been discovered at various points one hundred miles to the east of it, as far as Columbia county, and thence in a line, nearly parallel to the principal belt, to Alabama. The gold is found in both vein and deposit mines. In the former it generally occurs in quartzose veins, running through rocks of gneiss, mica schist, talcose schist, and chlorite schist. The quartz forming the veins is usually of a cellular structure, generally discoloured by iron, and with the cavities more or less filled with a fine yellow ochre. The gold, which varies much in the size of its particles, is found either in small scales, (its most usual form,) in the cavities or the fissures of the quartz, or in the yellow ochre, or in combination with the sulphurets of iron, of copper, and of lead, or united with silver. It sometimes, but rarely, exists in the adjoining schistose rocks.

"The deposit mines are of alluvial formation, obviously produced by the washing down of the detritus of the auriferous veins into the adjoining valleys. The schistose rocks, which are of a more perishable character, having crumbled away, and left the quartz veins exposed, the latter have fallen down from a want of support, and have been swept by torrents into the valleys below. The quartz pebbles, and the harder portions of the including rocks, and the gold, being heavy, would be deposited at the bottom of the streams, and would occur in the greatest quantity when there were the greatest inequalities. The lighter materials would at first be swept down to a lower point, or be deposited along the borders of the streams; but, with a change of the beds of the streams, or a diminution of their velocity, these materials would gradually accumulate over the original beds of pebbles and gold, and the valleys would ultimately present the appearance which they now do, of a stratum of several feet of allu-vial loam covering another of water-worn pebbles of quartz and schist, containing particles of gold, the whole resting on an original bed of schistose rocks, similar in constitution and dip to those of the surrounding hills. The quartz pebbles are usually flattened on the sides, indicating their compression in the veins, and are more or less water-worn, as they have for a longer or shorter period been exposed to the action of the currents of water."

The first discovery of gold in this state was made on Duke's Creek, Habersham county, in 1829. The mass weighed three ounces. After this, discoveries were rapidly made in all directions from Carolina to Alabama, and some of the mines were immensely rich. The gold obtained for the first few years was from the alluvion of the streams; after which many diluvial deposits were found, and subsequently many rich veins. The gold in the veins is generally imbedded in sulphuret of iron in quartz, sometimes in quartz alone, and, in a few instances, in micaceous and talcose slate, the auriferous pyrites being interspersed in minute crystals through the slate. The first-mentioned class are common, and abound everywhere, running parallel with the formation of the country, the general direction of which is northeast and southwest, corresponding with the Alleghany chain of mountains. These veins are usually enclosed in micaceous or talcose schist, some in chlorite and hornblende, rarely in gneiss or granite. In some instances the root of the vein is slate, and the floor granite or gneiss. The decomposition of the different strata varies from fifty to one hundred feet, and decreases as you near the mountains, where the overlying rocks terminate, and the veins cease to be auriferous. A few veins have been found which traverse the formation in which they are enclosed, and in every instance the gold is found to contain from fifteen to sixty-six per cent. of silver, whereas all parallel veins are alloyed with copper, from one-eighth to one-fortieth, and without a trace of silver. Of the former class is the Potosi mine, in Hall county, which runs northwest by west, is one foot wide, (average,) and was immensely rich in pockets. The first cropped out and extended about twelve feet deep by fifteen laterally, yielding over ten thousand pennyweights. Some ten feet from that, another pocket occurred, much richer, the gold being enclosed in felspar, with octahedral crystals of quartz radiating from it without a particle of gold. These veins are evidently of comparatively recent formation. Ore which yields twenty-five cents per bushel is considered profitable, provided the veins are large enough to furnish abundantly, and there is no extra expense. Where there is much water it requires expensive machinery, and the ore must be rich, and the vein of considerable size, to justify it. Many mines have and do yet yield much more—from fifty to one hundred cents per bushel, and a few even more, even reaching to several hundred dollars per bushel. Of such are the Calhoun and Battle Branch veins, and also the celebrated 1052 mine near Dahlonega. These are technically called pocket-veins, as the gold is found in limited portions of them, the rest without any. The greatest depths yet reached do not exceed eighty feet below the water-level, nor more than one hundred and forty feet below their outcrop; whereas, in the old world, they have gone more than two thousand feet. We consequently can form no opinion relative to their productiveness. Generally the mines are abandoned as soon as the water appears; the operators being men of but little capital, and ignorant of the proper mode of working below the water-level. Another and more powerful reason is, that, with but few exceptions, the veins become poorer as you descend, and below the water very poor.

The mode of working the mine or ores is by amalgamation. The ore is first reduced to powder, either wet or dry, by the action of stamps or pestles, weighing from one hundred to five hundred pounds; after which it passes through different-sized screens or grates, and then through various amalgamating machines, by which the quicksilver is made to take up the particles or dust of gold, forming an amalgam, which is distilled in a retort, saving the quicksilver for further use, and the mass of gold is melted in a crucible into bars or ingots for coining. Its average fineness is twenty-three carats. From the best information received, the amount obtained from 1829 to 1838 was sixteen million pennyweights, and from that time until 1849 four million; every year diminishing, notwithstanding the great improvements in machinery and increased practical knowledge.

But the future prosperity of Georgia is not so much assured by the production of her gold-bearing regions, or the operations of her industrious agriculturists, as by her wise and well-regulated system of railroads, and the admirable provision by which she has of late years encouraged manufactures generally, and in an especial manner those for the fabrication of cotton-cloths

—a branch of business for which the state is admirably adapted, from her immense facilities in the way of water-power.

Already, there are railroads stretching from Savannah to the Tennessee line, with branch roads, either finished or in contemplation, to Augusta, Athens, Atlanta, Macon, and Columbus; and in various portions of the state admitting of such a purpose, cotton-mills have been for a long time in successful operation.

These facilities for the transportation of staple productions, joined to the creation of a home-market, will gradually tend more and more to develop the latent resources of Georgia, and place the industrial position of the state upon a firm and indestructible basis.

True to the Union, notwithstanding her occasional difficulties with the federal government, she encouraged her sons to volunteer their services in those harassing campaigns in Florida, where the oozy bivouacs and the pestilential miasma of the everglades were far more destructive to human life than the weapons of the Seminoles. In the recent war with Mexico, also, the brave yeomanry of Georgia were among the foremost to respond to the call of their country, and were honourably distinguished by the prompt and gallant ardour with which they performed their various and responsible duties.

And here we bring this volume to a close, having been careful to omit no fact of importance, and to present as many points of interest in the narrative as strict truth to history would allow.

The authorities mainly relied upon in this work have been McCall's History of Georgia, Pickett's History of Alabama, White's Statistics of the State of Georgia, and Hildreth's History of the United States.

THE END.

STEREOTYPED BY L. JOHNSON AND CO.
PHILADELPHIA.

CATALOGUE
OF
VALUABLE BOOKS,
PUBLISHED BY
LIPPINCOTT, GRAMBO & CO.,
(SUCCESSORS TO GRIGG, ELLIOT & CO.)

NO. 14, NORTH FOURTH STREET, PHILADA.:

CONSISTING OF A LARGE ASSORTMENT OF

BIBLES, PRAYER-BOOKS, COMMENTARIES, STANDARD POETS,

MEDICAL, THEOLOGICAL, AND MISCELLANEOUS WORKS, ETC.,

PARTICULARLY SUITABLE FOR

PUBLIC AND PRIVATE LIBRARIES;

For Sale by Booksellers and Country Merchants generally throughout the United States.

THE BEST AND MOST COMPLETE FAMILY COMMENTARY.

The Comprehensive Commentary on the Holy Bible;

CONTAINING

THE TEXT ACCORDING TO THE AUTHORIZED VERSION,

SCOTT'S MARGINAL REFERENCES; MATTHEW HENRY'S COMMENTARY, CONDENSED, BUT CONTAINING EVERY USEFUL THOUGHT; THE PRACTICAL OBSERVATIONS OF

REV. THOMAS SCOTT, D.D.;

WITH EXTENSIVE

EXPLANATORY, CRITICAL, AND PHILOLOGICAL NOTES,

Selected from Scott, Doddridge, Gill, Adam Clarke, Patrick, Poole, Lowth, Burder, Harmer, Calmet, Rosenmueller, Bloomfield, Stuart, Bush, Dwight, and many other writers on the Scriptures.

The whole designed to be a digest and combination of the advantages of the best Bible Commentaries, and embracing nearly all that is valuable in

HENRY, SCOTT, AND DODDRIGE.

EDITED BY REV. WILLIAM JENKS, D.D.,

PASTOR OF GREEN STREET CHURCH, BOSTON.

Embellished with five portraits, and other elegant engravings, from steel plates; with several maps and many wood-cuts, illustrative of Scripture Manners, Customs, Antiquities, &c. In 6 vols. super-royal 8vo.

Including Supplement, bound in cloth, sheep, calf, &c., varying in

Price from $10 to $15.

The whole forming the most valuable as well as the cheapest Commentary in the world.

LIPPINCOTT'S EDITIONS OF

THE HOLY BIBLE,

SIX DIFFERENT SIZES.

Printed in the best manner, with beautiful type, on the finest sized paper, and bound in the most splendid and substantial styles. Warranted to be correct, and equal to the best English editions, at a much lower price. To be had with or without plates; the publishers having supplied themselves with over fifty steel engravings, by the first artists.

Baxter's Comprehensive Bible,

Royal quarto, containing the various readings and marginal notes, disquisitions on the genuineness, authenticity, and inspiration of the Holy Scriptures; introductory and concluding remarks to each book; philological and explanatory notes; tables of contents, arranged in historical order; a chronological index, and various other matter; forming a suitable book for the study of clergymen, Sabbath-school teachers and students.

The Oxford Quarto Bible,

Without note or comment, universally admitted to be the most beautiful family Bible extant.

Crown Octavo Bible,

Printed with large clear type, making a most convenient Bible for family use.

Polyglot Bible.

The Sunday-School Teacher's Polyglot Bible, with Maps, &c.

The Oxford 18mo. Bible.

This is an extremely handsome and convenient Pew Bible.

Agate 32mo. Bible,

Printed with larger type than any other small pocket edition extant.

32mo. Diamond Pocket Bible,

The neatest, smallest, and cheapest edition of the Bible published.

CONSTANTLY ON HAND,

A large assortment of BIBLES, bound in the most splendid and costly styles, with gold and silver ornaments, suitable for presentation; ranging in price from $10 00 to $100 00.

A liberal discount made to Booksellers and Agents by the Publishers.

ENCYCLOPÆDIA OF RELIGIOUS KNOWLEDGE;

OR, DICTIONARY OF THE BIBLE THEOLOGY, RELIGIOUS BIOGRAPHY ALL RELIGIONS, ECCLESIASTICAL HISTORY, AND MISSIONS.

In one volume, royal 8vo.

THE DIAMOND EDITION OF SHAKSPEARE.

(COMPLETE IN ONE VOLUME.)

INCLUDING A COPIOUS GLOSSARY.

UNIFORM WITH BYRON AND MOORE.

THE FOREGOING WORKS CAN BE HAD IN SEVERAL VARIETIES OF BINDING.

SCHOOLCRAFT'S GREAT NATIONAL WORK ON THE INDIAN TRIBES OF THE UNITED STATES.

WITH BEAUTIFUL AND ACCURATE COLOURED ILLUSTRATIONS.

HISTORICAL AND STATISTICAL INFORMATION

RESPECTING THE

HISTORY, CONDITION AND PROSPECTS

OF THE

Indian Tribes of the United States.

COLLECTED AND PREPARED UNDER THE DIRECTION OF THE BUREAU OF INDIAN AFFAIRS, PER ACT OF MARCH 3, 1847.

BY HENRY R. SCHOOLCRAFT, LL.D.

ILLUSTRATED BY S. EASTMAN, CAPT. U. S. A.

PUBLISHED BY AUTHORITY OF CONGRESS.

The Traveller's and Tourist's Guide

THROUGH THE UNITED STATES OF AMERICA, CANADA, ETC.

CONTAINING THE ROUTES OF TRAVEL BY STEAMBOAT, STAGE, AND CANAL; TOGETHER WITH DESCRIPTIONS OF, AND ROUTES TO, THE PRINCIPAL PLACES OF FASHIONABLE AND HEALTHFUL RESORT; WITH OTHER VALUABLE INFORMATION.

ACCOMPANIED BY

AN ENTIRELY NEW AND AUTHENTIC MAP OF THE UNITED STATES,

INCLUDING CALIFORNIA, OREGON, &c., AND A MAP OF THE ISLAND OF CUBA.

BY W. WILLIAMS.

THE POWER AND PROGRESS OF THE UNITED STATES.

THE UNITED STATES; Its Power and Progress.

BY GUILLAUME TELL POUSSIN,

LATE MINISTER OF THE REPUBLIC OF FRANCE TO THE UNITED STATES.

FIRST AMERICAN, FROM THE THIRD PARIS EDITION.

TRANSLATED FROM THE FRENCH BY EDMOND L. DU BARRY, M.D.

SURGEON, UNITED STATES NAVY.

IN ONE LARGE OCTAVO VOLUME.

BIGLAND'S NATURAL HISTORY.

OF ANIMALS, BIRDS, FISHES, REPTILES, AND INSECTS.

ILLUSTRATED WITH NUMEROUS AND BEAUTIFUL ENGRAVINGS.

BY JOHN BIGLAND,

Author of a "View of the World," "Letters on Universal History," &c.

Complete in one volume, 12mo.

GOLDSMITH'S ANIMATED NATURE

IN TWO VOLUMES, OCTAVO.

BEAUTIFULLY ILLUSTRATED WITH 385 PLATES.

CONTAINING A HISTORY OF THE EARTH, ANIMALS, BIRDS AND FISHES; FORMING THE MOST COMPLETE NATURAL HISTORY EVER PUBLISHED.

THE FARMER'S AND PLANTER'S ENCYCLOPÆDIA.

THE FARMER'S AND PLANTER'S ENCYCLOPÆDIA OF RURAL AFFAIRS.

BY CUTHBERT W. JOHNSON.

ADAPTED TO THE UNITED STATES BY GOUVERNEUR EMERSON.

Illustrated by seventeen beautiful Engravings of Cattle, Horses, Sheep, the varieties of Wheat, Barley, Oats, Grasses, the Weeds of Agriculture, &c.; besides numerous Engravings on wood of the most important implements of Agriculture.

IN ONE LARGE OCTAVO VOLUME.

THE AMERICAN GARDENER'S CALENDAR,

ADAPTED TO THE CLIMATE AND SEASONS OF THE UNITED STATES.

Containing a complete account of all the work necessary to be done in the Kitchen Garden, Fruit Garden, Orchard, Vineyard, Nursery, Pleasure-Ground, Flower Garden, Green-house, Hot-house, and Forcing Frames, for every month in the year; with ample Practical Directions for performing the same.

BY BERNARD M'MAHON.

Tenth Edition, greatly improved. In one volume, octavo.

MASON'S FARRIER AND STUD BOOK—NEW EDITION.

Price, $1.

THE GENTLEMAN'S NEW POCKET FARRIER:

COMPRISING A GENERAL DESCRIPTION OF THE NOBLE AND USEFUL ANIMAL,

THE HORSE;

WITH MODES OF MANAGEMENT IN ALL CASES, AND TREATMENT IN DISEASE.

BY RICHARD MASON, M.D.,

Formerly of Surry County, Virginia.

TO WHICH IS ADDED,

A PRIZE ESSAY ON MULES; AND AN APPENDIX,

Containing Recipes for Diseaes of Horses, Oxen, Cows, Calves, Sheep, Dogs, Swine, &c., &c.; with Annals of the Turf, American Stud-Book, Rules for Training, Racing, &c., &c.

WITH A SUPPLEMENT,

BY J. S. SKINNER,

Editor of the Farmers' Library, New York, &c., &c.

MASON'S FARRIER—FARMERS' EDITION.

Price, 62 Cents.

THE PRACTICAL FARRIER, FOR FARMERS:

COMPRISING A GENERAL DESCRIPTION OF THE NOBLE AND USEFUL ANIMAL,

THE HORSE;

WITH MODES OF MANAGEMENT IN ALL CASES, AND TREATMENT IN DISEASE.

TO WHICH IS ADDED,

A PRIZE ESSAY ON MULES; AND AN APPENDIX,

Containing Recipes for Diseases of Horses, Oxen, Cows, Calves, Sheep, Dogs, Swine, &c.

BY RICHARD MASON, M.D.

FORMERLY OF SURRY COUNTY, VIRGINIA.

In one volume, 12mo.; bound in cloth, gilt.

HINDS'S FARRIERY AND STUD-BOOK—NEW EDITION.

FARRIERY,

TAUGHT ON A NEW AND EASY PLAN:

BEING A

Treatise on the Diseases and Accidents of the Horse;

With Instructions to the Shoeing Smith, Farrier, and Groom; preceded by a Popular description of the Animal Functions in Health, and how these are to be restored when disordered.

BY JOHN HINDS, VETERINARY SURGEON.

With considerable Additions and Improvements, particularly adapted to this country,

BY THOMAS M. SMITH,

Veterinary Surgeon, and Member of the London Veterinary Medical Society.

WITH A SUPPLEMENT, BY J. S. SKINNER.

TO CARPENTERS AND MECHANICS.

JUST PUBLISHED.

A NEW AND IMPROVED EDITION OF

THE CARPENTER'S NEW GUIDE,

BEING A COMPLETE BOOK OF LINES FOR

CARPENTRY AND JOINERY;

Treating fully on Practical Geometry, Saffit's Brick and Plaster Groins, Niches of every description, Sky-lights, Lines for Roofs and Domes; with a great variety of Designs for Roofs, Trussed Girders, Floors, Domes, Bridges, &c., Angle Bars for Shop Fronts, &c., and Raking Mouldings.

ALSO,

Additional Plans for various Stair-Cases, with the Lines for producing the Face and Falling Moulds, never before published, and greatly superior to those given in a former edition of this work.

BY WM. JOHNSON, ARCHITECT,

OF PHILADELPHIA.

The whole founded on true Geometrical Principles; the Theory and Practice well explained and fully exemplified, on eighty-three Copper-Plates, including some Observations and Calculations on the Strength of Timber.

BY PETER NICHOLSON,

Author of "The Carpenter and Joiner's Assistant," "The Student's Instructor to the Five Orders," &c.

Thirteenth Edition. One volume, 4to., well bound.

SAY'S POLITICAL ECONOMY.

A TREATISE ON POLITICAL ECONOMY;

Or, The Production, Distribution and Consumption of Wealth.

BY JEAN BAPTISTE SAY.

FIFTH AMERICAN EDITION, WITH ADDITIONAL NOTES.

BY C. C. BIDDLE, Esq.

In one volume, octavo.

A BEAUTIFUL AND VALUABLE PRESENTATION BOOK.

THE POET'S OFFERING.

EDITED BY MRS. HALE.

With a Portrait of the Editress, a Splendid Illuminated Title-Page, and Twelve Beautiful Engravings by Sartain. Bound in rich Turkey Morocco, and Extra Cloth, Gilt Edge.

A Dictionary of Select and Popular Quotations,

WHICH ARE IN DAILY USE.

TAKEN FROM THE LATIN, FRENCH, GREEK, SPANISH AND ITALIAN LANGUAGES.

Together with a copious Collection of Law Maxims and Law Terms, translated into English, with Illustrations, Historical and Idiomatic.

NEW AMERICAN EDITION, CORRECTED, WITH ADDITIONS.

In one volume, 12mo.

The City Merchant; or, The Mysterious Failure.

BY J. B. JONES,

Author of "Wild Western Scenes," "The Western Merchant," &c.

ILLUSTRATED WITH TEN ENGRAVINGS.

In one volume, 12mo.

LAURENCE STERNE'S WORKS,

WITH A LIFE OF THE AUTHOR:

WRITTEN BY HIMSELF.

WITH SEVEN BEAUTIFUL ILLUSTRATIONS, ENGRAVED BY GILBERT AND GIHON, FROM DESIGNS BY DARLEY.

One volume, octavo; cloth, gilt.

RUSCHENBERGER'S NATURAL HISTORY.

COMPLETE, WITH NEW GLOSSARY.

THE ELEMENTS OF NATURAL HISTORY,

EMBRACING ZOOLOGY, BOTANY, AND GEOLOGY:

FOR SCHOOLS, COLLEGES, AND FAMILIES.

BY W. S. W. RUSCHENBERGER, M.D.

IN TWO VOLUMES.

WITH NEARLY ONE THOUSAND ILLUSTRATIONS, AND A COPIOUS GLOSSARY.

Vol. I. contains *Vertebrate Animals*. Vol. II. contains *Intervertebrate Animals, Botany, and Geology*.

The Mexican War and its Heroes;

BEING

A COMPLETE HISTORY OF THE MEXICAN WAR,

EMBRACING ALL THE OPERATIONS UNDER GENERALS TAYLOR AND SCOTT.

WITH A BIOGRAPHY OF THE OFFICERS.

ALSO,

AN ACCOUNT OF THE CONQUEST OF CALIFORNIA AND NEW MEXICO,

Under Gen. Kearney, Cols. Doniphan and Fremont. Together with Numerous Anecdotes of the War, and personal adventures of the Officers. Illustrated with Accurate Portraits and other Beautiful Engravings.

In one volume, 12mo.

EL PUCHERO; OR, A MIXED DISH FROM MEXICO.

EMBRACING GENERAL SCOTT'S CAMPAIGN, WITH SKETCHES OF MILITARY LIFE IN FIELD AND CAMP; OF THE CHARACTER OF THE COUNTRY, MANNERS AND WAYS OF THE PEOPLE, &c.

BY RICHARD M'SHERRY, M. D., U. S. N.

Late Acting Surgeon of Regiment of Marines.

In one volume, 12mo.

WITH NUMEROUS ILLUSTRATIONS.

MONEY-BAGS AND TITLES:

A HIT AT THE FOLLIES OF THE AGE.

TRANSLATED FROM THE FRENCH OF JULES SANDEAU.

BY LEONARD MYERS.

One volume, 12mo.

DODD'S LECTURES.

DISCOURSES TO YOUNG MEN.

ILLUSTRATED BY NUMEROUS HIGHLY INTERESTING ANECDOTES.

BY WILLIAM DODD, LL. D.

CHAPLAIN IN ORDINARY TO HIS MAJESTY, GEORGE THE THIRD.

FIRST AMERICAN EDITION, WITH ENGRAVINGS.

One volume, 18mo.

THE IRIS:

AN ORIGINAL SOUVENIR.

WITH CONTRIBUTIONS FROM THE FIRST WRITERS IN THE COUNTRY.

EDITED BY PROF. JOHN S. HART.

With splendid Illuminations and Steel Engravings. Bound in Turkey Morocco and rich Papier Mache Binding.

IN ONE VOLUME, OCTAVO.

The Western Merchant.

A NARRATIVE,

BY LUKE SHORTFIELD, A WESTERN MERCHANT.

In one volume, 12mo.

LONZ POWERS; OR, THE REGULATORS.

A ROMANCE OF KENTUCKY.

FOUNDED ON FACTS.

BY JAMES WEIR, ESQ.

IN TWO VOLUMES.

A MANUAL OF POLITENESS,

COMPRISING

THE PRINCIPLES OF ETIQUETTE AND RULES OF BEHAVIOUR

IN GENTEEL SOCIETY, FOR PERSONS OF BOTH SEXES.

18mo., with Plates.

BOOK OF POLITENESS.

THE GENTLEMAN AND LADY'S BOOK OF POLITENESS AND PROPRIETY OF DEPORTMENT,

DEDICATED TO THE YOUTH OF BOTH SEXES,

BY MADAME CELNART.

TRANSLATED FROM THE SIXTH PARIS EDITION, ENLARGED AND IMPROVED.

FIFTH AMERICAN EDITION.

One volume, 18mo.

SENECA'S MORALS.

BY WAY OF ABSTRACT TO WHICH IS ADDED, A DISCOURSE UNDER THE TITLE OF AN AFTER-THOUGHT.

BY SIR ROGER L'ESTRANGE, KNT.

A new and fine edition; one volume, 18mo.

A copy of this valuable little work should be found in every family library.

Bennett's (Rev. John) Letters to a Young Lady,

ON A VARIETY OF SUBJECTS CALCULATED TO IMPROVE THE HEART, TO FORM THE MANNERS, AND ENLIGHTEN THE UNDERSTANDING.

"That our daughters may be as polished corners of the temple.

THE AMERICAN CHESTERFIELD:

OR, "YOUTH'S GUIDE TO THE WAY TO WEALTH, HONOUR, AND DISTINCTION," &c.

In one volume, 18mo.

CONTAINING ALSO A COMPLETE TREATISE ON THE ART OF CARVING.

NEW SONG-BOOK.

Grigg's Southern and Western Songster;

BEING A CHOICE COLLECTION OF THE MOST FASHIONABLE SONGS, MANY OF WHICH ARE ORIGINAL.

In one volume, 18mo.

The Daughter's Own Book:

OR, PRACTICAL HINTS FROM A FATHER TO HIS DAUGHTER.

In one volume, 18mo.

THE LIFE AND OPINIONS OF TRISTRAM SHANDY, GENTLEMAN.

COMPRISING THE HUMOROUS ADVENTURES OF

UNCLE TOBY AND CORPORAL TRIM.

BY L. STERNE.

Beautifully Illustrated by Darley. Stitched.

A SENTIMENTAL JOURNEY.

BY L. STERNE.

ILLUSTRATED AS ABOVE BY DARLEY. STITCHED.

The beauties of this author are so well known, and his errors in style and expression so few and far between, that one reads with renewed delight his delicate turns, &c.

ROBOTHAM'S POCKET FRENCH DICTIONARY.

CAREFULLY REVISED,

AND THE PRONUNCIATION OF ALL THE DIFFICULT WORDS ADDED.

THE YOUNG CHORISTER;

A Collection of New and Beautiful Tunes, adapted to the use of Sabbath-Schools, from some of the most distinguished composers, together with many of the author's compositions.

EDITED BY MINARD W. WILSON.

THE GREEK EXILE:

Or, A Narrative of the Captivity and Escape of Christophorus Plato Castanis,

DURING THE MASSACRE ON THE ISLAND OF SCIO BY THE TURKS.

TOGETHER WITH VARIOUS ADVENTURES IN GREECE AND AMERICA.

WRITTEN BY HIMSELF.

One volume, 12mo.

General Scott and his Staff:

Comprising Memoirs of Generals Scott, Twiggs, Smith, Quitman, Shields, Pillow, Lane, Cadwallader, Patterson, and Pierce; Colonels Childs, Riley, Harney, and Butler; and other distinguished Officers attached to General Scott's Army.

TOGETHER WITH

Notices of General Kearney, Col. Doniphan, Colonel Fremont, and other Officers distinguished in the Conquest of California and New Mexico; and Personal Adventures of the Officers. Compiled from Public Documents and Private Correspondence.

WITH

ACCURATE PORTRAITS AND OTHER BEAUTIFUL ILLUSTRATIONS.

In one volume, 12*mo.*

THE LEGISLATIVE GUIDE:

Containing directions for conducting business in the House of Representatives; the Senate of the United States; the Joint Rules of both Houses; a Synopsis of Jefferson's Manual, and copious Indiçes; together with a concise system of Rules of Order, based on the Regulations of the United States Congress. Designed to economise time, secure uniformity and despatch in conducting business in all secular meetings, and also in all religious, political, and Legislative Assemblies.

BY JOSEPH BARTLETT BURLEIGH, LL.D.

In one volume, 12mo.

This is considered by our Judges and Congressmen as decidedly the best work of the kind extant. Every young man in the country should have a copy of this book.

THE FAMILY DENTIST,

INCLUDING THE SURGICAL, MEDICAL, AND MECHANICAL TREATMENT OF THE TEETH.

Illustrated with Thirty-one Engravings.

BY CHARLES A. DU BOUCHET, M. D.,

DENTAL SURGEON.

In one volume, 18*mo.*

MECHANICS

FOR THE MILLWRIGHT, ENGINEER, AND MACHINIST CIVIL ENGINEER AND ARCHITECT:

CONTAINING

THE PRINCIPLES OF MECHANICS APPLIED TO MACHINERY

Of American Models, Steam-Engines, Water-Works, Navigation, Bridge-building, &c., &c.

BY FREDERICK OVERMAN,

AUTHOR OF "THE MANUFACTURE OF IRON," AND OTHER SCIENTIFIC TREATISES.

Illustrated by 150 Engravings.

In one large 12mo. volume.

CALIFORNIA AND OREGON:

Or, Sights in the Gold Region, and Scenes by the Way.

BY THEODORE T. JOHNSON.

WITH A MAP AND ILLUSTRATIONS.

THIRD EDITION, WITH AN APPENDIX,

Containing Full Instructions to Emigrants by the Overland Route to Oregon.

BY HON. SAMUEL R. THURSTON,

Delegate to Congress from that Territory.

WILD WESTERN SCENES:

A NARRATIVE OF ADVENTURES IN THE WESTERN WILDERNESS.

Wherein the Exploits of Daniel Boone, the Great American Pioneer, are particularly described. Also, Minute Accounts of Bear, Deer, and Buffalo Hunts; Desperate Conflicts with the Savages; Fishing and Fowling Adventures; Encounters with Serpents, &c., &c.

BY LUKE SHORTFIELD,

Author of "The Western Merchant."

WITH SIXTEEN BEAUTIFUL ILLUSTRATIONS.

In one volume, 12mo.

POEMS OF THE PLEASURES:

CONSISTING OF

THE PLEASURES OF IMAGINATION, by Akenside; THE PLEASURES OF MEMORY, by Samuel Rogers; THE PLEASURES OF HOPE, by Campbell; and THE PLEASURES OF FRIENDSHIP, by M'Henry.

WITH A MEMOIR OF EACH AUTHOR,

Prepared expressly for this Work.

One volume, 18mo.

The Initials; A Story of Modern Life.

THREE VOLUMES OF THE LONDON EDITION COMPLETE IN ONE VOLUME, 12mo.

A new novel, equal to "Jane Eyre."

ARTHUR'S LIBRARY FOR THE HOUSEHOLD.

In Twelve handsome 18mo. volumes, bound in scarlet cloth, and each work complete in itself.

1. WOMEN'S TRIALS; OR, TALES AND SKETCHES FROM THE LIFE AROUND US.
2. MARRIED LIFE; ITS SHADOWS AND SUNSHINE.
3. THE TWO WIVES; OR, LOST AND WON.
4. THE WAYS OF PROVIDENCE; OR, "HE DOETH ALL THINGS WELL."
5. HOME SCENES.
6. STORIES FOR YOUNG HOUSEKEEPERS.
7. LESSONS IN LIFE, FOR ALL WHO WILL READ THEM.
8. SEED-TIME AND HARVEST; OR, WHATSOEVER A MAN SOWETH THAT SHALL HE ALSO REAP.
9. STORIES FOR PARENTS.
10. OFF-HAND SKETCHES, A LITTLE DASHED WITH HUMOR.
11. WORDS FOR THE WISE.
12. THE TRIED AND THE TEMPTED.

The above Series are sold together or separate, as each work is complete in itself. No family should be without a copy of this interesting and instructive Series. Price Thirty-seven and a Half Cents per Volume.

BALDWIN'S PRONOUNCING GAZETTEER.

A PRONOUNCING GAZETTEER:

Containing Topographical, Statistical, and other Information, of all the more important Places in the known World, from the most recent and authentic Sources.

BY THOMAS BALDWIN.

Assisted by several other Gentlemen.

To which is added an APPENDIX, containing more than TEN THOUSAND ADDITIONAL NAMES, chiefly of the small Towns and Villages, &c., of the United States and of Mexico.

NINTH EDITION, WITH A SUPPLEMENT,

Giving the Pronunciation of near two thousand names, besides those pronounced in the Original Work: Forming in itself a Complete Vocabulary of Geographical Pronunciation.

ONE VOLUME 12MO. — PRICE, $1 50.

FIELD'S SCRAP BOOK. — NEW EDITION.

Literary and Miscellaneous Scrap Book.

Consisting of Tales and Anecdotes—Biographical, Historical, Moral, Religious, and Sentimental Pieces, in Prose and Poetry.

COMPILED BY WM. FIELDS.

SECOND EDITION, REVISED AND IMPROVED.

In one handsome 8vo. Volume. Price, $2 00.

THE ARKANSAW DOCTOR.

THE LIFE AND ADVENTURES OF AN ARKANSAW DOCTOR

BY DAVID RATTLEHEAD, M. D.

"THE MAN OF SCRAPES."

With numerous Illustrations. Price Fifty Cents.

THE LADY KILLER.

BY REBECCA HICKS.

One Volume 12mo. Price Twenty-five Cents.

THIRTY YEARS WITH THE INDIAN TRIBES.

PERSONAL MEMOIRS OF A

Residence of Thirty Years with the Indian Tribes

ON THE AMERICAN FRONTIERS:

With brief Notices of passing Events, Facts, and Opinions.

A. D. 1812 TO A. D. 1842.

BY HENRY R. SCHOOLCRAFT.

One large 8vo. Volume. Price $3 00.

THE SCALP HUNTERS;

OR,

ROMANTIC ADVENTURES IN NORTHERN MEXICO.

BY CAPTAIN MAYNE REID,

Author of he "Rifle Rangers."

COMPLETE IN ONE VOLUME. PRICE FIFTY CENTS.

BOARDMAN'S BIBLE IN THE FAMILY.

The Bible in the Family:

OR, HINTS ON DOMESTIC HAPPINESS.

BY H. A. BOARDMAN.

PASTOR OF THE TENTH PRESBYTERIAN CHURCH, PHILADELPHIA.

One Volume 12mo.—Price One Dollar.

THE REGICIDE'S DAUGHTER:

A Tale of two Worlds.

BY W. H. CARPENTER,

AUTHOR OF "CLAIBORNE THE REBEL," "JOHN THE BOLD," &C., &C.

One Volume 18mo. Price Thirty-seven and a Half Cents.

Splendid Illustrated Books, suitable for Gifts for the Holidays.

The Iris: An Original Souvenir for any Year.

EDITED BY PROF. JOHN S. HART.

WITH TWELVE SPLENDID ILLUMINATIONS, ALL FROM ORIGINAL DESIGNS.

THE DEW-DROP: A TRIBUTE OF AFFECTION.

WITH NINE STEEL ENGRAVINGS.

GEMS FROM THE SACRED MINE.

WITH TEN STEEL PLATES AND ILLUMINATIONS.

THE POET'S OFFERING.

WITH FOURTEEN STEEL PLATES AND ILLUMINATIONS.

THE STANDARD EDITIONS OF THE POETS.

WITH ILLUSTRATIONS.

LORD AND LADY HARCOURT:
OR, COUNTRY HOSPITALITIES.

BY CATHARINE SINCLAIR,

Author of "Jane Bouverie," "The Business of Life," "Modern Accomplishments," &c., &c.

One Volume 12mo. Price 50 cents, paper; cloth, fine, 75 cents.

William's New Map of the United States,
ON ROLLERS.

SIZE TWO AND A HALF BY THREE FEET.

A new map of the United States, upon which are delineated its vast works of Internal Communication, Routes across the Continent, &c., showing also Canada and the Island of Cuba,

BY W. WILLIAMS.

This Map is handsomely colored and mounted on rollers, and will be found a beautiful and useful ornament to the Counting-House and Parlor, as well as the School-Room. Price Two Dollars.

THE ABBOTSFORD EDITION

OF

The Waverley Novels,

Printed upon fine white Paper, with new and beautiful Type,

FROM THE LAST ENGLISH EDITION,

EMBRACING

THE AUTHOR'S LATEST CORRECTIONS, NOTES, ETC.,

Complete in 12 volumes, demi-octavo, neatly bound in cloth,

With Illustrations,

FOR ONLY TWELVE DOLLARS,

CONTAINING

WAVERLEY, or 'Tis Sixty Years Since...THE FORTUNES OF NIGEL.
GUY MANNERING..........PEVERIL OF THE PEAK.
THE ANTIQUARY..........QUENTIN DURWARD.
THE BLACK DWARF..........ST. RONAN'S WELL.
OLD MORTALITY..........REDGAUNTLET.
ROB ROY..........THE BETROTHED.
THE HEART OF MID-LOTHIAN..........THE TALISMAN.
THE BRIDE OF LAMMERMOOR..........WOODSTOCK.
A LEGEND OF MONTROSE..........THE HIGHLAND WIDOW, &c.
IVANHOE..........THE FAIR MAID OF PERTH.
THE MONASTERY..........ANNE OF GEIERSTEIN.
THE ABBOT..........COUNT ROBERT OF PARIS.
KENILWORTH..........CASTLE DANGEROUS.
THE PIRATE..........SURGEON'S DAUGHTER, &c.

Any of the above Novels sold, in Paper Covers, at Fifty Cents each.

ALSO,

THE SAME EDITION

OF

THE WAVERLEY NOVELS,

In Twelve Volumes, Royal Octavo, on Superfine Paper, with

THREE HUNDRED CHARACTERISTIC AND BEAUTIFUL ILLUSTRATIONS.

ELEGANTLY BOUND IN CLOTH, GILT.

Price, Only Twenty-Four Dollars.

FROST'S JUVENILE SERIES.

TWELVE VOLUMES, 16mo., WITH FIVE HUNDRED ENGRAVINGS.

WALTER O'NEILL, OR THE PLEASURE OF DOING GOOD. 25 Engravings.
JUNKER SCHOTT, and other Stories. 6 Engravings.
THE LADY OF THE LURLEI, and other Stories. 12 Engravings.
ELLEN'S BIRTHDAY, and other Stories. 20 Engravings.
HERMAN, and other Stories. 9 Engravings.
KING TREGEWALL'S DAUGHTER, and other Stories. 16 Engr's.
THE DROWNED BOY, and other Stories. 6 Engravings.
THE PICTORIAL RHYME-BOOK. 122 Engravings.
THE PICTORIAL NURSERY BOOK. 117 Engravings.
THE GOOD CHILD'S REWARD. 115 Engravings.
ALPHABET OF QUADRUPEDS. 26 Engravings.
ALPHABET OF BIRDS. 26 Engravings.

PRICE, TWENTY-FIVE CENTS EACH.

The above popular and attractive series of New Juveniles for the Young, are sold together or separately.

THE MILLINER AND THE MILLIONAIRE.

BY MRS. REBECCA HICKS,

(Of Virginia,) Author of "The Lady Killer," &c. 1 vol. 12mo. Price, 37 1-2 cents.

STANSBURY'S

EXPEDITION TO THE GREAT SALT LAKE.

AN EXPLORATION OF THE VALLEY OF THE GREAT SALT LAKE OF UTAH,

CONTAINING ITS GEOGRAPHY, NATURAL HISTORY, MINERALOGICAL RESOURCES, ANALYSIS OF ITS WATERS, AND AN AUTHENTIC ACCOUNT OF

THE MORMON SETTLEMENT.

Also, A Reconnoissance of a New Route through the Rocky Mountains, with Seventy Beautiful Illustrations, from Drawings taken on the spot, and two large and accurate Maps of that region.

BY HOWARD STANSBURY,

CAPTAIN TOPOGRAPHICAL ENGINEERS. One Volume, Royal Octavo.

www.ingramcontent.com/pod-product-compliance
Lightning Source LLC
LaVergne TN
LVHW010141110826
845151LV00002B/395

9781425539115